# A
# CONFEDERATE
# TRILOGY
## FOR
# YOUNG READERS

---

The Life
of
Gen. Robert E. Lee
Lt. Gen. T. J. "Stonewall" Jackson
Major Gen. J. E. B. Stuart

by

## MRS. MARY L. WILLIAMSON

---

Harrisonburg, Virginia
SPRINKLE PUBLICATIONS
1989

# PREFACE TO THE NEW EDITION

In Hebrews 6:12 diligence in the Christian life is related to being "imitators of them who through faith and patience inherit the promises." The principle set forth is identified by the words of R. L. Dabney: "that the characters of his children, which exhibit the scriptural model, are given as examples, to be studied and imitated by us. He (God) would thus teach us more than those abstract conceptions of Christian excellence, which are conveyed by general definitions of duty; he would give us a living picture and concrete idea." The same thought is expressed by Jonathan Edwards when he wrote: "There are two ways of representing and recommending true religion and virtue to the world; the one by doctrine and precept; the other, instance and example."

The present generation of youth desperately needs mind and heart to be educated by the means of a careful study of the lives of proven men and women of God in history. That boys and girls aspire unto virtuous and distinctive masculinity and femininity, parents must set before their children legitimate heroes and heroines whose lives display compelling lessons and examples of manhood and womanhood.

In the providence of God the biographical records of many such men and women are still available to be read and studied. Yet, few parents seem to care. Fervent parental concern over computer literacy is common today. As common is the appalling parental indifference over biographical and historical illiteracy. While the former literacy may seem to hold the promise of marketable skills which will secure abundant mammon, the latter illiteracy direly impoverishes the same youth at the point of not having a clear view of distinctive manhood and womanhood. While history has unfolded page after page about those whose characters teach Christian graces and virtues, this generation seems to pay scant attention. The tragic results of such neglect are obvious. Late-twentieth century society is blighted with an epidemic of gender chaos. Men and women and, consequently, boys and girls, are groping in a unisex darkness that must be dispelled.

In the interest of shining upon youth the light of worthy examples, Sprinkle Publications has made available in one volume Mary L. Williamson's biographies of General Robert E. Lee, Lieutenant-General Thomas J. Jackson, and Major-General J. E. B. Stuart. Each of these biographies, originally written for children of elementary school age, is skillfully composed with a focus on character to which youth should aspire. Beyond informing children of the military histories of three of the most illustrious leaders of the Army of Northern Virginia, the author's aim is to "warm the hearts of rising generations to lives of courage and devotion."

Indeed, the lives of Lee, Jackson and Stuart are worthy of close study, not simply that they may be known, but that they may be imitated. A friend and biographer of Lee, J. William Jones, said: "If I have ever come in contact with a sincere, devout Christian, one who, seeing himself to be a sinner, trusted alone in the merits of Christ, who humbly tried to walk the path of duty, 'looking unto Jesus the author and finisher of our faith,' and whose piety was constantly exemplified in his daily life, that man was the world's great soldier and model man, Robert Edward Lee." From the life of Lee, the Christlike, Spirit-wrought virtues of humility, self-control, and dutiful obedience shine brightly.

The life of Jackson, succinctly described in the following words of B. M. Palmer, "Uniting the most beautiful simplicity with the most intense earnestness of character, with a religious consecration to duty as the regulative principle of his life, he was a true man in all the relations in which he moved," holds up to an age of unbelief and cynicism, a firm confidence in the providence of a present God and in the efficacy of prayer. Preeminently, Jackson was a man of prayer.

Stuart, a younger man of joyous temperament, converted as a college student and known at West Point as the "Bible class man," impressed his contemporaries with his purity of mind and heart. Such was his example that General Lee wrote of him, "To military capacity of a high order, he added the brighter graces of a pure life guided and sustained by the Christian's faith and hope." Of Stuart's manner with women, his principal early biographer and trusted staff officer, H. B. McClellan, wrote that he was "pure in thought and action."

May it be that the moral excellencies illustrated in the lives of these three men leave a lasting impression upon the hearts of all who read these accounts. And, under the blessing of God, may each reader exercise the intellectual and moral faculties to the end that Christ, the fountain from which such excellencies flow, be sought and found.

George McDearmon
Ballston Lake Baptist Church
Ballston Lake, New York
1989

**UNVEILING OF LEE MONUMENT**
At Richmond, Va., Friday, May 29, 1890.

# THE LIFE

OF

# GEN. ROBERT E. LEE,

## FOR CHILDREN,

### IN EASY WORDS.

ILLUSTRATED.

---

MRS. MARY L. WILLIAMSON.

---

Harrisonburg, Virginia

SPRINKLE PUBLICATIONS

1989

Sprinkle Publications
P. O. Box 1094
Harrisonburg, Va. 22801

# PREFACE.

In preparing the "Life of Lee for Children," for use in the Public Schools, I beg leave to place before teachers good reasons for employing it as a supplementary reader.

First, I urge the need of interesting our children in history at an early age. From observation I find that the minds of children who study history early expand more rapidly than those who are restricted to the limits of stories in readers. While teaching pupils to read, why not fix in their minds the names and deeds of our great men, thereby laying the foundation of historical knowledge and instilling true patriotism into their youthful souls?

Secondly, In looking over the lives of our American heroes we find not one which presents such a picture of moral grandeur as that of Lee. Place this picture before the little ones and you cannot fail to make them look upward to noble ideals.

This little book is intended as auxiliary to third readers. I have used the diacritical marks of Webster, also his syllabication. In compiling this work I referred chiefly to Gen. Fitzhugh Lee's "Life of Lee," and Rev. J. William Jones' "Personal Reminiscences of R. E. Lee."

MARY L. WILLIAMSON.

NEW MARKET, VA.,
September 28, 1898.

# The Sword of Robert Lee.

Words by MOINA.     Music by ARMAND.

Forth from its scabbard, pure and bright,
    Flashed the sword of Lee!
Far in the front of the deadly fight,
High o'er the brave, in the cause of right,
Its stainless sheen, like a beacon light,
    Led us to victory.

Out of its scabbard, where full long
    It slumbered peacefully—
Roused from its rest by the battle-song,
Shielding the feeble, smiting the strong,
Guarding the right, and avenging the wrong—
    Gleamed the sword of Lee!

Forth from its scabbard, high in air,
    Beneath Virginia's sky,
And they who saw it gleaming there,
And knew who bore it, knelt to swear
That where that sword led they would dare
    To follow and to die.

Out of its scabbard!  Never hand
    Waved sword from stain as free,
Nor purer sword led braver band,
Nor braver bled for a brighter land,
Nor brighter land had a cause as grand,
    Nor cause a chief like Lee!

Forth from its scabbard!  All in vain!
    Forth flashed the sword of Lee!
'Tis shrouded now in its sheath again,
It sleeps the sleep of our noble slain,
Defeated, yet without a stain,
    Proudly and peacefully.

# The Life of Gen. Robert E. Lee.

## CHAPTER I.

### Birth and Youth.

ROBERT EDWARD LEE was born at Stratford, Westmoreland county, Virginia, on the 19th of January, 1807.

His father, General Henry Lee, had been a great chief in Washington's army. They sometimes call him "Light-Horse Harry Lee." While with Washington, he was ever in front of the foe, and his troopers were what they always should be—the eyes and ears of the army.

After the war he was Governor of Virginia, and then a member of Congress. It was he who said in a speech made before Congress after the death of Washington, that he was "First in war, first in peace, and first in the hearts of his countrymen." He also said, "Virginia is my country; her will I obey, however sad the fate to which it may subject me."

The long line of Lees may be traced back to Launcelot Lee, of Loudon, in France, who went with William the Conqueror upon his expeditior to England; and when Harold had been slain upon the bloody field of Hastings, Launcelot was given by William the Conqueror an estate in Essex. From that time the name of Lee is ever an honorable one in the history of England.

In the time of the first Charles, Richard Lee came to the New World and found a home in Virginia. He was a man of good stature, sound sense, and kind heart. From him the noble stock of Virginia Lees began. He was the great-great-grandfather of Robert, who was much like him in many ways.

Robert's mother was Anne Hill Carter, who came from one of the best families of Virginia. She was a good and noble woman, who lived only to train her children in the right way.

Stratford, the house in which Robert was born, is a fine old mansion, built in the shape of the letter H, and stands not far from the

STRATFORD.

banks of the Potomac River and near the birthplace of Washington. Upon the roof were summer houses, where the band played, while the young folks walked in the grounds below, and enjoyed the cool air from the river and the sweet music of the band.

He had two brothers and two sisters. His brothers were named Charles Carter and Sidney Smith, and his sisters Anne and Mildred.

When Robert was but four years of age his father moved to Alexandria, a city not very far from the Stratford House, where he could send his boys to better schools. But he was not able to stay with them and bring them up to manhood. Shortly after he had moved to Alexandria, he was hurt in Baltimore by a mob of bad men, and he was never well again.

When Robert was six years old, his father went to the West Indies for his health. While there he wrote kind letters to his son, Charles Carter Lee, and spoke with much love of all. Once he said, "Tell me of Anne. Has she grown tall? Robert was always good." He wished to know, also, if his sons rode and shot well, saying that a Virginian's sons should be taught to ride, shoot, and tell the truth.

When he had been there five years, and only grew worse, he made up his mind to return home. But he grew so ill that he was put ashore on Cumberland Island at the home of a friend. He soon gave up all hope of life. At times his pain was so great that he would drive his servants and every one else out of the room. At length an old woman, who had been Mrs. Greene's best maid, was sent to nurse him. The first thing General Lee did when she came into the room was to hurl his boot at her head. Without a word, she picked up the boot and threw it back at him. A smile passed over the old chief's face as he saw how brave she was, and from that time to the day of his death none but Mom Sarah could wait on him. Two months after the sick soldier landed he was dead. His body was laid to rest amid the cedars and flowers of the South, and it has never been moved to Virginia.

MOM SARAH.

At this time Robert was only eleven years old.    If he was a good boy, it was his mother who kept him so, for he never knew a father's care.    His mother once said to a friend, "How can I spare Robert!    He is both a son and a daughter to me."

About that time the girls and other boys were away from home, and she had no one but Robert to care for her.    He took the keys and "kept house" for her when she was sick, and also saw to all of her outdoor work.    He would run home from school to ride out with her, so that she might enjoy the fresh air and sunshine.    When she would complain of the cold or draughts, he would pull out a great jackknife and stuff the cracks with paper, for the coach was an old one.

So he grew up by her side, a good and noble boy.    At first he went to school to a Mr. Leary, who was ever his firm friend.    Then he went to the school of Mr. Benjamin

H. Hallowell, who always spoke of him as a fine young man.

Robert was fond of hunting, and would sometimes follow the hounds all day. In this way he gained that great strength which was never known to fail him in after life.

The old home, in Alexandria, where his mother had lived, was always a sacred place to him. Years after, one of his friends saw him looking sadly over the fence of the garden where he used to play. "I am looking," he said, "to see if the old snow-ball trees are still here. I should be sorry to miss them."

When he was eighteen years old, he went to West Point to learn to be a soldier. He was there four years, and in that time never got a bad mark or demerit. His clothes always looked neat and clean, and his gun bright. In short, he kept the rules of the school and studied so well that he came out second in his class.

When he came home from West Point, he found his mother's old coachman, Nat, very

UNCLE NAT.

ill. He took him at once to the South and nursed him with great care. But the spring-time saw the good old slave laid in the grave by the hand of his kind young master.

Not very long after, his dear mother grew quite ill. He sat by her bedside day and night, and gave her all her food and medicine with his own hand. But his great care and love could not save her. He was soon bereft of her to whom he used to say he "owed everything."

Some one has said, "Much has been written of what the world owes to 'Mary, the mother of Washington'; but it owes scarcely less to 'Anne, the mother of Lee.'"

---

Gĕn'-er-al, the head of an army.

Ex'-pe-dĭ'-tion, a voyage ; a trip, with an aim in view.

Stăt'-ūre, height.

Drȧughts (drȧfts), currents of air.

Tell what you remember about—

    Robert's father.

    Robert's mother.

    The situation of his home.

    Robert's kindness to his mother.

    His life at West Point.

## CHAPTER II.

### A Young Engineer.

In 1829, when twenty-two years old, Robert entered the Engineer Corps of the United States, and thus became Lieutenant Lee.

ROBERT E. LEE,
Lieut. of Engineers.

It is the duty of these engineers in time of peace, to plan forts, to change the course of rivers which make sand-banks at wrong places, and to do other work of the same kind. Lieutenant Lee was sent at once to Hampton Roads, in Virginia, to build strong works, not dreaming that in after years it would be his fate to try to pull them down.

Lieutenant Lee was married on the 30th of June, 1831, to Mary Custis, who was the great-granddaughter of Mrs. Washington, and the only child of George Parke Custis, the adopted son of Washington. She lived at a fine old place on the Virginia bank of the Potomac River, called Arlington. At this time Lieutenant Lee was very handsome in face and tall and erect in figure.

Two years after his marriage he was sent to the city of Washington. This change was pleasant to him, for he was then near the home of his wife.

In 1837 he was sent to St. Louis to find means to keep the great Mississippi River in its own bed. It was a hard task, but he at last forced the mighty river into the channel he wished. While at work, some men, who did not know what great things he could do, tried to drive his workmen away, and even brought up cannon. Lee did not mind them, but went on with his work,

ARLINGTON.

and soon had the great river to flow in the right place.

From St. Louis he was sent to New York to plan and build new forts to protect that great city. He was now a captain of engineers, and was soon to try the horrors of war.

In 1846, a war broke out between the United States and Mexico. "Engineers are of as much use to an army as sails to ships." They have to make roads and bridges, to plant big guns and draw maps, and guide the men when going to fight.

At first, Captain Lee was sent to join General Wool, in the north of Mexico. Not long before the battle of Buena Vista (Bwā́-nă̈-vees-tă̈), General Wool sent Lee to see where Santa Anna, the general of the Mexicans, had placed his army. News had come that he was not far off.

Lee rode, with only one man to guide him, into the mountains. After he had been riding for some hours, he saw on a hill-side

MEXICO.

the smoke of fires, and objects which he thought were tents. He went on, in a very cautious way, till he had gotten quite near. Then, he saw the white objects were only flocks of sheep and herds of cattle and mules on the way to market. He found out from the men driving them that Santa Anna had not crossed the mountains, and then went back to his friends, who thought that they would never see him again.

Though he had ridden forty miles that night, he rested but three hours before taking a troop of horsemen and going far into the mountains to find out just where Santa Anna had gone with his army.

Soon after this brave deed, Captain Lee was sent to join General Scott in the south of Mexico. He was put to work at Vera Cruz (Vā-rä-kroŏs), a large town on the coast. There was a high wall, with strong forts around Vera Cruz. General Scott wished to take this city from the Mexicans. So Captain Lee had to plant big guns and build forts; and to do this he worked night and day.

As they were short of men, he was told to take some sailors from a man-of-war to help with the work. These men began to complain loudly. "They did not enlist to dig dirt, and they did not want to work under a landlubber anyhow." Their captain said to Lee, "The boys don't want any dirt to hide behind; they want to get on the *top*, where they can have a fair fight." Lee quietly showed his orders, and told the old "salt" he meant to carry them out, and pushed on the work 'mid curses both loud and deep.

Just as the work was done, the Mexicans began to fire their guns at that point, and these brave sons of the sea were glad enough to hide behind the "bank of dirt." Not long after, their captain met Captain Lee and said, "I suppose the dirt did save some of my boys. But I knew that we would have no use for dirt-banks on shipboard. that there what we want is a clear deck and an open sea. And the fact is, Captain, I don't like this land fighting anyway; *it 'aint clean.*"

Vera Cruz was taken by General Scott in two weeks' time. Then the men went on over hills and vales, till they came to the strong fort on Cerro Gordo. Captain Lee then found a way to lead the Americans to the rear of the Mexicans, who soon broke and fled.

While this battle was raging, Captain Lee heard the cries of a little girl, and found by the side of a hut a Mexican drummer boy. His arm had been badly hurt and a large Mexican, who had been shot, had fallen on him. Captain Lee stopped, had the big Mexican thrown off of the boy, and the little fellow moved to a place of safety.

His little sister stood by. Her large black eyes were streaming with tears, her hands were crossed upon her breast, and her hair in one long plait reached to her waist. Her feet and arms were bare. She was very thankful to Captain Lee for saving her brother.

In a letter to his son from this place, he says: "I thought of you, my dear Custis,

CAPTAIN LEE RESCUING DRUMMER BOY.

on the 18th in the battle, and wondered, when the musket balls and grape were whistling over my head, where I could put you, if with me, to be safe. I was truly thankful you were at school, I hope, learning to be good and wise. You have no idea what a horrible sight a battle-field is."

From Cerro Gordo, they went on fighting battles until they came to the large and rich city of Mexico.

On this march, Captain Lee was always at the front to guide the men. Once, when one part of General Scott's army had lost its way, General Scott sent *seven* engineers to guide it into the right road. They had to cross a huge, rough bed of lava and rock. *Six* of them went back to camp, saying that they could not get across; but, Captain Lee pressed on in the dark, alone and on foot, and brought the men out in safety. General Scott once said that it was the greatest feat done by any *one man* during the war.

There were many battles fought, but at last the city of Mexico was taken by General Scott. In after years, this great man was heard to say that his great success in Mexico was largely due to the skill and valor of Robert E. Lee, and that he was the *best soldier* that he ever saw in the field.

In the midst of all this fighting, his boys were ever in his thoughts. This is a part of what he wrote to his son Custis on Christmas-Eve, 1846:

"I hope good Santa Claus will fill my Rob's stocking to-night; that Mildred's, Agnes's, and Anna's may break down with good things. I do not know what he may have for you and Mary, but if he leaves you one-half of what I wish, you will want for nothing. I think if I had one of you on each side of me, riding on ponies, I would be quite happy."

Not long after, he wrote to his boys thus:

"The ponies here cost from ten to fifty dollars. I have three horses, but *Creole* is my pet. She is a golden dun color, and takes me over all the ditches I have yet met with."

When the war was at last ended, in 1848, Captain Lee went home for a short rest, after which he was sent to West Point, as the Superintendent of the Academy from whose walls he had gone forth twenty-three years before. His duty was to watch over the studies and training of the boys who would one day be officers in the army.

————————

Corps (kōre), a body of troops.

Of'ficer, one who has charge of soldiers.

Lävȧ, melted matter flowing from a volcano.

Fēat, a great deed.

Lieuten'ant (lutĕn'ant), an officer next below a captain.

Tell me—

When Robert became Lieutenant Lee.

Whom he married.

Where he was sent in 1837.

What war broke out in 1846.

About a great feat performed by Captain Lee.

Where he was sent in 1848.

## CHAPTER III.

### A Cavalry Officer.

AFTER being three years at West Point, Captain Lee was sent to Texas as Lieutenant-Colonel (kûrnel) of the Second Regiment of Cavalry. Cavalrymen are soldiers who fight on horseback and who carry sabers, and pistols, and short guns, called carbines.

Colonel Lee did not wish to leave the Engineer Corps, as he had become very fond of the work, and had won a high rank in it; but, as he had been promoted to a higher place, he thought it best to take it. When at West Point, he had been a fine horseman. He was still fond of horses and liked to see them fed and well taken care of. Though now forty-six years of age, he still had a firm seat in the saddle and rode well. His regiment was sent to the new State of Texas, where his duty was to watch the Indians and keep them from killing the whites.

I have no doubt that Colonel Lee enjoyed

LEE CHASING THE INDIANS.

riding over the vast plains of Texas, but life in the forts was not very pleasant to such a man as Lee. The forts were in the midst of dreary plains, and there were only a few men

at each post.   The scouting parties were led
by lieutenants, and the higher officers would
remain at the forts to see that all went right.
Such a lonely life did not suit our hero, but
he made the best of it.

Near  his  first  post, Camp  Cooper,  was
an   Indian   Reserve,   where   the   Indians
would   come   to   be   fed   by   the   Government.   When it was  cold  and  food  was
scarce,  they  would  come  in;  but  when
the grass grew in the spring and the game
was fat, they would go off and become wild
and  savage  enough  to  kill  those  who  had
been kind to them.

Catumseh,  a  Comanche  chief,  was  at  the
Reserve   when   Lee   was   at   Camp   Cooper.
Lee thought it would be better to visit him
and tell him that he would trust him as a
friend so long as he behaved; but if he did
not  behave  he  would  take  him  for  a  foe.
Catumseh was not much pleased with Lee's
speech,  but  gave  an  ugly  grunt  and  said
that,  as  he  had  *six*  wives,  he  was  a  "big

Indian." Lee had better "get *more wives* before he talked." This visit did not do much good. Catumseh was no doubt taking the measure of Lee's scalp, while Lee was displeased with the sly and filthy savage.

The Comanche Indians were then the fiercest tribe in that region. They ate raw meat, slept on the ground, and were great thieves and murderers. They were fine horsemen, and moved swiftly from place to place on their ponies.

In June, 1856, Lee was sent with four companies of his regiment on an expedition against the Comanches, but they could not be found. The wily savages had fled to their desert retreats, where foot of pale face had never trod.

From Camp Cooper he writes to Mrs. Lee:

"My Fourth-of-July was spent after a march of thirty miles in one of the branches of the Bra'zos, under my blanket, which rested on four sticks driven in the ground, as a sun-shade. The sun was fiery hot, the air like a furnace, and the water salt; still my love for my country was as great, my faith in her future as true, as they would have been under better circumstances."

The change of weather in Texas is sometimes very great.

In another letter, he tells his wife about a cold wind or norther. "I came here in a cold norther, and though I pitched my tent in the most sheltered place I could find, I found this morning, when getting up, my bucket of water, which was close by my bed, so hard frozen that I had to break the ice before I could pour the water into the basin."

While Colonel Lee rode with his troopers from fort to fort, a dreadful disease broke out among them. Many died, but Colonel Lee did not catch the disease, though he lived among his men and ran great risks. In these sad times, his thoughts were ever with his dear ones at home.

In a letter dated Camp Cooper, June 9,

1857, he tells about the sickness of the troopers:

"The great heat has made much sickness among the men. The children, too, have suffered. A bright little boy died from it a few days since. He was the only child, and his parents were much grieved at his loss * * *. For the first time in my life, I read the service of our Church over the grave to a large number of soldiers." A few days after, he again read the service over a little boy who had died with the disease.

In a long letter from Fort Brown, Texas, December, 1856, he says:

"I thought of you and wished to be with you." He wrote again: "Though absent, my heart will be in the midst of you; I can do nothing but love and pray for you all. My daily walks are alone, up and down the banks of the river, and my chief pleasure comes from my own thoughts, and from the sight of the flowers and animals I meet with here."

In the midst of this wild, lonely life he was ever true to his faith in Christ, which he had professed after the Mexican war.

There was at Arlington a large yellow cat, called Tom Tita. All the family were fond of him, and Colonel Lee among the rest. This led him to write home about the cats he saw in his travels. He

TOM TITA.

told once of a cat called by his mistress Jim Nooks. He was a great pet, but at last died from eating too much. He had coffee and cream for breakfast, pound cake for lunch, turtle and oysters for dinner, buttered toast and Mexican rats, taken raw, for supper. He was very handsome, but his "beauty could not save him." The kindness of his mistress was his ruin.

Again he told his little girl about a cat which was dressed up. He had two holes bored in each ear, and in each wore bows of pink and blue ribbon.    He was snow-white and wore a gold chain on his neck.    His tail and feet were tipped with black, and his eyes of green were truly cat-like.

In the summer of 1857, he was made Colonel (kûr'nel) of his regiment.    The next fall his father-in-law, Mr. Custis, died, and Colonel Lee went home for a short time. Mr. Custis left Arlington and the rest of his land to Mrs. Lee, and he also willed that at the end of five years all of his slaves should be set free.    He had chosen Colonel Lee to see that his will was carried out.

Colonel Lee stayed as long as he could with his lonely wife, and then went back to his post in Texas.    It must have been far from easy for him to go back to the wild, hard life on the plains.    There were then no railroads.    The United States mail was carried on mules, by armed soldiers who rode in a gallop from place to place.    Often they were slain by the Indians, who would scalp them and leave their bodies to be found by the troopers as they chased the savages back to their retreats.

Two years more were spent in Texas, when, in October, 1859, we find him again at home, and taking part in a great tragedy.

A man, named John Brown, made a plan to set free the negro slaves who were then in the South, and to kill all the whites. This plot did not succeed, and John Brown and his men took refuge in the Round House at Harper's Ferry. Colonel Lee, who was then at home on a furlough, was ordered to take a band of soldiers and capture these bold men. He went at once to Harper's Ferry and quickly took them prisoners. They were then tried and hung for treason.

Just here, I must tell you that the slaves were blacks, or negroes, who had first been brought to this country from Africa, in 1619, by the Dutch, and sold to the Virginia planters. At first, the planters bought them out of pity, as they were badly treated by the Dutch. But after a time it was found

COL. R. E. LEE AT JOHN BROWN'S FORT, HARPERS FERRY.

that the negroes worked well in the corn and tobacco fields, and that they made money for their masters.

Many men at the North were sea-going men, and they soon found out that, by sailing over the ocean to Africa and catching the blacks, they could sell them at a great profit to themselves. This they did, and men both at the North and South bought them, though, even then, there were some people at the South who thought it wrong to buy and sell human beings.

In the State of Georgia it was for a time against the law to hold negro slaves.

After a while, it was found that the climate at the North was too cold for the negro to thrive. It did not pay the men at the North to keep them, and so they were sold to the Southern planters.

In the South, the climate was hot, like that of their native Africa, so they did well in that sunny land.

In 1808, it was made unlawful to bring

any more slaves from Africa to the United States. The people at the South were glad that the trade in slaves was stopped, but the Northern traders were of course sorry that they could make no more money in that way.

When the negroes were first brought from Africa, they were heathen savages; but, after a few years, they learned the speech and customs of the whites; and, more than all, the worship of the true God. In thinking of this, we have to admit that slavery must have been permitted by the Lord in order to bring a heathen people out of darkness into the light of the Gospel.

There were now four millions of negroes in the South. There was great love between the blacks and their masters, as we have seen when John Brown tried to get the former to rise up and slay the whites. For years, there had been a feeling in the North that it was wrong to own slaves, and some of the people began to hate the South and to try to crush it.

The South felt that they owned the slaves under the law, or Constitution of the United States, and that they ought to be let alone. They also claimed that the slaves, as a class, were better treated than any other working people in the world. They, moreover, said that the Southern States had a perfect right to go out of the Union, if they wished, and set up a government for themselves. This the North denied; and thus they quarreled about the rights of States, and slavery, and other things, until they began to think of war.

In a short time after the John Brown Raid, Colonel Lee was back at his post in Texas, but he was much troubled at the state of his dear country. He loved the Union and had lived nearly all his life in its service; but he knew that Virginia was in the right, and that he could not fight against his native State.

So, when the war came, he left the United States Army to fight for Virginia and the South.

He was offered the chief command of the United States Army if he would remain in the "Union" service. He knew that if he went with the South he would lose his rank, and also his lovely home—Arlington, but " 'none of these things moved him'; his only wish was *to know, that he might walk the path of duty.*"

He said to Mr. Blair, who came to offer him the command of the army: "If I owned the four millions of slaves in the South, I would give them all up to save the Union, but how can I draw my sword upon Virginia, my native State?" So, when Mr. Lincoln called for troops to send against the South, Lee turned his back upon "wealth, rank, and all that a great power could give him, and offered his stainless sword to his native State." His great soul was wrung with grief, but he obeyed the call of duty.

He went at once to Richmond, and was

made Major-General of the Virginia troops. His three sons also joined the Confederate army.

General Lee was now fifty-four years old. He had been thirty-two years in the service of the United States.

The great "Civil War" now began. The eleven Southern States which had left the "Union" were now called "The Confederate States of America"; Mr. Jefferson Davis was made President of them, and Richmond in Virginia was made the capital city.

----

Sā'bers, swords with broad blades.

Furlough (fûr'lō), a leave of absence.

Trea'son (trē'zon), the act of being false to one's country.

Promō'ted, raised to a higher rank.

Rĕg'iment, a body of troops under a colonel.

Trăg'ĕdy, an action in which the life of a person is taken.

VIRGINIA STATE CAPITOL, FORMERLY OCCUPIED BY THE CONFEDERATE CONGRESS.

[43]

What do you know about—

    Cavalrymen?

    Colonel Lee's life in Texas?

    Catumseh?

    The Comanche Indians?

    The negroes?

    John Brown?

    The wish of Lee?

    What he deemed his duty?

    The great " Civil War "?

## CHAPTER IV.

### A Confederate General.

In this little book I cannot tell all that happened during the Civil War, but only as much as will relate to our hero, General Lee.

There were now two governments—one at the North; the other at the South. Mr. Abraham Lincoln was President of the North, or Federals, while Mr. Jefferson Davis was the President of the South, or Confederates. The first thought of the North was to defend Washington, their capital city; while the South was just as busy taking care of Richmond, and getting arms and troops ready for war.

In this war, brother fought against brother, and friend against friend. It was a time of great trouble all over the land. At the North, one hundred thousand men were enlisted in three days. At the South, the feeling was more intense. Men rushed to arms from all parts of the country.

You must notice that from the first of the war, the South was much poorer in the number of men and arms than the North. There were at the North eighteen millions of whites; while at the South, there were only six millions. Through all the South, there could be found only fifteen thousand new rifles and about one hundred thousand old muskets.

The Federals wore a uniform of blue, while the Confederates were clad in gray; hence they were sometimes called "the blue" and "the gray."

The first blood which flowed in this war was shed in Baltimore. The Sixth Massachusetts Regiment, as it was passing through the city on its way south, was attacked by a band of men who loved the South and could not bear to see them marching on to fight their brethren. In the fierce street fight which followed, several men were killed. This happened on April the 19th, 1861.

GEN. R. E. LEE IN WEST VIRGINIA.

The first gun of the war was fired at half-past four o'clock April 12, 1861, at Fort Sumter, in South Carolina. This fort was taken by the Confederates after a fight of thirty-four hours, in which no one was hurt on either side.

During the first months of the war, General Lee was kept in Richmond to send Virginia men, who came to fight for the South, to the places where they were most needed. All around Richmond were camps, where men were trained for war. The largest of these camps was called "Camp Lee," after our hero. But in July, 1861, Lee was sent to Western Virginia, and was, for the first time, commander of troops in the field.

Just then, there were heavy rains and a great deal of sickness among the men of his small army, so that he was not able to attack the enemy, as he had planned.

After some time, it was thought best to give up Western Virginia, and General Lee went back to Richmond, where he stayed

only a short time. In November, 1861, he
was sent south to build a line of forts along
the coasts of South Carolina and Georgia.
In four months' time he did much to show
his skill as an engineer.

But a large Northern army, under General
McClellan, was at the gates of Richmond, and
Lee was sent for to take charge of all the
armies of the South. Very soon, a battle
was fought at Seven Pines, May 31st, which
stopped General McClellan's "On to Richmond." In that battle General Johnston,
the commanding general, was badly wounded,
and General Lee was put in his place. Lee
was swift to plan and as swift to act. His
task was hard. The hosts of the North
were at the gates of Richmond. The folks
on the house-tops could see their camp-fires
and hear the roar of their cannon. Lee at
once began to make earth-works, and to
place his men for battle. Every day, now, a
fine-looking man, clad in a neat gray uniform,
might be seen riding along the line.

He wished to know what was going on in the camp of the foe, and now the right man came forward. His name was J. E. B. Stuart, best known as Jeb Stuart. He led his brave troopers quite around the army of the North and found out all that Lee wished to know. He was ever after this, until his death, the "eyes and ears" of Lee.

"Stonewall" Jackson now came from the Valley with his brave men, and Lee at once began the "Seven Days' Battle." Stuart was "the eyes and ears" of Lee, and Jackson was his "right arm," as you will learn before you get through with this little book.

For seven days the battle went on, and at last the Army of the Potomac, under General McClellan, was forced back to the James river, and Richmond was saved from the foe by the skill of Lee and the valor of his men.

Lee now marched north towards Washington City, and in August, 1862, met the army of General Pope and fought the Second Battle of Manassas. Lee had made a bold plan to put the army of Pope to flight. He sent Stonewall Jackson fifty-six miles around to the rear of Pope, while he (Lee) kept him in check in front.

Jackson's men marched so fast that they were called "foot cavalry." They ate apples and green corn as they marched along, for they had no time to stop. Only one man among them knew where they were going. Little cared they, for Stonewall Jackson led the way.

On the evening of the second day, Jackson, with twenty thousand men, was between Pope and Washington city. Lee was in front of Pope with the rest of the army.

General Jackson fell upon Manassas Junction and took three hundred prisoners and many car-loads of food and clothes. After the men had eaten what food they wanted, they burned the rest and moved away.

Jackson found a good position from which to fight, and when Pope's men came up was ready for them. They fought all day, and when the powder and shot gave out the Southern men fought with stones.

All this time Lee, with most of the men, was coming round to help Jackson. How eagerly Jackson looked for help! He had only twenty thousand men against three times that many. At last Lee came up, and the battle was won (August 30th). Many brave men were killed on both sides, but Lee was the victor. In three months' time he had driven the foe from Richmond, and was now in front of Washington with his army.

He now sent General Jackson to Harper's Ferry, where he took as prisoners twelve thousand men of the North, September 15th. Jackson then hurried back to Lee, who had crossed the Potomac and gone over into Maryland, on September 5, 1862.

At Sharpsburg sometimes called Antietam (Ante'tam), he again met the fresh army of McClellan and fought one of the most bloody battles of the war. Lee had only half as

LAST MEETING OF LEE AND JACKSON.

[53]

many men as McClellan, but when, after the
battle, Lee thought it best to return to Virginia, McClellan did not follow him. Lee
led his army back to Virginia without the
loss of a gun or a wagon, and they rested
near Winchester, Virginia.

General Lee, in his tent near Winchester,
heard of the death of his daughter Annie.
She had been his dearest child, and his grief
at her death was great; but he wrote thus
to Mrs. Lee:

"But God in this, as in all things, has
mingled mercy with the blow by selecting
the one best prepared to go. May you join
me in saying 'His will be done!'"

It was now McClellan's turn to attack
Lee, but he was slow to move—so slow that
Mr. Lincoln sent him word "to cross the
Potomac and give battle to the foe, and
drive him south." But still he did not
move, and Lee, who was also wanting to
move, sent Jeb Stuart over into Maryland to
find out what McClellan was doing. That

gallant man again went around the whole Northern army, and came back safe to Lee, having found out what Lee wished to know.

The Northern army now came back to Virginia and Lee moved to Fredericksburg, a town on the Rappahannock river.

Burnside was now put at the head of the Northern army in the place of General McClellan, whom Mr. Lincoln accused of being too slow.

Lee placed his men on the heights above the river, on the south side, while Burnside's hosts were on Stafford Heights and the plains below.

At daylight on December 13, 1862, the battle began, and was fought bravely by both sides. But Burnside's men had little chance, since Lee's men from above poured the shot and shell so fast that they could not move forward.

The noise of this battle was terrible, as there were three hundred cannon roaring at once.

Cooke, a great writer, tells us that as Burnside's guns were fired directly at the town, the houses were soon on fire and a dense cloud of smoke hung over its roofs and steeples. Soon the red flames leaped up high above the smoke and the people were driven from their homes. Hundreds of women and children were seen wandering along the frozen roads, not knowing where to go.

General Lee stood upon a ridge which is now called "Lee's Hill," and watched this painful scene. For a long time he stood silent, and then, in his deep, grave voice, said these words, which were the most bitter that he was ever known to utter: "These people delight to destroy the weak, and those who can make no defence; it just suits them."

When the day was done, Lee was again victor.

In less than *six months* Lee had fought *four* great battles—all victorious to his arms,

LEE AT FREDERICKSBURG.

except that of Sharpsburg, which was neither a victory nor defeat. The Southern army was now full of hope and courage. At the battle of Fredericksburg, Lee had only sixty thousand men, while Burnside's army numbered over one hundred thousand. In this battle Lee lost five thousand men, while twelve thousand of Burnside's men lay stark and cold upon the bloody field.

Lee grieved over the loss of his brave men, and for the good people of Fredericksburg who had lost their homes by fire during the fight. He now waited day after day for Burnside to attack, but in vain. At length Lee went into winter quarters in a tent at the edge of an old pine field near Fredericksburg, and began to get ready for fight when the spring came. It was at this time that among a number of fowls given to Lee, was a fine hen which began the egg business before her head came off, and Bryan, Lee's servant, saved her for the egg which he found each day in the General's tent. Lee would

leave the door of the tent open for the hen
to go in and out. She roosted and rode in
the wagon, and was an eye-witness of the

GEN. LEE'S HEN.

battle of Chancellorsville. She was also at
the battle of Gettysburg; but when orders
were given to fall back, the hen could not
be found. At last, they saw her perched on
top of the wagon, ready to go back to her
native State.

In 1864, when food began to get scarce

and Bryan was in sore need for something
nice for guests, he killed the good old
hen unknown to her master. At dinner,
General Lee thought it a very fine fowl, not
dreaming that Bryan had killed his pet.

It was now time for Lee to carry out the
will of old Mr. Custis and set free his slaves.
Many of them had been carried off by the
Northern men, but now he wrote out the
deed and set them free by law. He wrote
thus of them to Mrs. Lee:

"They are all entitled to their freedom,
and I wish them to have it. Those that
have been carried away I hope are free and
happy."

He had set free his own slaves years before.

Lee had proved so great a leader that the
people of the South began to look to him
with great love and hope.

During these battles, of which I have told
you, one-half of the Southern men were in
rags, and many were without shoes. Yet
shoeless, hatless, ragged and starving, they

followed Lee and fought his battles. Their pet name for him was "Marse Robert." They knew that their great chief cared for them, and would not send them into danger if he could help it; and it was no fault of his if their food was scant and poor. They learned to love and trust him. "Marse Robert says so," was their battle-cry.

---

Prĕs'ident, the head of a free people.
Mēr'cy, kindness.
Găl'lant, brave ; daring in fight.
Vĭc'tor, one who wins.
Posĭ'tion, place.

Tell about—
    The two governments.
    The first blood shed.
    The first gun fired.
    "Camp Lee."
    Where General Lee was first sent.
    The "On to Richmond."
    Jeb Stuart.    "Stonewall" Jackson.
    The Second Battle of Manassas.
    Sharpsburg.    Fredericksburg.
    The will of Mr. Custis.
    The soldiers' love for Lee.

## CHAPTER V.

### A Confederate General.

(*Continued.*)

WHEN the spring of 1863 came, the two armies were still in sight of each other near Fredericksburg. A new man, General Hooker, sometimes called "Fighting Joe," had been put at the head of the army of the North. Take note that he was the fourth general that President Lincoln had sent forth within a year to conquer Lee.

Lee watched his new foe, and when he had found out his plans was ready for him. He fell back to a place called Chancellorsville, and there, in the midst of a dense forest, the fight took place (May 2, 3).

While the battle was going on, Lee sent Jackson to the rear to cut Hooker off from a ford in the river. Jackson's men moved through the forest so swiftly and with so little noise that they fell upon Hooker's men with a loud yell before he knew they were near. They rushed out like a thunder-bolt and swept down upon the line like a flash of lightning. The foe did not wait, but turned and fled.

It was now nearly dark, and, as Jackson rode forward to view the way, he was shot by his own men, who, in the dim light, thought that he and his aids were a squad of Northern cavalry. He was shot in three places—in his right hand, his left forearm, and again in the same limb near the shoulder. He was placed in a litter and taken from the field. All care was taken of this great and good man, but he died the next Sunday. His last words were:

"Order A. P. Hill to prepare for action. Pass the infantry to the front. Tell Major Hawkes"—he stopped and then said, as if the fight was over, "Let us pass over the river and rest under the trees."

Thus passed away the great Stonewall Jackson, the "right arm of Lee."

For two days after Jackson was wounded, the fight went on and raged with great fury. General Hooker was struck by a piece of wood split off by a cannon ball, and for a time was thought dead.

Lee made bold plans and his brave men carried them out. Stuart, who had taken Stonewall Jackson's command, led his men to battle, singing "Old Joe Hooker, won't you come out of the wilderness."

At last the battle of Chancellorsville was won and Hooker was forced back to his old camp at Fredericksburg.

Chancellorsville was Lee's greatest battle, but its glory was clouded by Jackson's death. General Lee wrote to his wife, May 11, 1863:

"You will see we have to mourn the loss of the good and great Jackson. * * I know not how to replace him, but God's will be done."

In this battle Lee had only fifty-three

GEN. STONEWALL JACKSON

thousand men, one-third as many men as Hooker.

In June, 1863, Lee again crossed the Potomac and met an army under General Meade at Gettysburg, in Pennsylvania.

Lee had two reasons for this move. One was to get food for his men and horses; and the other to draw the Northern army away from its strong forts around Washington city. He gave strict orders to his men not to steal and rob. This is a part of his order:

"The commanding general thinks that no greater disgrace could befall the army, and through it our whole people, than to commit outrages on the innocent and defenceless. * * * It must be remembered that we make war only upon *armed men*."

This order, with its noble Christ-like spirit, will remain the "undying glory of Lee"; for all his property had been taken by the Federals. His wife and daughters were homeless, yet he did not fail to return good for evil.

When Lee started into Maryland, he sent Jeb Stuart on ahead to guard the right flank of his army. By some mishap, he crossed the Potomac too far to the east, and soon found that the whole Federal army was between him and General Lee. By hard fighting and riding he at last joined Lee at Gettysburg, but not until after the fight had begun. Lee was thus without his "eyes and ears," as we have called General Stuart, and could not tell just where the foe was. Neither Lee nor Meade had planned to fight at Gettysburg, but they fell upon each other pretty much like two men groping in the dark.

For the first two days (July 1, 2) Lee's men drove back the enemy. On the third day, at 1 o'clock P. M., Lee began to fight with one hundred and fifty big guns. For two hours the air was alive with shells. Then, out of the woods swept the Confederate battle line, over a mile long, under General Pickett. A thrill of wonder ran along the Federal lines as that grand column of fifteen thousand men marched, with ragged clothes, but bright guns and red battle-flags flying, up the slope of Cemetery Ridge. Down upon them came shot and shell from guns on the heights above and round them.

The line was broken, but on they went. They planted their Confederate flags on the breast-work; they fought hand to hand and killed men at the cannon with the bayonet; but down from the hill rushed tens of thousands of Federals, and many who were not killed were taken prisoners. Few got back to tell the story. That night the stars looked down upon a field of dead and dying men and also upon a sad general. Lee's orders had not been obeyed, and, for the first time, he had been foiled.

Lee afterwards said to a friend, "Had I had Stonewall Jackson at Gettysburg, I would have won a great victory."

He had made a bold plan to attack early in the day; but it was not done, and thus Meade got time to bring up his troops.

Meade did not attack Lee, who rested that night upon the same ground as the night before.

Lee now had but little powder and shot. On the next day, the 4th of July, he started his long trains of wounded and prisoners towards Virginia; and, at the same time, buried his dead. That night, in a storm, the army began its homeward march, and reached the Potomac river to find it too high to cross. Calm and brave, Lee sent his wounded over in boats and got ready for Meade. But Meade was in no mood to attack Lee and came up slowly.

While waiting for the river to fall, Lee heard of the capture of his son Gen. W. H. F. Lee.

On the 13th, Lee's men began to cross the river, and by the next night they were again safe in Virginia.

The men lost at Gettysburg were never replaced, for the South had sent forth all her fighting men and had no more to give.

The rest of the year passed without any great battle. Lee's chief concern was to get food and clothes for his men and to watch Meade, who would not give battle.

About this time the city of Richmond presented to Lee a house. This he kindly but firmly refused to take, and begged that what means the city had to spare might be given to the families of his poor soldiers.

Late in November, General Meade moved towards Lee, who had built strong forts at Mine Run. But Meade found the forts too strong for attack and withdrew during the night.

The next year a new man was sent against Lee—Ulysses S. Grant. Lee had now only sixty-two thousand men to meet Grant, who had *one hundred and twenty-five thousand* men, and a wagon train that reached sixty-five miles.

With this large army, Grant crossed the Rapidan river, and marched on to give Lee battle. Lee did not wait for Grant, but went forward and met his hosts in a place called the Wilderness, which was a vast forest full of underbrush, and with only narrow roads here and there. It was a bad place in which to fight a battle, for no man could see but a few yards around him. Cannon and horsemen were of no use, because they could not move through the tangled bushes.

Grant did not know that Lee's men were so near. But when they rushed into these wilds and boldly began the fight he had to give battle. For two days, May 5th and 6th, 1864, two hundred thousand men in blue and gray fought breast to breast in the thickets. Men fell and died unseen, their bodies lost in the bushes and their death-groans drowned in the roar of battle.

In the midst of these horrors, the woods caught on fire and many of the wounded were burnt alive. Lee, however, pressed forward, and when night closed had taken a portion of the Federal breast-works.

During the fight of the 6th, General Lee

placed himself at the head of some men from Texas to lead the charge. "Hurrah for Texas!" he cried, and ordered the charge. But the soldiers, anxious for their dear general, shouted, "Lee to rear!" A gray-haired soldier seized his bridle, saying, "General Lee, if you do not go back, we will not go forward!" So General Lee reined back his horse and the brave Texans swept on to victory and death.

On the morning of the 7th, Grant made no motion to attack Lee, but that night marched towards Spotsylvania Court-House. Lee at once found out his plans and began a race to reach there first. When the front of Grant's army reached the Court-House the next morning, they found Lee's men behind breast-works and ready for the fight. Lee had gotten between Grant and Richmond! That evening the two great armies were again facing each other on the banks of the Po river. Here they threw up breast-works, which may yet be seen.

For twelve days, Grant made many attacks upon Lee's lines. Early on the morning of the 12th his men made an opening in Lee's lines and poured in by thousands. Lee's men

LEE IN FRONT OF HIS TROOPS.

ran up quickly and soon a most terrible fight took place. The trenches ran with blood and the space was piled with dead bodies, whose lips were black with powder from biting cartridges.

Though Grant held that position, he could not break through the second line. The little army in gray stood as firm as the mountains.

In the fight of which I have just told you, General Lee again rode in front, with hat off, to lead the charge; but General Gordon dashed up and said:

"These are Virginians and Georgians who have never failed. Go to the rear, General Lee."

Then he said to the men:

"Must General Lee lead this charge?"

"No! No!" they cried; "we will drive them back if General Lee will go to the rear."

They rushed off and once more hurled back the Federal troops.

Grant now sent his cavalry general, Sheridan, on a raid near Richmond. A fierce battle was fought at Yellow Tavern, in which the famous Jeb Stuart was wounded so that he died the next day.   Alas for Lee! Jackson and Stuart were both gone.

Grant again moved to the rear, and Lee next moved to the North Anna river.   While Grant was again trying to flank, Lee got to the old works at Cold Harbor.   Grant made an attack at daylight.   His troops, sinking into a swamp, were killed by thousands, while Lee lost but few men.

A second assault was ordered, but the men would not move forward.   About thirteen thousand of their comrades had been killed in less than half an hour, and they could no longer stand the awful fire.

We are told by General Fitzhugh Lee that Lee's men were hungry and mad.   One cracker to a man, with no meat, was a luxury.   One poor fellow, who had his cracker shot out of his hand before he could eat it, said: "The next time I'll put my cracker in a safe place down by the breastworks where it won't get wounded, poor thing!"

Lee again stood in Grant's way to Richmond. In the battles from the Wilderness to Cold Harbor, Grant had lost sixty thousand men, while Lee's loss was eighteen thousand.

Just before the battle of Cold Harbor, Grant had looked for Sigel to move up the Valley and fall upon Lee's rear. But Sigel was met at New Market on May 15th by Breckenridge with five thousand troops, among which was a band of cadets from the Virginia Military Institute at Lexington. These boys fought like heroes, fifty of them being killed and wounded. Sigel was sent running back down the Valley, and Breckenridge then marched to the help of Lee.

Grant then, on the night of June 12th, began to move his army south of the James river to march towards Petersburg, a city about twenty-one miles south of Richmond.

The famous General Beauregard (Bo′regard) was at Petersburg with only about two thousand men, as he had sent the most of his troops to the north side of the James river to the help of Lee.

Against these, on the 15th, General Grant sent eighteen thousand men.

Beauregard held these men in check until Lee sent troops to aid him. Lee then came up with the main army, and Grant, having lost ten thousand men, now began to make trenches and build forts to protect his men, as he was going to lay siege to Petersburg, the key to Richmond.

Lee had to defend both Richmond and Petersburg with lines thirty-five miles long, against Grant's army, which was twice as large as his own. In fact, Grant had all the men that he asked for; while Lee's ranks were thin and food was scarce. A fourth of a pound of meat and one pound of flour was all that each soldier had for one day.

In this stress, it is said that Lee thought it best to give up Richmond and march south to join the army there. I do not know the truth of that statement. At any rate, he did not go, but went to work to make his lines stronger and to get in food for his men. One of his great cares was to keep Grant from getting hold of the railroads which brought food from the South and other parts of the country.

Just here, it will be well to give you some of the war prices at that time. Flour brought, in Confederate money, two hundred and fifty dollars per barrel; meal, fifty dollars; corn, forty; and oats, twenty-five dollars per bushel. Brown sugar cost ten dollars per pound; coffee, twelve dollars; tea, thirty-five dollars; and they were scarce and hard to get. Woolen goods were scarce; calico cost thirty dollars per yard, and lead pencils one dollar a-piece. Women wore dresses that were made of cloth spun, woven and dyed by their own hands. Large thorns were used for pins and hair-pins, and shoes were made with wooden soles. Hats were made by girls out of wheat straw, plaited into a braid and then sewed into shape.

Those were indeed hard times; but in spite of want and care, the spirits and courage of the Southern people did not flag.  All food that could be spared was sent to Richmond, and every one hoped for the best.

Time after time Grant's men made attacks upon Lee's works, but were always sent back faster than they came, by his watchful men.

The shells from Grant's big guns fell into the city of Petersburg day after day, bursting into the churches and houses, and making the people flee for their lives.

One day, as General Lee was sitting on a chair under a tree at his headquarters, the "Clay House," the balls fell so thick about him that his aids begged him to seek a safer place.  He at last mounted his horse and rode away.  A moment after, a gay young soldier sat down in the chair and tilted it back, saying, "I'll see if I can fill Lee's place for awhile."  Just then a ball struck the front round of the chair and cut it in twain. If Lee had been there, with the chair upon the ground, he would have been badly hurt. All thanked God that he was safe.

On June 22d, the Confederates under General Mahone made a sally from their lines and gave the Federals a great surprise. As the Southern shot and shell burst upon them, they fled back into their lines and the Confederates brought off two thousand prisoners, four cannon and eight flags.

On the same day, there was a fight at Reams' Station, in which the Federals were put to flight and lost twelve guns and one thousand men.

All this time, Grant was making earthworks and forts, and at last carried out a very cruel plan. From a spot out of sight, he had a mine dug until it reached under one of the Confederate forts. In that hole he had caused to be placed a blast of eight thousand pounds of powder. His plan was to blow a hole in Lee's lines and then rush in with a large band of men and take the city.

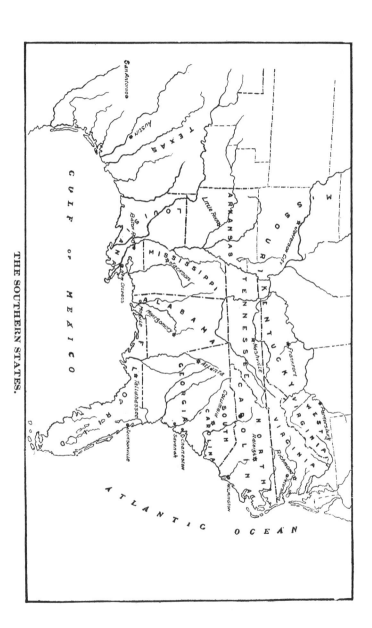

THE SOUTHERN STATES.

General Lee found out that they were digging the mine and where it was, and had a
strong line made in the rear, while big guns
were placed so as to fire across the breach
when the mine was sprung.

At that time there were only thirteen
thousand men in the trenches at Petersburg,
as General Lee had been forced to send some
of his troops to the north of the James to
check a move which Grant had made on
purpose to draw off Lee's men from the mine.

Just at dawn, July 30th, the blast was
fired. A great roar was heard, and then
two hundred and fifty-six men from South
Carolina and twenty-two from Petersburg,
with guns, large masses of earth, stones and
logs, were thrown high into the air. A
breach one hundred and thirty-five feet long,
ninety feet wide, and thirty feet deep, had
been made in the Confederate lines. Those
near the spot were at first stunned, and
those far away could not think what the
noise meant.

Grant's guns fired at once all along the line, and a band of men marched out to rush in through the breach. When they had rushed across the space to the gap, they found a deep pit at their feet.

EXPLOSION OF THE CRATER.

The Confederates had now gained their wits, and at once opened fire. The storm of shot and shell forced the Federals down into the pit for shelter; but when there, they could not get out. Band after band of Federals were sent forward to charge the works, but they either fell into the Crater or ran back to their own lines.

Two hours had now passed, when black troops were sent to seize the guns which were doing such deadly work. They marched bravely up, but the Confederate fire was too hot for them and they ran for their lives— some into the Crater, and some back to their own lines. White troops were again sent forward, but they, too, were driven back. All this time the Crater was full of wounded, struggling and dying men, upon whom the hot sun beat and shot poured down.

Soon General Lee rode up, and by his orders, General Mahone, with Weisiger's and Wright's brigades, came up and charged with a yell upon the Federals who had for the first time reached the breast-works. There was a fierce hand-to-hand fight, but the Federals were quickly forced back.

All honor is due to the few men who had so bravely held the breach until help came.

Just at this time a white flag was seen to

float above the side of the Crater, which told
that some were alive down there and ready
to give up.

In this strange fight Grant lost about four
*thousand* men and Lee about four *hundred.*

The pluck and skill of Lee and a few men
had foiled a well-laid plan and showed what
these brave heroes could do after years of toil
and battle.

Lee now thought that if he would again
send troops to threaten Washington, he
might cause Grant to move some of his
large army there, and thus give him (Lee) a
chance to hurl back the hosts of Grant from
Richmond. So he sent General Early down
the Valley into Maryland with only ten thousand men.

They went as fast as they could, and on
July 9th met, at Monocacy Bridge, General
Lew Wallace with seven thousand men.
Having whipped him and taken from him
two thousand men, Early marched on to
Washington.

On the 10th, his troops marched thirty miles, and on the 11th were in front of Washington. But his force was too small and too much worn out to try to attack the city. He coolly camped in front of it all day, and at night after a fight with some Federal troops sent to catch him, went back into Virginia.

This raid of Early's did not move Grant. He left Mr. Lincoln to take care of Washington and kept the most of his men massed in front of Lee's lines.

It was about this time that the Federal General Sheridan passed up the Valley and burned two thousand barns filled with wheat and hay, and seventy mills filled with flour. He also drove off and killed four thousand head of stock. The boast was that ''if a crow wants to fly down the Valley he must carry his food along.''

This was a part of the plan to crush and starve Lee, for a great part of his flour and meat was sent from the Valley.

After many trials, on August 18th Grant at last got hold of the Weldon railroad, which brought supplies from the south. This was a great blow to Lee.

In the fall of this year, when meat was scarce, General Wade Hampton sent a note to General Lee, telling him that there was a large drove of beeves in the rear of Grant's army and asked leave to take a force of horsemen and drive out the cattle. General Lee at last told him to go, but urged him to take great care not to be caught.

The men were well on their way when day broke, and rode on until dark, when they came to a halt in a road overhung by the branches of trees. Here they slept, men and horses, till just at dawn they sprang to their saddles, and with the well-known yell dashed into the camp of the foe. The Federals made a good fight for their meat; but at last fell back, and the Confederates captured and drove out more than two thousand beeves. These they brought safe into camp after having two fights and riding one hundred miles.

This fresh meat was a great treat to Lee's men and the cause of much fun.

Lee's lines were so close to Grant's at one point that the men would often call over to each other. The Federals called the Confederates Johnny Rebs, while the Con-

JOHNNY REB AND BILLY YANK.

federate name for the Federals was Billy Yanks. On the day after the beef raid, one of Grant's men called out:

"I say, Johnny Reb, come over. I've got a new blue suit for you."

"Blue suit?" growled out Johnny.

"Yes," said the other, "take off those

greasy butternut clothes.    I would, if I were you.''

''Never you mind the *grease*, Billy Yank,'' drawled out the Confederate, ''I got *that out'n them beeves 'o yourn.*''

Pop! went the Federal's gun, and the Confederate was not slow to pop back at him.

General Lee's life was now full of care; as soon as one attack on his lines was over, another was begun.    He lived in a tent and would go down to the trenches himself to see how his men were getting on.

An old soldier relates that one day he came into the trenches when the firing was quite rapid.    The men did not dare to cheer, lest they might bring a hotter fire from the foe, but they crowded around him and begged him to go back.    But he calmly asked after their health and spoke words of cheer.    Then he walked to a big gun and asked the lieutenant to fire, so that he might see its range and work.    The officer said, with tears in his eyes, ''General, don't order me to fire this gun while you are here. They will open fire over there with all those big guns and you will surely get hurt. Go back out of range and I'll fire all day." General Lee was greatly touched by this, and went back, while the men quickly fired off the huge gun.

Lee needed not only men, but food for those he had. Many men died from cold and want.

The winter of 1864 and '65 was a sad one for Lee and the South. There were no more men in the South to take the place of those who had been killed.

The corn and wheat of the South had been burnt and the cattle killed by the Northern armies. The people sat down to empty tables and had no more food to send their men.

Mrs. Lee, in her sick chair in Richmond, "with large heart and small means" knit socks, which she would send at once to the bare-footed men.

On January 10, 1865, General Lee writes to Mrs. Lee:

"Yesterday three little girls walked into my room, each with a small basket. The eldest had some fresh eggs, the second some pickles, and the third some pop-corn, which had grown in her garden.   *   *   They had with them a young maid with a block of soap made by her mother. They were the daughters of a Mrs. Nottingham, a refugee from Northampton county.   *   *   I had not had so nice a visit for a long time. I was able to fill their baskets with apples, and begged them to bring me hereafter nothing but kisses, and to keep the eggs, corn, etc., for themselves."

Lee's men were ragged and starving, but they fought on till April 1st, 1865, when, at Five Forks, the left wing of Grant's large army swept around the right and rear of Lee, and made him give up Richmond and Petersburg.

When the Southern troops were leaving

Richmond, by law of Congress the tobacco houses were set on fire to keep them from falling into the hands of the foe. The fire spread, and Mrs. Lee's house was in danger of being burnt. Friends came in and wished to move her to a place of safety, but she was loath to go. The fire had no terror for her as she thought of her husband with his band of ragged, starving men marching with their "faces turned from Richmond." White clouds of dense smoke, with the light of fire in their folds, hung above the city as the Federal army, with waving flags and clashing music, marched in and stacked arms in the Capitol Square.

In the meantime, Lee marched on towards Amelia Court-House, where he had ordered meat and bread to be sent for his men. But when he got there he found that it had been sent elsewhere, and now real want set in. His men had nothing to eat but corn, which they would parch at night and eat as they marched along. General Lee's plan had

been to march south and join General Johnston, but some time had been lost in looking
for food, and General Grant's hosts were near
at hand.

So Lee fell back towards Lynchburg, but
on April 9th, 1865, being entirely surrounded
by Grant's vast army, he and his few ragged
men surrendered to General Grant at Appomattox Court-House. Lee had only *eight
thousand* men, while Grant's army numbered
about *two hundred thousand.*

In all these battles, of which I have told
you, General Lee had never been really defeated; but he gave up at last because he
had no more men and no more food. The
Northern generals had all the men and food
they asked for, as they had the world to
draw from; but the South, being blockaded,
or shut in by Northern ships of war, could
not get what she needed from other lands.

Lee did all that courage and genius could
do against such odds, and was, without doubt,
the greatest commander of his time.

Colonel Venable, an officer on General Lee's staff, tells this story of the surrender: "When I told General Lee that the troops in front were not able to fight their way out, he said 'Then, there is nothing left me but to go and see General Grant, and I would rather *die a thousand deaths.'*"

Another officer says that when Lee was thinking of the surrender he exclaimed, "How easily I could get rid of all this and be at rest! I have only to ride along the lines and all will be over. But," he added quickly, "*it is our duty to live,* for what will become of the *women* and *children* of the South if we are not here to support and protect them?"

So, with a heart bursting with grief, he once more did his *duty*. He went at once to General Grant and surrendered himself and his few remaining men.

By the terms of the surrender, Lee's men gave up their fire-arms, but all who had horses took them home, "to work their little farms."

General Grant, it must be said, was most kind to General Lee and his men. He did not ask for General Lee's sword, nor did Lee offer it to him; neither did he require Lee's men to march up to stack their guns between ranks of Federals with flags flying and bands playing. Lee's men simply went to places which were pointed out and stacked their guns. Their officers then signed a parole not to fight again against the *United States.* They were then free to go back to their homes, which, in some cases, were burnt— blight and want being on every side.

After all, Grant did not go to Lee's camp or to Richmond to exult over the men who had so often met him in battle; but he mounted his horse, and, with his staff, rode to Washington. Before going, he sent to Lee twenty-five thousand rations; for, as I have told you, Lee's men had nothing to eat but parched corn.

After the surrender, Lee rode out among his men, who pressed up to him, eager to "touch his person, or even his horse," and tears fell down the powder-stained cheeks of the strong men.   Slowly he said:

"Men, we have fought the war together;

LEE LEAVING APPOMATTOX C. H.

I have done my best for you; my heart is too full to say more."

"And then in silence, with lifted hat, he rode through the weeping army towards his home in Richmond."

As General Lee rode on towards Richmond he was calm, and his thoughts dwelt much more on the state of the poor people at whose houses he stopped than upon his own bad fortune. When he found that all along the road the people were glad to see him and gave him gladly of what they had to eat, he said, "These good people are kind— too kind. They do too much—more than they are able to do—for us."

At a house which he reached just at night, a poor woman gave him a nice bed; but, with a kind shake of the head, he spread his blanket and slept upon the floor.

The next day he stopped at the house of his brother, Charles Carter Lee; but, when night came, left the house and slept in his old black wagon. He could not give up at once the habits of a soldier.

When, at last, the city of Richmond was in sight, he rode ahead with a few of his officers. A sad sight met his view. In the great fire of the 3d of April, a large part of the city had been burned, and, as he rode up Main street, he saw only masses of black ruins.

As he rode slowly, some of the people saw him, and at once the news flashed through the streets that General Lee had come.

The people ran to greet him, and showed by cheers and the waving of hats and hand-kerchiefs how much they loved him.

General Lee now went home and there again took up his duty. He had fought for the South, which had failed to gain the victory. He thought that it was now the duty of every good man to avoid hate and malice and do all that he could to build up the waste places of his dear land. He had been a soldier for forty years, and, for the first time since manhood, was in private life.

He now enjoyed the company of his wife and children, and as long as he kept his parole and the laws in force where he lived, was thought to be safe. There were, how-ever, steps taken to try him for treason; but General Grant went to the President and told him that his honor was pledged for the safety of General Lee, and that he wished him to be let alone. So, General Grant's request was granted and no trial took place.

After some months the Lee family left Richmond and went to live at the house of a friend in Powhatan county.

The spring and summer of 1865 was spent by our hero in taking the rest which he so much needed.

---

Rĕf'ugee', one who leaves home for safety.
Siēġe, the act of besetting a fortified place.
Hûrled, thrown.
Gēnius, a great mind.
Surrĕn'der, the act of yielding to another.

What do you remember about—
    Chancellorsvïlle?
    The death of General Jackson?
    Gettysburg?
    The Wilderness?
    "Lee to the rear?"
    Cold Harbor?
    The siege of Richmond and Petersburg?
    The surrender?
    General Grant's kindness?

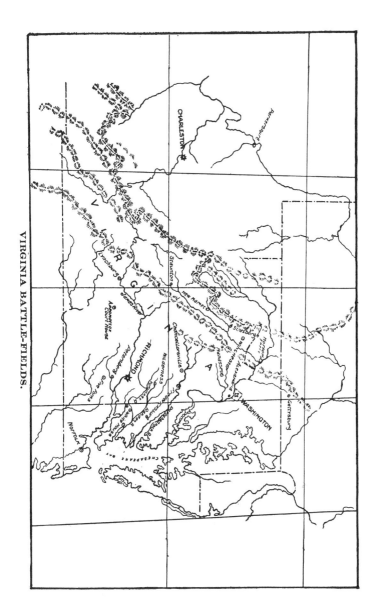

VIRGINIA BATTLE-FIELDS.

# CHAPTER VI.

## A College President.

In October, 1865, General Lee became President of Washington College, in Lexington, Virginia. Many other places of trust were offered him, but he chose to lead the young men of the South in the paths of peace and learning, as he had so nobly done in times of war.

General Lee rode on his war-horse, Traveler, from Powhatan county to Lexington in four days. As he drew rein in front of the village inn, an old soldier knew him, gave the military salute, and, placing one hand upon the bridle and the other upon the stirrup, stood and waited for him to dismount.

On October 2d, 1865, General Lee took the oath of office, before William White, Esq., justice of the peace. The General stood, dressed in a plain suit of gray, his arms folded, and his eyes calmly fixed upon Judge Brockenbrough, as he read the oath of office.

The great chief was now changed into a college president. "I have," said he, "a task which I cannot forsake." That task was not easy, for the college had lost much during the war and now had to be built up in every way.

**WASHINGTON & LEE UNIVERSITY AND COLLEGE CHAPEL.**

He went to work with great skill and energy, and soon all felt that a great man was leading them.

Some one has aptly said, "Suns seem larger when they set;" so it was with Lee. At this time of his life he appears nobler and grander than ever before. In his quiet study, away from the noise of the world, he gave his time and talents to the young men of his dear South. His earnest wish was to make Washington College a great seat of learning, and for this he worked and made wise plans.

In March, 1866, he went to Washington city to appear as a witness before the committee which was inquiring into the state of things in the South. This was his first visit to any of the cities since the war, and it caused much comment.

General Fitz. Lee tells us that the day after his return, he proposed a walk with one of his daughters, who said, in fun, that she did not admire the new hat which he was about to put on. "You do not like my hat?" said he; "why, there were a thousand people in Washington the other day admiring this hat." This was the only time that he spoke of the crowds of people who sought him while in that city.

When his nephew, General Fitz. Lee,

wrote to know what he thought of having the Southern dead moved from the field of Gettysburg, he said, "I am not in favor of moving the ashes of the dead unless for a worthy object, and I know of no fitter resting-place for a soldier than the field on which he so nobly laid down his life."

It is sometimes asked if General Lee was content in the quiet of his home at Lexington. This is what he wrote to a friend:

"For my own part, I much enjoy the charms of civil life, and find, too late, that I have wasted the best years of my life."

In his life as College President, duty was, as ever, his watchword. He knew each student by name, and just how well he studied.

Once, when asked how a certain young man was getting along, he said: "He is a very quiet and orderly young man, but *he seems very careful not to injure the health of his father's son.* Now, I do not want our young men to injure their health, but I want them to come as near it as possible."

One of his friends relates that, even amidst this busy life at college, he found time to be the most polite gentleman in town. "How often have I seen him," says this friend, "in the stores and shops of Lexington, talking pleasantly with each new comer; or, walking a mile through mud and snow to call on some humble family, who will hand it down as an event in their lives that they had a visit from General Lee!"

Seeing, during the first year, that the college chapel was not large enough, he at once began to plan for a new one. He chose the site for it in front of the other houses, so that it might be in full view. He then had the plan drawn under his own eye, and did not rest until it was finished and opened for the service of God.

In this chapel his body now rests, as I shall tell you hereafter.

Early in 1870, in the midst of these labors, his health began to fail. There was a flush upon his cheek, and an air of weari-

ness about him which alarmed his friends.
Rheumatism of the heart and other parts of
the body had set in, and in March, 1870, he
went south ''to look upon other scenes and
enjoy the breezes in the 'land of sun and
flowers.'"    His daughter Agnes went with
him.

On this trip he once more went to see his
father's grave, on an island off the coast
of Georgia, where, you remember, General
Henry Lee was taken when so ill on board
ship, and where he died.   They placed fresh
flowers upon the grave, which they found in
good order, though the house had been burnt
and the island laid waste.

His health seemed better when again at
home; but soon his step was slower, and the
flush upon his cheek began to deepen.    '' A
noble life was drawing to a close.''

On the morning of October 12, 1870, the
news flashed over the wires that General
Lee was dead.   He had taken cold at a vestry meeting.   The church was cold and

**GRAVE OF LEE'S FATHER.**

damp, and a storm was raging outside. He grew chilly, and when he reached home was unable to speak.

Mrs. Lee wrote thus of his last hours:

"My husband came in while we were at tea, and I asked where he had been, as we had waited some time for him. He did not reply, but stood up as if to say grace. No words came from his lips, but with a sad smile he sat down in his chair."

He could not speak! A bed was at once brought to the dining-room, and the doctors sent for. At first he grew better, but soon a change came for the worse.

He rarely spoke except when sleeping, and then his thoughts were with his much-loved soldiers on the "dreadful battle-fields." Among his last words were, "Tell Hill he must come up."

Once when General Custis Lee said something about his getting well, he shook his head and pointed upward. When his doctor said, to cheer him, "How do you feel to-day, General?" General Lee said slowly, "I feel better."

The doctor then said:

"You must make haste and get well. Traveler has been standing so long in the stable that he needs exercise."

The General made no reply, but shook his head and closed his eyes. Once or twice he put aside his medicine, saying, "It is no use."

On October 10th, about midnight, he was seized with a chill and his pulse became feeble and rapid. The next day he was seen to be sinking. He knew those around him, but was not able to speak. Soon after nine o'clock on the morning of the 12th, he closed his eyes on earthly things and his pure soul took its flight to God.

It was thought that the strain and hardships of war, with sorrow for the "Lost Cause" and the griefs of his friends, had caused his death. Yet, to those who saw his calmness in all the trials of life, it did not seem true that his great soul had been worn away by them.

The college chapel was chosen by Mrs. Lee as a burial place for her husband, and one-and-a-half o'clock P. M. on the 13th of October was the time fixed on for moving the remains to the chapel, where they were to lie in state until Saturday, the 15th of October, the day for the burial.

At the hour named, a long procession, with Professor J. J. White as chief marshal, was formed. Old soldiers formed an escort of honor. Just after the escort came the hearse, preceded by the clergy and twelve pall-bearers. In rear of the hearse, Traveler, the iron-gray war-horse of General Lee, was led by two old soldiers. Then followed a long line of students, cadets and people.

The body was borne to the college chapel and laid in state upon the dais, the people passing slowly by, that each one might look upon the face of the dead. The body was clad in a simple suit of black and lay in a coffin, strewed by loving hands with rare, pale flowers. The chapel was then placed in charge of the guard of honor. This guard of students kept watch by the coffin day and night.

On the 14th, a funeral service was held in the chapel; and on the 15th of October, as I have said, the body was borne to the tomb. The flag of Virginia hung at half-mast above the college and a deep gloom rested upon all.

As the procession moved off, the bells of the town began to toll, and the Virginia Military Institute battery fired minute-guns. All was simple and without display. Not a flag was to be seen along the line. The Rev. J. William Jones tells us as follows:

"The old soldiers wore their citizen's dress, with black ribbon in the lapel of their coats; and Traveler, with trappings of mourning on his saddle, was again led by two old soldiers. The Virginia Military Institute was very beautifully draped, and from its turrets hung at half-mast, and draped in mourning, the flags of all the States of the late Southern Confederacy.

"When the procession reached the Institute, it passed the corps of cadets drawn up in line, and a guard of honor presented arms as the hearse went by. When it reached the chapel, where a large throng had gathered, the students and cadets, about six hundred and fifty strong, marched into the left door and aisle past the remains and out by the right aisle and door to their proper place.

"The rest of the line then filed in, the family, with Drs. Barton and Madison, and Colonels W. H. Taylor and C. S. Venable, members of General Lee's staff during the war, were seated just in front of the pulpit, and the clergy and the Faculties of the College and Institute had places on the platform.

"The coffin was again covered with flowers and evergreens.

"Then the Rev. Dr. Pendleton, the dear friend of General Lee, his Chief of Artillery during the war, and his rector the past five years, read the beautiful burial service of the Episcopal Church. There was no sermon, and nothing said besides the simple service, as General Lee had wished.

"When the body had been placed in the vault, the chaplain read the concluding service from the bank on the southern side of the chapel, and then the grand old hymn,

'How firm a foundation, ye saints of the Lord,' was sung by the people.

"The vault is of brick and just reaches the floor of the library. Upon the white marble are these words:

> "'ROBERT EDWARD LEE,
> Born January 19, 1807;
> Died October 12, 1870.'"

The white marble top has now been replaced by the beautiful recumbent statue by Valentine, a Virginia sculptor.

All the South mourned for Lee. Bells were tolled in cities and villages, and meetings were held to express the grief of the people.

RECUMBENT STATUE OF LEE.

This is what a little girl wrote to Mrs. Lee:

"I have heard of General Lee, your husband, and of all his great and noble deeds during the war. I have also heard lately of his death. I have read in the papers that collections are being made for the Lee monument.  I have asked my mother to let me send some money that I earned myself.  I made some of the money by keeping the door shut last winter, and the rest I made by digging up grass in the garden.  I send you all I have.  I wish it was more.  I am nine now.

"Respectfully,

"MAGGIE MCINTYRE."

Many noble men and women also wrote to Mrs. Lee, and money was given, until now there are two beautiful statues of General Lee—one in Lexington, where he is buried, and the other in Richmond, the city he fought so hard to save.

Virginia mourned for her noble son.  The State Legislature passed a bill making January 19th, the birthday of Robert E. Lee, a legal holiday.

On that day, all over the South, meetings are held in memory of him, speeches are made by great men, and children recite poems which honor his name and deeds.

Perhaps no man has ever lived, so great, so good, so unselfish as Lee. Duty was the key-note of his life. In the midst of his greatness he was humble, simple and gentle. He loved little children wherever he met them.

"One day, during the war, a number of little girls were rolling hoops on the side-walks in Richmond, when General Lee came riding towards them. They stopped playing to gaze at so great a man. To their surprise, he threw his rein to his courier, dismounted, and kissed every one of them. Then mounting, he rode away, with a sunny smile of childhood in his heart and plans of great battles in his mind."

" While in Petersburg, in the winter of 1864, he went to preaching one day at a crowded church, and saw a little girl, dressed in faded garments, standing just inside the door and looking for a seat. 'Come with me, my little lady,' said the great soldier, 'and you shall sit by me.' Thus the great chief and poor child sat side by side."

Once when riding in the mountains with one of his daughters, they came upon a group of children who ran at the sight of him. General Lee called them back and asked:

"Why are you running away? Are you afraid of me?"

"Oh! no, sir; but we are not dressed nice enough to see you."

"Why, who do you think I am?"

"You are General Lee. We know you by your picture."

So great was the love of the people for Lee that, after the war, almost every home had some picture of the great chief.

General Lee knew all the children in Lexington whom he met in his walks and rides, and it was charming to see their joy when he would meet them.

Once, when calling upon the widow of

General A. P. Hill, her little girl met him at the door and held out her puppy which she had named after our hero. "O, General Lee," she cried, "here is 'Bobby Lee'; do kiss him." The great man made believe to kiss him and the child was delighted.

In one of the Sunday-schools of Lexington a prize was offered to the child who should bring in the most pupils.

A little boy of five went for his friend, General Lee, to get him to go to his school. When told that General Lee went to another school, he said with a deep sigh, "I am very sorry. I wish he could go to our school, and be my new scholar."

General Lee thought it quite funny, and said kindly;

"Ah! C——, we must all try to be *good Christians*—that is the great thing. I can't go to your school to be your new scholar to-day. But I am very glad you asked me. It shows that you are zealous in a good cause, and I hope that you will ever be so as you grow up. And I do not want you to think that I am too old to go to Sunday-school. No one is ever too old to study the truths of the Bible."

When he died, all the schools of Lexington were closed, and the children wept with the grown people when they heard that their kind friend was dead.

A gentleman tells this story, which is quite in keeping with General Lee's way of pleasing children :—

"When my little girl, about four years old, heard of General Lee's death, she said to me, 'Father, I can never forget General Lee. I asked, 'Why?' 'Because, when Maggie and I were playing at the gate the other day, and General Lee was riding by, he stopped and took off his hat and bowed to us and said, 'Young ladies, don't you think this is the prettiest horse you ever saw?' And we said it was a very pretty horse. 'Oh, no,' he said; 'I want to know whether Traveler is not the very prettiest

[118]

horse you ever saw in your life.' And when we looked at him, and saw how white and gay he was, we said, 'Yes.' Then he laughed and said, 'Well, if you think he is so pretty, I will just let you kiss him'; and then he rode off smiling, and I don't believe I can ever forget that."

Another gentleman, who was clerk of the faculty at Washington College, says that General Lee was very careful about little things. One day the clerk wrote a letter to some one at General Lee's request, in which he used the term "our students." When General Lee looked at it, he said that he did not like the phrase "our students." He said that we had no property rights in the young men, and he thought it best to say, "*the* students," not "*our* students." The clerk struck out with his pen the word "our" and wrote "the." He then brought the letter to General Lee. "This will not answer," said he. "I want you to write the letter over." So the clerk had to make a fresh copy.

One day General Lee directed him to go to the Mess Hall and measure for a stove-pipe. "Set the stove in its place on its legs," he said, "and measure the height to a point opposite the flue-hole, and then the space from the joint to the wall." The man returned with the measure. "Did you set the stove on its legs?" asked the General. The clerk replied no; that the legs were packed up inside the stove, and that he simply allowed for the legs. "But I told you to put the stove on its legs and then measure. Go back and do as you were told," said the General, who was always kind but meant to be obeyed.

The same gentleman remembers this amusing incident:—

One day they saw a gentleman coming up the lawn, and wondered who he was. General Lee shook hands with him as though he knew him, and chatted for some time. He tried in vain to remember his name. In the meantime Rev. J. William Jones, whose month it was to lead the services in the chapel, came up and whispered to General Lee to introduce the strange clergyman to him, so that he might ask him to conduct the services in his place. But General Lee, with his own ready tact, said: "Mr. Jones, it is time for service; you had better go in the chapel."

After service, when he could do so without being heard, General Lee asked Mr. Jones to find out the stranger's name. He had met him in the Mexican war but could not recall his name. Mr. Jones did so, and General Lee, standing near, heard it, and then, without making it known that he had forgotten his friend of the Mexican war, introduced him to those who were near. He could not think of hurting the clergyman's feelings by letting him know that he had been forgotten.

General Lee was always careful not to injure what belonged to others.

"A Southern Girl" tells this story of him:

"When in Maryland, he gave strict orders that no harm should be done to property, and was once seen to get down from his horse and put up a fence-rail that his men had thrown down."

This story of General Lee went the rounds of the Southern newspapers in 1864:—

"On the train to Petersburg, one very cold morning, a young soldier, with his arm in a sling, was making great efforts to put on his overcoat. In the midst of his trouble, an officer rose from his seat, went to him and kindly helped him, drawing the coat gently over the wounded arm, and then with a few kind words went back to his seat.

"Now, the officer was not clad in a fine uniform with a gilt wreath on his collar and many straps on his sleeves, but he had on a plain suit of gray, with only the three gilt stars which every Confederate colonel could wear. And yet, he was no other than our chief general, Robert E. Lee, who is not braver than he is good and modest."

In the winter of 1864, some of the cavalry were moved to Charlottesville, in order to get food for their horses, and not having much to do, the officers began to attend dances. General Lee, hearing of this, wrote to his son Robert thus:—

"I am afraid that Fitz was anxious to get back to the ball. This is a bad time for such things. * * There are too many Lees on the committee. I like them all to be at battles, but I can excuse them at balls."

It is said that during the seven days' battle, of which I have told you, he was sitting under a tree, the shades of evening hiding even the stars on his coat collar, when a doctor rode up and said:

"Old man, I have chosen that tree for my field hospital and I want you to get out of the way."

"I will gladly give way when the wounded

come up, but in the meantime there is plenty
of room for both of us," was the reply.

The angry man was about to make some
retort when a staff officer rode up and spoke
to his "old man" as General Lee.

The doctor then began to make excuse for
his rudeness, but General Lee said quietly:

"It is no matter, Doctor; there is plenty
of room till your wounded come up."

This story is often told of him: In 1864,
when General Lee was on the lines below
Richmond, many soldiers came near him
and thus brought to them the fire of the foe.
He said to the soldiers: "Men, you had better go into the back-yard; they are firing up
here and you might get hurt."

The men obeyed, but saw their dear General walk across the yard and pick up some
object and place it in a tree over his head.
They found out that the object he had risked
his life for was only a little bird which had
fallen out of its nest. God had given the
stern chief a heart so tender that he could

pause amid a rain of shot and shell to care for a tiny fallen birdling.

General Lee dearly loved his horses. Once, when at the springs, he wrote to his clerk in Lexington and sent this message to his horse, Traveler: "Tell him I miss him dreadfully."

Traveler lived only two years after the death of his master. In the summer of 1872, when he was fifteen years old, the fine, faithful animal, that had carried the General through the storms of war and the calm of his latter years, died of lock-jaw in Lexington. He was noted for his springy walk, high spirit, and great strength. When a colt, he was called Jeff. Davis. The General changed his name to Traveler. He was his most famous war-horse.

In the summer of 1862, General Lee owned a beautiful war-horse called Richmond, given to him by some friends in the city of Richmond. But, to the grief of his master, this pet was short-lived; and what he writes after his loss, sounds almost as if he were looking back to the death of a friend:

"His labors are over, and he is at rest. He carried me very faithfully, and I shall never have so beautiful an animal again."

General Lee was noted for his want of hatred towards any one. He called the Northern soldiers "those people." Once, in the midst of a fierce battle, he said to his son Robert, who was bravely working at a big gun, "That's right, my son; drive those people back." When told of Jackson's fatal wound, his eye flashed fire and his face flushed as he thought of his great loss; but he quietly said:

"General Jackson's plans shall be carried out. Those people *shall be* driven back *to-day.*"

The Rev. J. William Jones says—that one day after the war, as he went up the street, he saw General Lee standing talking to a poor man. As the man walked away he said to him: "That is one of the old soldiers, and added, 'he fought on the other side; but we must not think of that.'"

After the war, when at the springs, a lady friend pointed to a man near by and said to General Lee, "That is General ——, of the Federal Army. He is having quite a dull time. He is here with his daughters, but we do not care to have anything to do with them."

"I am glad that you told me," said General Lee; "I will see at once that they have a better time."

After that he took pains to make friends with "those people," and so set the fashion for others. General —— and his daughters were soon having "a better time."

General Lee was more than brave and tender; he was meek, yet with a heart big enough to love every one of his soldiers, and great enough to plan long marches and glorious battles.

After the battle of Gettysburg, one of his officers rode up and told him that his men were for the most part killed or wounded. Lee shook hands with him and said: "All this has been my fault. It is *I* who have lost this fight, and you must help me out as best you can."

PICKETT'S RETURN AFTER THE BATTLE OF GETTYSBURG.

Not once did Lee cast the blame where it belonged, but rode among his men with such words of cheer as these: "All this will come right in the end." "We want all good and true men just now." "All good men must rally." In this way he closed up his broken lines, and showed such a brave front that Meade did not deem it well to renew the fight.

Once, when some friends were at his house in Richmond, the Rev. Dr. —— spoke in sharp terms of the way in which the North had acted. General Lee said, "Well! it matters little what they may do to me; I am old, and have but a short time to live at best."

When Dr. —— got up to go home, General Lee went with him to the door and said to him, "Doctor, there is a good book which I read, and which you preach from, which says, 'Love your enemies, bless them that curse you, do good to them that hate you.' Do you think your speech just now quite in that spirit?"

When Dr. —— made some excuse, General Lee said: "I fought the people of the North because I believed that they were seeking to wrest from the South her rights. * * * I have never seen the day when I did not pray for them."

One day during the war, as they were looking at the hosts of the foe, one of his generals said, "I wish those people were all dead!" General Lee, with that grace which was his own, said, "How can you say so?

9

Now, I wish that they would all go home and leave us to do the same.''

At the close of the war, some of our best men went to seek homes in other lands. This, General Lee deemed wrong. He thought that the men of the South should stay at home and build up what had been laid waste by war. He wrote to one of his friends thus: '' She (Virginia) has need for all of her sons, and can ill afford to spare you.'' Once more he wrote: ''I think the South needs the aid of her sons more than at any time of her history. As you ask, I will state that I have no thought of leaving her.''

In a word, the welfare of the impoverished, desolated South was his chief concern. He kept in sight the honor of the South, but not that hate to the North which brought no good.

A lady who had lost her husband in the war, and had brought her two sons to college, spoke in sharp terms of the North to General Lee. He gently said: ''Madam, do not train up your children as foes to the Government of the United States.  *  * We are one country now.  Bring them up to be Americans." Thus did this grand man, with a sad heart, try to do his duty at all times and on all occasions.

Though meek in the way I have told you, General Lee was at the same time too proud to take the aid which, from time to time, his friends would offer him.  They knew that he had lost his "all" by the war, and felt that he should now be helped, so that he might pass his days without care.  But this proud man would take no aid.  When, in a quiet way, the trustees of the college gave the house in which he lived to Mrs. Lee, and also the sum of three thousand dollars each year, he wrote, in Mrs. Lee's name, a kind but firm letter and declined the gift.

After his death, they again deeded the home to Mrs. Lee and sent her a check for a large sum of money.  But she, with the pride of her husband, sent back the check and would not let the funds of the college be taken for her use.

General Lee was always neat in his attire. This trait was the cause of much comment at the time of the "surrender."

General Sharp, of the Federal Army, says:

"It was late in the day when it was known that General Lee had sent for General Grant. The surrender took place in the left-hand room of an old house which had a hall-way through it. In that room were a few officers, of whom I was one.

"A short space apart sat two men. The larger and taller of the two was the more striking. His hair was as white·as snow. There was not a speck upon his coat; not a spot upon those gauntlets that he wore, which were as bright and fair as a lady's glove. That was Robert E. Lee. The other was Ulysses S. Grant. His boots were muddy, and he wore no sword.

**LEE AND GRANT.**

[133]

"The words that passed between Lee and Grant were few. General Grant, while the men wrote out the terms of the surrender, said: 'General Lee, I have no sword; I rode all night.' And General Lee, with the pride which became him well, made no reply, but in a cold, formal way, bowed.

"Then General Grant, in the attempt to be polite, said: 'I don't always wear a sword.'

"Lee only bowed again.

"Some one else then said: 'General Lee, what became of the white horse you rode in Mexico? He may not be dead yet; he was not so old.'

"General Lee again bowed and said: 'I left him at the White House, on the Pamunkey river, and I have not seen him since.'

"Then there were a few words, which we could not hear, spoken in a low tone of voice between Grant and Lee.

"At last, when the terms of surrender had all been signed, Lee arose, cold and proud, and bowed to each man on our side in the room. And then he went out and passed down that little square in front of the house, and mounted the gray horse that had carried him all over Virginia.

"When he had gone we learned what the low-toned words had meant. General Grant turned and said: 'You go and ask each man that has three rations to turn over two of them, and send them on to General Lee. His men are on the point of starvation.'"

This calm, proud man was the same who a few hours before had said: "Then there is nothing left me but to go and see General Grant, and I would rather die a thousand deaths." His superb, proud mien won from the foe only praise and respect.

I must here give you General Fitzhugh Lee's picture of the two generals at that time:

"Grant, not yet forty-three years old, five

feet eight inches tall, shoulders slightly stooped, hair and beard nut-brown, wearing a dark-blue blouse; top-boots, pants inside; dark thread gloves; without spurs or sword, and no marks of rank save the straps of a general.

"Lee, fifty-eight years old, six feet tall, hair and beard silver-gray; a handsome uniform of Confederate gray, buttoned to the throat, with three stars on collar, fine top-boots with spurs, new gauntlets, and at his side a splendid sword." Lee wore his best in honor of the cause for which he fought.

General Lee never touched tobacco, brandy or whiskey; he was always a sober man. Just as he was starting to the Mexican war, a lady in Virginia gave him a bottle of fine old whiskey, saying that he would be sure to need it, and that it was very fine. On his return home he sent the bottle, unopened, to his friend to convince her that he could get along without whiskey.

General Lee once proposed to treat some

of his officers, saying, "I have a demijohn which I know *is of the best.*" The demijohn was brought, and the cups, held out for the treat, were filled to the brim—not with old "Rye," but with fresh buttermilk, which a kind lady had sent. The General seemed to enjoy the joke hugely.

Being once asked to a fine dinner, he refused all the good dishes, and said to the lady of the house: "I cannot consent to be feasting while my poor men are nearly starving."

It was his way to send any nice thing he might have to the sick and wounded in the hospitals.

A lady relates that when her brother was badly wounded near Petersburg, he was taken to a tent near a hospital, out of range of the fire of the foe. One day General Lee came riding up and went in to see the wounded man. He took him gently by the hand and told him to cheer up and get well; that he had use for all brave men like him. Then he drew two fine peaches from his pocket and laid them on the side of the cot.

Tears trickled down the wounded man's pale cheeks as he listened to these kind words, and felt that his chief cared so much for him, a private soldier.

Near the close of the war, when meat had become quite scarce, an aide of President Davis', being at headquarters, was asked to dine. The meal spread on the rough board was corn-bread, and a small piece of meat in a large mess of greens. The aid saw that the meat was not touched, though General Lee had asked all to take a piece of it. When the meal was over, the aide asked one of the men why the meat was not eaten. The reply was, that it had been loaned by a friend to cook with the greens, and had to be returned.

It was General Lee's wish to fare just as his men did. When, during the siege of Petersburg, Mrs. Lee, fearing the great strain would be too much for him begged him to take more care of his health, he wrote : "But what care can a man give to himself in time of war?" He then went on to say that he lived in a tent in order to be near his men and the officers with whom he had to act; that he had been offered rooms by kind friends, but that he could not turn their homes into a camp.

An English officer wrote this account of Lee's headquarters in 1862: "Lee's headquarters I found were only seven or eight pole-tents, with their backs to a stake-fence, while a little stream of good water flowed close by. In front of the tents were three wagons, and a number of horses roamed over the fields. No guards were seen near, and no crowd of aids swarmed about. A large farm-house stood close by, which would have made a good home for the General, but Lee does not let his men rob or disturb the people, and likes to set them a good example."

It was in this way that he gained the great love of his men.

A short time after the surrender, two ragged Confederates, just from prison in the North, waited upon the General and said that there were sixty other fellows around the corner who were too ragged to come. They had sent these two to offer their loved chief a home in the mountains of Virginia. "We will give you," said one of them, "a good house and a fine farm. We boys will work for you and you shall never want."

Tears came to the eyes of General Lee as he told them that he must decline their gift. The offer of these men was but the feeling of the whole South. Though poor themselves, they would have given him houses, lands and money had he let them.

Just after the war, General Lee received the following letter from one of his old soldiers:

" Dear General :

" We have been fighting hard four years, and now the Yankees have got us in Libby Prison.

They are treating us awful bad. The boys want you to get us out if you can ; but if you can't, just ride by the Libby and let us see you and give you a cheer. We will all feel better for it."

This letter touched the tender heart of Lee, as well as this story which was told to

LIBBY PRISON.

him by Rev. J. William Jones: After the war, the latter was riding along a road one day, when he saw a young man plowing in a field, guiding the plow with one hand, for on the other side was an empty sleeve.

He soon saw that the man plowing was a soldier whom he had known, and stopped to speak to him. In fact, he had known the

young man from boyhood; how, at the first
tap of the drum he had gone to fight for his
native State; and how he had been maimed
for life, and had gone home to find that he
must work with one arm for his bread, as his
fortune had been wrecked by the war. When
he told the young man how sad it made him
to see him thus, the latter said: "Oh! it is
all right. I thank God that I have *one* arm
left, and can use it for those I love."

When the Rev. Mr. Jones told this to
General Lee, his face flushed, and he said:
"What a noble fellow! But it is just like
one of our soldiers. The world has never
seen nobler men than those who belonged to
the Army of Northern Virginia."

The real corner-stone of Lee's life was
his trust in God. Whatever came to him he
always said, "God's will be done."

The death of the wife of his son, General
W. H. Fitzhugh Lee, gave General Lee much
grief. The former General was wounded and
taken prisoner. While in prison his lovely

wife died.   In this bitter grief, General Lee
wrote to his son these words:

"My whole trust is in God, and I am
ready for whatever He may ordain."

While the army was at Mine Run, in November, 1863, and a battle was at hand,
General Lee, with a number of officers riding
down the line of battle, came upon a party
of soldiers who were holding a prayer-meet-
ing.   The shooting had begun along the
lines, the cannon were already roaring, and
the mind and heart of the great chief were
on the battle.   Yet, as he saw these men
bent in prayer, he dismounted and joined in
the simple worship.   So these humble men
led the devotions of their loved General.

One day in 1865, while riding along the
lines with his staff, General Lee met the Rev.
J. William Jones, who was giving tracts to
the men in the trenches.   He at once reined
in his horse and spoke to this "man of God,"
while the officers crowded around.

General Lee asked if he ever had calls for

prayer-books, and said that if he would come to his headquarters he would give him some—that a friend in Richmond had given him a new book; and upon his saying to his friend that he would give his old book, that he had used ever since the Mexican war, to some soldier, the friend offered him a dozen new books for the old one.  He had, of course, taken so grand an offer, and now had twelve, in place of one, to give away.

When the Rev. Mr. Jones called, General Lee was out, but had left the books for Mr. Jones with one of his staff.  He had written on the fly-leaf of each book, "Presented by R. E. Lee."

We are sure that if any of these books were saved amid the din and stress of war, they are now much prized by those who own them.

These are some of the words which General Lee would use when his army had gained the day: "Thanks be to God."  "God has again crowned the valor of our troops with success."

Again, upon a fast-day, he said in an order, "Soldiers! let us humble ourselves before the Lord our God, asking, through Christ, the forgiveness of our sins."

With the close of the war, the piety of this great man seemed to increase. His seat at church was always filled, unless he was kept away by sickness, and he was ever ready for good works. He did not find fault with preachers, as so many do, but was most fond of those who were simple and true to the teachings of the Bible.

Once he said to a friend: "Do you think that it would be any harm for me to hint to Mr. —— that we should be glad if he made his *morning prayers* a little short? You know our friend makes this prayer too long. He prays for the Jews, the Turks, and the heathen, and runs into the hour for our College recitations. Would it be wrong for me to hint to Mr. —— that he confine his morning prayers to us *poor sinners at the College*, and pray for the Turks, the Jews,

10

the Chinese, and other heathen some other time?"

General Lee was a constant reader of the Bible. One of his friends relates that, as he watched beside his body the day after death, he picked up from the table a well-worn pocket Bible, in which was written in his own hand, "R. E. Lee, Lieutenant-Colonel of U. S. Army." This little book had been the light of his pathway through many trials.

General Lee gave freely of his small means to his church and to the poor. At a vestry meeting which took place the evening of his illness, the sum of fifty-five dollars was needed for the pay of the Rector. Though he had before given his share, General Lee said in a low voice, "I will give the sum." These were the last words he spoke to the vestry, and this giving was his last public act.

His love for his wife and children is shown by the tender, loving letters he wrote when away from them. During the Civil War his anxiety for them was great.

Just before the Northern army crossed the Potomac, in 1861, Mrs. Lee left her beautiful home, Arlington, and came South. Arlington was at once seized by the Northern Government, and the grounds were taken for a burial-place for the Northern soldiers.

Mrs. Lee and her daughters then sought a home at the "White House," on the Pamunkey river, where Washington married the "Widow Custis," and which had been left by Mr. Custis to

RESIDENCE OF GENERAL LEE IN RICHMOND.

one of General Lee's sons. Mrs. Lee and her daughters were soon driven from there by the hosts of McClellan, and the house was burned to the ground. At last, they found a home in Richmond, where they lived until the close of the war.

Mrs. Lee's health had failed, but a large part of her time was spent in knitting socks for the poor bare-footed soldiers of the South. Her brave daughters, also, knit socks, and nursed the sick and wounded soldiers.

MARY CUSTIS LEE.

Those were sad times, and the Lee family suffered most heavily.

The death of her noble husband was a great shock to Mrs. Lee, who was then not able to walk without aid. She did not survive him many years, and now rests beside him in the College chapel at Lexington, Virginia. Their daughter Agnes, who died shortly after her father, is buried in the same place.

Close by is the grave of Stonewall Jackson. How meet that these two friends and heroes should rest so near each other!

The blue mountains of their loved Virginia keep "watch and ward" over their graves; and each year, pilgrims from every part of the land come to visit their tombs and place fresh flowers and green wreaths upon them.

General Custis Lee was made President of the College in his father's place. The College is now called the "Washington and Lee University," after Washington and Lee, the two great names in the history of our country.

------

Cŏn'cōurse, a crowd of people.

Cou'rier (kōō'rier), a man who carries an order for an officer.

Pĭl'grim, a traveler to holy places.

Tell me—

> What General Lee became in 1865.
> Something about his work.
> His visit to the South in 1870.

His illness and death.

What day is kept throughout the South in memory of Lee?

About Mrs. Lee.

The tomb of Lee.

Washington and Lee University.

LEE'S COURT OF ARMS.

# CHAPTER VII.

## A People's Hero.

AFTER the death of General Lee, many speeches were made in his praise, and many letters were written telling of the sorrow of his friends. These letters came not only from the South, but from the North, and other lands.

The New York *Sun* thus closes its notice:

"His death will awaken great grief through the South, and many people in the North will drop a tear of sorrow on his bier. * * * In General Lee, an able soldier, a sincere Christian, and an honest man has been taken from earth."

The New York *Herald* said these kind words of him:

"In a quiet autumn morning, in the land he loved so well, and, as he held, he had served so faithfully, the spirit of Robert E.

GENERAL ROBERT E. LEE.

Lee left the clay which it had so much ennobled, and traveled out of this world into the great and unknown land. * * *

"Not to the Southern people alone shall be limited the tribute of a tear over the dead Virginian. Here in the North, forgetting that the time was when the sword of Robert E. Lee was drawn against us, we have long since ceased to look upon him as the Confederate leader, but have claimed him as one of ourselves; for Robert Edward Lee was an American, and the great nation which gave him birth would to-day be unworthy of such a son if she looked upon him lightly."

The Pall Mall *Gazette*, London, England, said :

"The news from America, that General Robert E. Lee is dead, will be received with great sorrow by many in this country, as well as by his fellow-soldiers in America.

"It is but a few years since Robert E. Lee ranked among the great men of his time. He was the able soldier of the Southern

Confederacy, the leader who twice threatened, by the capture of Washington, to turn the tide of success and cause a revolution which would have changed the destiny of the United States."

The London *Standard* gave this tribute to Lee:

"A country which has given birth to men like him, and those who followed him, may look the chivalry of Europe in the face without shame; for the lands of Sidney and of Bayard never brought forth a nobler soldier, gentleman and Christian, than Robert E. Lee."

He was called "the great captain of his age"—"the great general of the South"—"a good knight, noble of heart and strong of purpose, and both a soldier and a gentleman."

These beautiful words were said of him in a speech soon after his death:

"General Lee's fame is not bounded by the limits of the South, nor by the continent.

I rejoice that the South gave him birth. I rejoice that the South will hold his ashes. But his fame belongs to the human race. Washington, too, was born in the South and sleeps in the South, but his fame belongs to mankind. We place the name of Lee by that of Washington. They both belong to the world.

"There is one thing more I wish to say before I take my seat. General Lee's fame ought to rest on its true foundation. He did not draw his sword in the cause of slavery—he did not seek to overthrow the Government of the United States. He drew it in the defense of constitutional liberty. That cause is not dead, but will live forever."

General W. Preston spoke of him thus:

"I knew him first when he was a captain. * * At that time, General Scott had decided upon General Lee as a man who would make his mark if he were ever called upon to do great work. He never drank, he never swore an oath, but there was never a dispute among gentlemen in which his voice was not more potent than any other; his rare calmness and dignity were above all. When the war came on, he followed his native State, Virginia. * * Scott maintained that Lee was the greatest soldier in the army. * *

"I remember when Scott made use of these words: 'I tell you one thing, if I were on my death-bed, and knew that a battle was to be fought for my country, and the President were to say to me, 'Scott, who shall command?' I tell you that, with my dying breath, I would say Robert Lee. Nobody but Robert Lee! Robert Lee, and nobody but Lee!'"

These extracts would not be complete without this one, bearing upon his life as a teacher:

"And it is an honor for all the colleges of the South, and for all our schools, that this pure and bright name is joined by the will of him that bore it with the cause of education. We believe that, so long as the name of Lee is cherished by Southern teachers, they will grow stronger in their work. They will be encouraged to greater efforts when they remember that Lee was one of their number, and that his great heart, that had so bravely borne the fortunes of an empire, bore also, amid its latest aspirations, the interests and hopes of the teacher."

A great public honor was paid to our hero when the bronze statue by Mercié (Mersea) was unveiled in Richmond.

Shortly after the death of General Lee, a few ladies met in a parlor in Richmond and formed a society known as the Ladies' Lee Monument Association. Their plan was to erect a monument in Richmond to the memory of the great chief, and to collect funds for this purpose from the entire South. They began at once their labor of love. Though the South was at that time very poor, the people gave gladly of their small means until the Ladies' Association had collected over fifteen thousand dollars.

Almost at the same time, another "Lee Monument Association" was formed of the old soldiers and sailors of the Confederacy, which had General Jubal A. Early for its president. The ladies of the Hollywood Memorial Association were asked to help, and they proved great workers in the cause.

I cannot tell you the many ways in which these and other societies worked to raise the money, but at last there was enough in the treasury to erect the statue.

In the meantime, General Fitzhugh Lee was made Governor of Virginia, and he at once began to take measures to bring about the erection of the monument. By his efforts a "Board of Managers" was appointed, whose work was to choose the design, the artist, and the site for the monument. The Allen lot, in the western part of the city, was at last chosen for the site, and was accepted as the gift of Mr. Otway Allen, June 18th, 1887. It was then the duty of the Board to find a sculptor worthy to execute this great work.

After many trials, the Board selected Monsieur Mercie, a Frenchman, who was both a painter and a sculptor of note. In the summer of 1887, the best photographs of General Lee, as well as one of his shoes and his uniform, were sent to the sculptor. A small spur, such as General Lee wore, was taken over to France by Miss Randolph, who was one of the Board of Managers. Monsieur Mercie told her that when General Lee's shoe was sent to him, there was no one in his household, except his twelve-year-old boy, with a foot small enough to wear it.

In working out the likeness to General Lee, Monsieur Mercié had the good fortune to have Miss Mary Lee, who was then in Paris, as a critic of his work.

On the 27th of October, 1887, the corner-stone was laid with splendid rites, and on the 3rd of May, 1890, the statue reached Richmond by way of New York. It was packed in three boxes. On the 7th of May, each box was placed in a separate wagon, from which waved the flags of Virginia and the Confederacy. Then, one wagon was drawn by men of the city, one by old soldiers, and one by women and girls—the fine lady and her humble sister standing shoulder to shoulder. They went through the city, pulling the ropes amid the cheers of twenty thousand people, until they came to the spot where the statue was to stand. Such was their love for Lee! The monument in all is about sixty-one feet in height, and cost sixty-five thousand dollars. It shows the General mounted upon his war-horse, Traveler. His feet touch the stirrups lightly, after the manner of the Southern horsemen. He is clad in a plain uniform. A sash girds his waist, and the sword of a cavalry officer hangs from his side. He holds the bridle reins in his left hand, while in his right is his hat, which he grasps as if he had just taken it off to acknowledge the cheers of his men, through whose ranks we may suppose him to be passing.

The day decided upon for unveiling the statue was Friday, May 29th, 1890.

From North, South, East and West, people thronged to do honor to the great chief.

All the city was then thinking of one man—Lee, just as, twenty-five years before, all their hopes had turned to him.

On that day, the sun rose bright and the people with it. Soon, the noise of tramping feet and the tap of the drum were heard, and ere long the glitter of bayonets, the flashing of sabers and the waving of flags told that the line was forming. The streets were crowded, and rang with cheers as some noted soldier rode by or an old Confederate flag was waved.

At noon, the long line was formed on Broad street, and the parade began. Every window, doorway, and even the house-tops along the line of march, were filled with people eager to see the great parade, which

11

stretched through the streets four miles in moving mass.

General Fitzhugh Lee, nephew of the hero who had been one of his most daring cavalry generals during the war, and who had formerly been Governor of Virginia, was chief marshal of the parade. Cheer after cheer arose as he rode by, wearing the slouch hat of a cavalryman. "Our Fitz," as his men loved to call him, "was himself again."

The guests rode in open carriages, and among them were Misses Mary and Mildred Lee; and General W. H. Fitzhugh Lee, wife and sons. They were followed by band after band of volunteer troops from all the Southern States, in the following order: South Carolina, North Carolina, Mississippi, Texas, Maryland, District of Columbia, Alabama, West Virginia and Virginia. Behind these marched the veterans—men who had fought in the Civil War, and who came from all parts of the South. Brave men were there from Texas, the far-off "Lone Star State." With the veteran troops from Louisiana was "the old war-horse" Longstreet, who had led the First Corps of the Army of Northern Virginia; and at the head of the Georgia men was the tried and true Gordon. Gallant sons of Florida, Mississippi and Alabama were in line with the brave men of North and South Carolina. Veterans from Arkansas, Tennessee, Kentucky, Maryland, West Virginia and Virginia were also there to honor the memory of their leader.

Whenever and wherever these veterans were seen, they were greeted with hearty cheers. Some were clad in their old gray uniforms, faded and worn, and in many cases, full of bullet-holes. Here and there along the line could be seen the old and tattered flags of the Confederacy.

After the veterans, came the civic orders in Richmond, the students of Washington and Lee University, and the corps of cadets from the historic Virginia Military Institute.

The cross-bars and battle-flags of the Confederacy floated in the breeze by the side of the "Stars and Stripes," which meant that the people of the United States were one nation.

As the line moved along the streets decked with floating flags and gay bunting, the sound of the many feet was lost in loud and hearty cheers that arose from doors, house-tops and crowded sidewalks.

At last, the throng at the grandstand heard the roll of the drum and the nearing din of the parade, and soon the bright line swept into view. The crowd was so dense that persons on the grandstand could not be seen by those on the ground. Ringing cheers arose, not once, but time and time again, as the great men took their places on the stand, and it was as late as 3:45 o'clock P. M. when Governor McKinney stepped forward to make the opening speech.

Then there was prayer by Rev. Dr. Minnigerode, who was rector of St. Paul's church during the war, at which church General Lee worshiped when in Richmond.

When the prayer ended, the band played Dixie, the war-song of the South, with whose strains the old soldiers had so often been thrilled as they marched into battle. Then there was a great noise which at last wore itself away, and General Early rose and spoke a few words of cheer to the old soldiers.

The orator of the day was Colonel Archer Anderson, who pictured scene after scene in the life of General Lee with great force and clearness. Again the grand hero seemed to live and act in their midst—to lead them on to victory or to teach them how to bear defeat.

When the speaker took his seat, amid cheers, General Joseph E. Johnston arose and with two old soldiers marched to the base of the monument. Each of the soldiers carried a battle flag, tattered and torn by shot and shell. When the monument was reached, General Johnston pulled the rope, and one part of the veil fell off. Another pull brought off the rest of the veil, and the splendid statue was in plain view of the eager multitude. A score of old soldiers mounted its base and waved their old Confederate flags in loyal, eager love for their dead chief. Mighty cheers broke from the watching throng, like the wild breaking of a storm, but at last they died away.

Up there, against the blue sky, kissed by the rays of the setting sun, in the midst of his own people, was the matchless face and form of Lee.

Some wept, others shouted, but all thanked God that he had given to America such a son as Lee.

Seldom had men looked on such a scene before. At last the crowd went slowly away, leaving their hero in bronze to keep silent watch over the city he loved so well. Beneath him were the homes of his friends, and beyond, in "Hollywood" and "Oak-wood," Richmond's "cities of the dead," were the graves of his fallen heroes, and far away, across and a-down the James, were his battlefields.

As time rolls on, statue and city will pass away. But the name and virtues of Robert E. Lee will never die, for they are written in the history of his country and in the Book of Life, and will live beyond the shores of Time.

---

Monsieur (mōsyur′), a French word for Mr.

Sincēré′, honest.

Acknowledge (aknŏl′eg), to own a gift or favor.

Pōt′ent, strong, having power.

Sĭd′ney, an English patriot.

Bayard (bä′yär′), a French hero.

Pa′triot, one who loves his country.

Tell about—

A great honor paid to Lee.

The laying of the corner-stone.

The monument.

The parade.

The unveiling.

The undying fame of Lee.

# GENERAL R. E. LEE'S

# Farewell Address to His Soldiers.

HEADQUARTERS ARMY NORTHERN VIRGINIA,

APPOMATTOX C. H., April 10, 1865.

**General Orders No. 9.**

After four years of arduous service, marked by unsurpassed courage and fortitude, the ARMY OF NORTHERN VIRGINIA has been compelled to yield to overwhelming numbers and resources.

I need not tell the survivors of so many hard-fought battles, who have remained steadfast to the last, that I have consented to this result from no distrust of them ; but, feeling that valor and devotion could accomplish nothing that would compensate for the loss that must have attended a continuance of the contest, I determined to avoid the useless sacrifice of those whose past services have endeared them to their countrymen.

By the terms of the Agreement, Officers and men can return to their homes and remain until exchanged. You will take with you the satisfaction that proceeds from the consciousness of duty faithfully performed, and I earnestly pray that a merciful God will extend to you His blessing and protection. With an unceasing admiration of your constancy and devotion to your Country, and a grateful remembrance of your kind and generous consideration for myself, I bid you all an Affectionate Farewell.

R E Lee

# THE LIFE

OF

# GEN. THOS. J. JACKSON

"Stonewall"

# FOR THE YOUNG,

(FOURTH READER GRADE)

## IN EASY WORDS.

## ILLUSTRATED.

❧ ❧ ❧

## BY MRS. MARY L. WILLIAMSON.

❧ ❧ ❧

Harrisonburg, Virginia

## SPRINKLE PUBLICATIONS

## 1989

Sprinkle Publications
P. O. Box 1094
Harrisonburg, Virginia 22801

'04–1–F. Co.

*DEDICATED*

*TO ALL YOUTHS WHO*

*ADMIRE THE CHRISTIAN VIRTUES*

*AND MILITARY GENIUS OF*

*THOMAS J. JACKSON.*

# PREFACE.

Continuing the argument set forth in the "Life of Gen. Lee for Children," that we can advance primary education and impress lessons of morality upon children in no better way than to place before them the careers of our great men, I now give, in simple words, the "Life of Gen. Thos. J. Jackson."

In this brief sketch of our great Southern hero, I have endeavored to portray, amid the blaze of his matchless military genius, the unchanging rectitude of his conduct, the stern will-power by which he conquered all difficulties, his firm belief in an overruling Providence, and his entire submission to the Divine Will. These traits of character were the corner-stones upon which he reared the edifice of his greatness, and upon which the young people of our day will do well to build.

Teachers may introduce this book as a supplementary reader into the fourth grade, as I have been careful to employ as few words as possible outside of the vocabulary of that grade.

In preparing this work, I used chiefly as reference and authority the Life of Lieut.-Gen. Thomas J. Jackson, by Prof. R. L. Dabney, D. D., who was, for a time, Jackson's chief of staff, and who had personal knowledge of his character and military exploits.

Acknowledgment is due Col. James H. Morrison for valuable assistance rendered, and to Mrs. Thomas J. Jackson, of Charlotte, N. C., and Mr. M. Miley, of Lexington, Va., for furnishing valuable illustrative matter.

I am also indebted to the kindness of Messrs. Paxton and Henkel, the editors, respectively, of the *Rockbridge County News* and the *Shenandoah Valley*, for files of their reliable journals, containing accounts of the more recent events recorded in the last chapter.

MARY LYNN WILLIAMSON.

NEW MARKET, VA.,

# Stonewall Jackson's Way.

DES RIVIERES.

Come! stack arms, men; pile on the rails,
   Stir up the camp-fires bright;
No matter if the canteen fails,
   We'll make a roaring night.
Here Shenandoah brawls along,
There lofty Blue Ridge echoes strong
To swell the brigade's rousing song
   Of "Stonewall Jackson's Way."

We see him now—the old slouched hat
   Cocked o'er his eye askew;
The shrewd, dry smile, the speech so pat,
   So calm, so blunt, so true.
The "Blue Light Elder" knows them well:
Says he, "That's Banks—he's fond of shell;
Lord save his soul! we'll give him—." Well,
   That's Stonewall Jackson's Way.

Silence! ground arms! kneel all! caps off!
   "Old Blue Light's" going to pray;
Strangle the fool who dares to scoff!
   Attention! it's his way:
Appealing from his native sod,
*In forma pauperis* to God—
"Lay bare thine arm. stretch forth thy rod;
   Amen!" That's Stonewall Jackson's Way.

He's in the saddle now. Fall in!
   Steady! the whole brigade!
Hill's at the ford, cut off! We'll win
   His way out ball and blade.
What matter if our shoes are worn?
What matter if our feet are torn?
Quick step! we're with him e'er the morn!
   That's Stonewall Jackson's Way.

The sun's bright glances rout the mists
   Of morning—and. by George!
There's Longstreet struggling in the lists,
   Hemmed in an ugly gorge.
Pope and his columns whipped before.—
"Bay'nets and grape!" hear Stonewall roar;
"Charge, Stuart! pay off Ashby's score!"
   Is "Stonewall Jackson's Way."

# Life of Gen. T. J. Jackson.

## CHAPTER I.

### An Orphan Boy.

THOMAS JONATHAN JACKSON was born January 21, 1824, at Clarksburg, West Virginia, which state was then a part of old Virginia. He sprang from Scotch-Irish stock. His great-grandfather, John Jackson, was born in Ireland, but his parents moved to the city of London when John was only two years old. John Jackson grew up to be a great trader. In 1748 he came to the New World to make his fortune, and landed in the State of Maryland. Not long after, he married Elizabeth Cummins, a young woman who was noted for her good looks, fine mind, and great height.

John Jackson with his wife soon moved West, and at last took up lands in what is now known as Upshur county, West Virginia. As land was then cheap, he soon owned a

*House in which Jackson was Born, Clarksburg, Va.*

large tract of country, and was a rich man for those times. He was greatly aided by his brave wife, Elizabeth. In those days the Indians still made war upon the whites, who would flee for safety into the forts or strongholds. It is said that in more than one of those Indian raids Elizabeth Jackson aided in driving off the foe.

*Father of "Stonewall" Jackson.*

When the great Revolutionary war came on, John Jackson and several of his sons marched to the war; and at its close came back safe to their Virginia home. In these lovely and fertile valleys, John Jackson and his wife Elizabeth passed long and active lives. The husband lived to be eighty-six years old, while his wife lived to the great age of one hundred and five years. Her strength of body and mind fitted her to rear a race of mighty men.

Thomas Jonathan was the great-grandson of these good people. His father, Jonathan Jackson, was a lawyer. He is said to have been a man of good mind and kind heart. Thomas's mother was Julia Neale, the daughter of a merchant in the then village of Parkersburg, on the Ohio river. Mrs. Jackson was good and beautiful. Thomas had one brother, Warren, and two sisters, Elizabeth and Laura. Not long after the birth of the baby Laura, Elizabeth was taken sick with fever and died. Her father, worn out with nursing, was also taken ill; and two weeks after her death he was laid in a grave by her side.

After his death it was found that he had left no property for his widow and babes.

They were now without a home, and the Masonic Order gave the widow a house of one room. Here she sewed, and taught school, caring as well as she could for her little fatherless children.

In the year 1830 she married Mr. Woodson, a lawyer, who was pleased with her youth and beauty. Her children—Warren, Thomas, and Laura—were now claimed by their father's family, who did not like the second marriage of the mother.

As her new husband was not a rich man, she was at last forced to give them up. Little Jonathan, then only seven years old, was placed behind good, old "Uncle Robinson," the last of his father's slaves, and sent away to his aunt, Mrs. Brake, who lived about four miles from Clarksburg.

After being one year at his aunt's he was sent for to see his mother die. Death for her had no sting; and Thomas, long years after, said that her dying words and prayers had never been erased from his heart. She was laid to rest not far from the famous Hawk's Nest, on New river, West Virginia.

Jonathan was then a pretty child, with rosy cheeks, wavy brown hair, and deep-blue eyes. It is said of him that, as a child, he was strangely quiet and manly. The sadness of his young life made him grave and thoughtful beyond his years. When he was but eight years old he went one day to the home of his father's cousin, Judge John G. Jackson, in Clarksburg.

While eating his dinner, he said to Mrs. Jackson in a quiet way, "Uncle and I don't agree. I have quit him and shall not go back any more." His kind cousin tried to show him that he was in fault and that he should go back to his Uncle Brake. He only shook his head and said more firmly than ever, "No, uncle and I don't agree. I have quit him and shall not go back any more." It seems that his uncle had tried to govern him by force rather than through his sense of right and wrong. So, this strange child calmly made up his mind not to stay where there would be constant warfare.

From Judge Jackson's he went that evening to the home of another cousin, who also tried to persuade him to return to his Uncle Brake. But Jonathan only said, "I have quit there. I shall not go back there any more." The next morning he set out alone and on foot, and went eighteen miles to the home of his uncle, Cummins Jackson, the half-brother of his father.

There he found his brother Warren, and soon felt quite at home with his kind uncle and aunts. His Uncle Cummins was a bachelor, who owned a fine farm and mills, and was one of the largest slave-owners in Lewis county.

He was quite fond of his little nephew, and took pains to teach him all the arts of country life. He treated him more as an equal than as a child, for he saw at once the noble nature with which he had to deal. He also sent Thomas and Warren to the nearest

county school, but Warren, now a bold lad
of fourteen years, did not like such restraint.
He at last induced Thomas to go with him
from their uncle's home to seek their fortunes
in the great West.

After stopping for a time at the home of
their uncle on the Ohio river, they went
down that river, and for some months were
not heard from.

In the fall of that year, they returned to
their kind friends, ragged, and ill with chills
and fever.

Their story was that they made a raft
and floated down to one of the lonely islands
in the Mississippi river near the Kentucky
shore, where they cut wood for steamboats
on the river. Here they spent the summer
alone, with little food, in the midst of a
dense forest surrounded by the turbid, rush-
ing waters of the great Mississippi.

At last, illness forced them to seek their
way homeward; and Thomas boldly said
that he was going back to his good Uncle

*Warren and Thomas on the Ohio river*

(17)

Cummins. Warren stopped at the home of his Uncle Brake, but disease had laid so firm a hold upon him that, after lingering a few years, he died, aged about nineteen.

Thomas and Laura were now all that were left of the little family. They lived together for several months at their Uncle Cummins's, and it is told of Thomas that he was very fond of his little sister. Across the brook from the house was a large grove of sugar-maple trees where they would go to play "making sugar." It was a great pleasure to Thomas to build bridges for his little sister to walk on in crossing the stream, and many were the delights of the cool and fragrant forests. But in a short time Laura was sent to live with her mother's friends in Wood county, and Thomas was left alone. Though they could not live together, Thomas always cherished the warmest love for his sister, and the very first money he ever earned was spent in buying a silk dress for her.

Thomas now went to school to Mr. Robert

P. Ray. He showed no aptness for any study except arithmetic. When called upon to recite a lesson, he would flatly say that he did not understand it and, therefore, was not ready; nor would he go to the next lesson until he had learned the first perfectly. Thus, he was always behind his class. He was never surly at school, but was always ready for a merry romp or play. When there were games of "bat and ball" or "prisoner's base," he was sure to be chosen captain of one side, and that side generally won.

As long as he was treated fairly by his playmates, he was gentle and yielding; but, if he thought himself wronged, he did not hesitate to fight it out. It is said that he would never admit that he had been beaten in a fray, and was always ready to renew the contest when his foe assailed him again.

In the summer, Thomas worked on the farm and became of use to his uncle in many ways. One of his most frequent tasks was to haul great logs of oak and pine from the wood to the saw-mill.   He, thus, became a famous driver of oxen, and was known throughout the country-side as a young man of great strength and courage.

So his life was passed, from nine to sixteen, between the school and the farm.   He was then like his father, of low stature, but he afterwards grew tall like the men of his mother's race.

About this time, he was made constable of one-half of Lewis county.   We see him now with his bag of bills and account books going up and down the hills of Lewis county. In this work he had to be firm and exact, for it was now his task to collect money due for debts.

This story is told of his nerve and skill in doing this unpleasant duty.   A man who owed a debt of ten dollars promised to pay it at a given time.   The day came and the man failed to keep his word.   Young Jackson paid the money out of his own purse, and then watched for the man who would

not pay his debt. The very next morning
the man came riding up the street on a good
horse. Jackson at once taxed him with not
keeping his word, and was going to take the
horse for the debt, when the latter resisted,
and a fierce fight took place in the street.
In the midst of the fray the man mounted
his horse and was riding off.

Jackson, however, sprang forward and
seized the bridle. Seeing that he could get
the man off the horse in no other way, he
led it to the low door of a stable near by.
The man cuffed him right and left, but Jackson clung to the bridle, and pulled the horse
into the stable. The man was thus forced
to slide off to keep from being knocked off;
and Jackson got the horse.

Though this life in the open air was good
for the health of our hero, it did not benefit
his morals. He was kept much from home,
and was thrown with the worst class of
people in the county.

His aunts had now married, and his Uncle

Cummins was keeping "bachelor's hall." He ·also kept race horses, and none save Thomas could ride for him if a contest was close.

It was said through all that country that if a horse could win, he would do so if young Tom Jackson rode him in the race.

It is sad to think of this young man thrown upon the world without mother or sister or any human influence, save his own will, to keep him in the right way. But in this wild, rough life the great wish of his heart was to reach that condition from which he had been thrust when left a poor orphan boy. And even now the great God, who has said that He will be a father to the fatherless, was opening up a way to a great and notable career.

---

Constable (kun'-sta-ble), an officer of the peace.

Nŏ-ta-ble, wonderful.

Ca-reer', a course.

In'-flu-ence, power not seen.

Do you remember—

The name of Thomas's father?

The place of his birth?

His early loss of father and mother?

His life at Uncle Cummins's?

The story told of him when constable?

The wish of his heart in the midst of his wild, rough life?

# CHAPTER II.

## A Cadet.

In 1842, the place of a cadet in the great academy at West Point became vacant. In that school or academy the young men of the United States are trained to become soldiers. Thomas at once sought and secured the place, and very soon set out on horse-back to Clarksburg, where he would take the coach going to Washington.

He was clad in home-spun clothes, and his whole wardrobe was packed in a pair of saddle-bags.

When he reached Clarksburg, he found that the coach had passed by; but he rode on until he overtook it and then went on to Washington city.

He was kindly met by his friend Mr. Hays, member of Congress from his district,

3

who took him at once to the Secretary of War. The latter was so pleased with his manly bearing and direct speech that he ordered his warrant to be made out at once.

Mr. Hays wished him to stay in Washington for a few days in order to see the sights of the city, but he was content to climb to the top of the dome of the Capitol, from which he could view the whole scene at once. He was then ready to go on to West Point for examination. His great trouble now was the thought that he might not know enough to stand that examination.

Mr. Hays wrote to his friends at the academy and asked them to be easy in examining the mountain boy, who wished so much to be a soldier; and it is said that they asked him no very hard questions.

Thomas was now eighteen years old. He had a fresh, ruddy face, and was strong and full of courage.

The fourth-class men at this school were called by their school-mates "plebs," and

*View of West Point from Fort Putnam.*

were made to sweep and scrub the barracks and to do other tasks of the same kind. The third-class men would play pranks upon the new boys, some of which were quite hard to bear. Now, when they saw this country boy in his home-spun clothes, they thought that they would have rare sport out of him. But such were his courage and good temper that they soon let him alone.

He now studied hard, for, being behind his class, he had double work to do. He once said to a friend that he studied very hard for what he learned at West Point.

Just as when he was a boy, if he did not understand the lesson of the day, he would not pass over it to the next, but would work on until he knew all about it.

It was often the case that when called to the black-board to recite, he would say that he was still at work on the last lesson. This, of course, caused him to get low marks, but he was too honest to pretend to know what he did not understand at all. His teachers judged his mind sound and strong, but not quick. What he lacked in quickness, he made up in steady work; so, at the end of the fourth year, he graduated seventeenth in his class.

During the second year at West Point, he grew, as it were, by a leap to the height of six feet; and in his cadet uniform was very fine-looking.

He was neat in his attire, and kept his gun clean and bright.

It is said that one day during this year, he found that his bright musket had been stolen, and that a foul and rusty one had been put into its place.

He told the captain of his loss, and gave him a mark by which his gun might be known. That evening it was found in the hands of a fellow-cadet who had stolen it and then told a falsehood to shield himself from punishment.

Jackson had been angry because of his musket, but now he was deeply vexed at the falsehood, and asked that the cadet should be sent away, as he was unfit to remain at the academy. The friends of the boy at last prevailed upon him to waive his right of pressing the charge, and the erring cadet was let alone. Not long after, the cadet again broke the rules of the school and was sent away in disgrace.

From this we see that Jackson had at that time a hatred of all that was low and wicked.

He now wrote, in a blank book, a number of maxims as rules for his life. They touched on morals, manners, dress, the choice of friends, and the aims of life. One of these rules every boy should keep in mind. It was this :

"You may be whatever you resolve to be."

We shall see that this was indeed the guiding star of his life. Whatever he willed to do he always did by sheer force of endeavor.

At this time it is plain that it was his purpose to place his name high up on the roll of earthly honor. Beneath his shy and modest manners, there burned the wish to be truly great. His life was not yet ruled by love of Christ, but it shows some of the highest and noblest aims.

Jackson was twenty-two years old when he left West Point, June 30, 1846. He then took the rank of second lieutenant of artillery in the United States army. The artillery is that branch of an army which fights with cannon, or big guns. At that time a war was going on between the United States and Mexico. General Scott was then going to the seat of war to take the chief command of the army of the United States; and Jackson, the young lieutenant, was sent to join him in the south of Mexico.

———————

Ca-det' (kā-det'), a military pupil.
Warrant (wŏr'-rant), a certificate.
Max'-im (măks-im), a wise saying.
Mor'als (mŏr-als), conduct.
Waive (wāv), to give up.

Tell what you remember about—

> Jackson's going to West Point.
> His life at West Point.
> The cadet who stole his musket.
> The important maxim.
> His age and rank when he left West Point.
> The war which was going on at that time.

## CHAPTER III.

### A Major of Artillery.

On the 9th day of March, 1847, thirteen thousand five hundred troops were landed in one day from the American fleet upon the sea-shore near Vera Cruz (Vā-rä Kroos).

This fine army, with its waving flags and bright guns, presented a scene of splendor which Lieutenant Jackson never forgot.

General Scott's plan was to take the city of Vera Cruz by storm, and then march over the hills and valleys and lofty mountains to the City of Mexico.

This was a hard task, and cost many lives, as I will show you.

On the 13th of March, General Scott had placed his men all around the city of Vera Cruz and was ready for battle. On the 29th of March, after a fierce battle, the city was

*Bird's-Eye View of City of Mexico.*

taken by the Americans. This was the first battle in which our hero took part, and it is said that he fought bravely.

From Vera Cruz, the army marched on until it came to a mountain, on the crest of which was the strong fort of Cerro Gordo (Sĕr'-rō Gôr'-dō). Here, our troops were led by Captain Robert E. Lee, of the engineers, over a rough road planned by him, to the rear of the Mexicans. The Americans being in front of the Mexicans and also behind them, the latter were soon put to flight, leaving many men and guns on the battle-field.

After this battle, Jackson was placed in the light artillery, which used small cannon and moved rapidly from place to place.

This change was just what young Jackson wished, for though more dangerous, the light artillery service gave him a better chance to win the honors for which his soul thirsted.

Santa Anna, the general of the Mexicans, now brought forward another large army and placed it on the mountain heights of Cherubus'co. Here, a fierce fight took place, and the Mexicans were again driven back.

As a reward for his brave conduct in this fight, our hero was given the brevet rank of captain of artillery. The army then marched on over the mountains to the strong castle of Chapultepec (Chä-pool'-tā-pĕk'). This castle was built upon a high hill guarding the plain which led to the City of Mexico. The level plain at the foot of the mountain was covered with crops of corn and other grain, and with groves of trees. Here and there were deep and wide ditches which the farmers had dug for drains. These ditches the artillery and horsemen could not cross; in fact, the growing crops so concealed them that the men could not see them until they had reached their brinks.

Within the castle of Chapultepec were swarms of Mexican soldiers, while around its base were cannon, so placed as to sweep every road that led up to it.

On the 13th of September the assault was made on three sides at the same time. Jackson was sent with his men and guns to the northwest side. Two regiments of infantry, or footmen, marched with him.

They pushed forward, pouring shot and shell at the foe, until they were quite close to their guns, and at so short a range that Jackson in a few moments found a number of his horses killed and his men struck down or scattered by the storm of grapeshot.

Just at this time, General Worth, seeing how closely Jackson was pressed, sent him word to fall back. Jackson, however, replied that if General Worth would send him fifty more men he would march forward and take the guns which had done such deadly work.

While the troops were coming up, it is said that Jackson lifted a gun by hand across a deep ditch, and began to fire upon the Mexicans with the help of only one man, the rest of his command being either killed, wounded, or hidden in the ditch.

*Jackson moving cannon across a ditch.*

Soon another cannon was moved across the ditch, and in a few moments the foe was driven back by the rapid firing of these two guns.

By this time, the men storming the castle on the other two sides had fought their way in, and the Mexicans began to fall back upon the City of Mexico.

Orders had been given that when this move took place, the artillery must move forward rapidly and scatter the ranks of the foe. In an instant Jackson's guns were thundering after the Mexicans, fleeing through the gates into the city.

The next morning, September 14th, the gates were forced and the Americans marched into the city of Mexico.

For his brave conduct in the battle of Chapultepec, Jackson was raised to the rank of major.

In after years, when he was modestly telling of this battle, a young man cried out, "Major, why did you not run when so many of your men and horses were killed?" He replied, with a quiet smile, "I was not ordered to do so. If I had been *ordered* to run I should have done so."

Once, when asked by a friend if he felt no fear when so many were falling around him, he said that he felt only a great desire to perform some brave deed that would win for him lasting fame. At that time, his thoughts were chiefly fixed upon the faithful performance of his duty, and gaining honor and distinction thereby.

In the beautiful City of Mexico, the American army now rested from warfare. Some months passed before Jackson's command was ordered home. His duties being light, he began the study of the Spanish language, and was soon able to speak it well. He greatly enjoyed the fine climate of Mexico, and admired the beauty and grace of her women.

For the first time in his life, he began to think of religion and to study the Bible in search of the truth.

On May 26th, 1848, a treaty of peace was made between the United States and Mexico, and the war being over, the American troops were sent home.

Major Jackson's command was sent to Fort Hamilton, about seven miles from the city of New York. While there, he was baptized and admitted to his first communion in the Episcopal Church.

4

After he had been at Fort Hamilton two years, Major Jackson was sent to Fort Meade, near Tampa Bay, on the west coast of Florida. While at this place, on the 28th of March, 1851, he was elected professor of natural and experimental philosophy and artillery tactics in the Military Institute at Lexington, Virginia.

---

Bre-vĕt', a commission which gives an officer a rank above his pay.

As-sault', an attack, a violent onset.

Clī'mate, the prevailing state with regard to heat and cold, &c.

What do you remember about—

The landing of troops at Vera Cruz?

The assault upon the castle of Chapultepec?

The taking of the City of Mexico by the Americans?

The new rank of Jackson?

His life in the City of Mexico?

What he once said about running?

What happened at Fort Hamilton?

The position which he accepted March 27th, 1851?

## CHAPTER IV.

### A Professor.

In writing of Major Jackson as a professor, it seems highly appropriate to mention

*Entrance to the Virginia Military Institute Grounds.*

the circumstances leading to his appointment to that position.

Reared in adverse circumstances, which prevented him in early youth from receiving the benefits of a good common-school educa-

tion, by his own efforts, mainly, he fitted
himself to enter the United States Military
Academy at West Point.    His first year's
course would have discouraged him in prose-
cuting his studies had he not been conscious
that there was that within, which, if properly
nurtured, would lead to ultimate success.
In his second year, he raised his general
standing from 51 to 30; in the third, from
30 to 20, and in the fourth, his graduating
year, from 20 to 17.    His upward progress
attracted attention, and one of his associates
remarked: "Had Jackson remained at West
Point upon a course of four years' longer
study, he would have reached the head of his
class."

His advancement in the Mexican war,
rising rapidly from brevet second lieutenant
of artillery to brevet major, was no less
marked than that at the academy, and his
gallant and meritorious services had been
heralded to the world through the official
reports of his superiors.

General Francis H. Smith, superintendent of the Virginia Military Institute, in "Institute Memorial," writes:

"It is not surprising that, when the Board of Visitors of the Virginia Military Institute were looking about for a suitable person to fill the chair of Natural and Experimental Philosophy and Artillery, the associates of this young and brave major of artillery should have pointed him out as worthy to receive so distinguished an honor. Other names had been submitted to the Board of Visitors by the Faculty of West Point, all of men distinguished for high scholarship and for gallant services in Mexico. McClellan, Reno, Rosecrans, afterward generals in the Northern army, and G. W. Smith, who afterward became a general in the Confederate army, were thus named. But the peculiar fitness of young Jackson, the high testimonials to his personal character, and his nativity as a Virginian, satisfied the Board that they might safely select him for the vacant chair without seeking candidates from other States. He was, therefore, unanimously elected to the professorship on the 28th of March, 1851, and entered upon the duties of his chair on the 1st of September following.

"The professorial career of Major Jackson was marked by great faithfulness, and by an unobtrusive, yet earnest spirit. With high mental endowments, *teaching* was a new profession to him, and demanded, in the important department of instruction assigned to him, an amount of labor which, from the state of his health, and especially from the weakness of his eyes, he rendered at great sacrifice.

"Conscientious fidelity to duty marked every step of his life here, and when called to active duty in the field he had made considerable progress in the preparation of an elementary work on optics, which he proposed to publish for the benefit of his classes.

"Strict, and at times stern, in his disci-

*Virginia Military Institute Barracks (fore-shortened)*

(47)

pline, though ever polite and kind, he was not always a popular professor; but no professor ever possessed to a higher degree the confidence and respect of the cadets for his unbending integrity and fearlessness in the discharge of his duty. If he was exact in his demands upon them, they knew he was no less so in his own respect for and submission to authority; and, thus, it became a proverb among them, that it was useless to write an excuse for a report made by Major Jackson. · His great principle of government was, that *a general rule should not be violated for any particular good;* and his animating rule of action was, that *a man could always accomplish what he willed to perform.*

"Punctual to a minute, I have known him to walk in front of the superintendent's quarters in a hard rain, because the hour had not quite arrived when it was his duty to present his weekly class reports.

"For ten years, he prosecuted his unwearied labors as a professor, making during this period, in no questionable form, such an impress upon those who from time to time were under his command, that, when the war broke out, the spontaneous sentiment of all cadets and graduates was, *to serve under him as their leader.*"

An incident is related by General Smith in the same work, which shows clearly how Jackson was looked upon in the community in which he resided:

"He left the Virginia Military Institute on the 21st of April, 1861, in command of the corps of cadets, and reported for duty at Camp Lee, Richmond. Dangers were thickening rapidly around the State. Invasion by overwhelming numbers seemed imminent. Norfolk, Richmond, Alexandria, and Harper's Ferry were threatened. Officers were needed to command at these points. The Governor of Virginia nominated Major Jackson as a colonel of volunteers. His nomination was immediately and unanimously confirmed by the Council of State.

and sent to the Convention then in session. Some prejudice existed in that body from the supposed influence of the Virginia Military Institute in these appointments, and the question was asked by various members, 'Who is this Thomas J. Jackson'? A member of the Convention from the county of Rockbridge, Hon. S. McDowell Moore, replied: 'I can tell you who he is. *If you put Jackson in command at Norfolk, he will never leave it alive unless you order him to do so.*' Such was the impress made upon his neighbors and friends in his quiet life as a professor at the Military Institute."

In accepting the position of professor, he was again stepping higher. In active warfare an officer may advance rapidly, but in times of peace he lives quietly at a military post and simply rusts out. Ill-health, brought on mainly by exposure in the Mexican War, caused Major Jackson to resign his commission in the army; but in all probability, had this not been the case he would have aban-

doned army life, because he felt that by
close study and application, he could reach
a much higher degree of mental excellence
than he had attained; and the position of
professor would enable him to do this, for he
knew that the best way to learn was to
teach.

In consequence of the weakness of his
eyes, his great will-power had now to be
exerted to the utmost, because he could not
use his eyes at night.    In order to do himself
and his classes justice, each morning after
class hours, he would carefully read over the
lessons for the next day, and, at night after
his simple supper, he would quietly sit with
his face to the wall and go over in his mind
the lessons read that day.    In this way he
made them his own, and was prepared to
teach the next day.    This training was of
great use to him in his after life as a soldier.
The power of his mind was such that while
riding, in later years, at the head of his army,
he could study the movements of the foe, and

plan his own with as much care and skill as in the quiet of his study at home.

The statement made by General Smith respecting the desire of the cadets to serve under Major Jackson in the war shows how popular he was, and this estimate of his powers could have been produced only by their knowledge of his great worth.

"Old Jack" was the name given to the Major by the cadets, but it was never used derisively. Pranks were played in Major Jackson's section room by the cadets, but more for their own amusement than for any other purpose. They well knew the consequences if caught, but were willing to run the risk for the sake of fun.

Cadet Abe Fulkerson once wore a collar made out of three fourths of a yard of linen, (for no other purpose than to produce a laugh) and it made even "Old Jack" laugh—that is, smile, which he would not have done if the size, shape, or color of collars had been fixed by the Institute regulations.

Cadet Davidson Penn, with an uncom-
monly solemn face and apparently in good
faith, once asked Major Jackson, "Major, can
a cannon be so bent as to make it shoot
around a corner?" The Major showed not
the slightest sign of impatience or of merri·
ment, but after a moment of apparently
sober thought, replied, "Mr. Penn, I reckon
hardly."

It has been said that Major Jackson never
smiled or laughed. It has just been shown
that he smiled *once*, and there is no doubt
but that if he could have been seen when he
read the excuse mentioned below, not only
would another smile have been seen, but a
good, hearty laugh heard. At artillery drill
one evening Major Jackson had given the
command, "Limbers and caissons pass your
pieces, trot, march!" Cadet Hambrick failed
to *trot* at command and was reported. The
next day the following excuse was handed
in: Report, "Cadet Hambrick not trotting
at artillery drill." Excuse, "I am a natural

pacer." These three incidents are recounted by Dr. J. C. Hiden, of Richmond, Virginia.

Cadet Thos. B. Amiss, who was afterwards surgeon of one of Jackson's Georgian regi-

*Professor Jackson's Class-room, Virginia Military Institute.*

ments, tried a prank for the double purpose of evading a recitation and creating a laugh. He was squad-marcher of his section, and after calling the roll and making his report to the officer of the day, he turned the section over to the next man on the roll, took his place in ranks, and cautioned the new squad-marcher not to report him absent. While the squad-marcher was making his report to Major Jackson whose eyes seemed always riveted to his class-book when this was being done, Amiss noiselessly climbed to the top of a column that stood nearly in the center of the room. Having received the report, Major Jackson commenced to call the names of those whom he wished to recite at the board, commencing with Amiss; not hearing Amiss respond, he asked, "Mr. Amiss absent?" The squad-marcher replied, "No, sir." The Major looked steadily along the line of faces, seemed perplexed and cast his eyes upwards, when he spied the delinquent at the top of the column. The Major, for a moment, gazed at the clinging figure and said, "You stay there," and Amiss had to remain where he was until the recitation was over. He was reported, court-martialed, received the maximum number of demerits, and had a large number of extra tours of guard duty assigned him, during the walking of which in the lone hours of the night, he had ample time to repent of his folly.

When the class that graduated in 1860 commenced its recitations under Major Jackson, a sudden end was made to all kinds of merriment in his class-room. A member of the class, who is now a member of Congress from Virginia, concealed a small music-box under his coatee and carried it into the class-room. After the recitation had commenced he touched a spring and the room was filled with sweet, muffled strains of music. Major Jackson did not hear, or if he did, took no notice of it. The cadet, finding that his music was not duly appreciated, commenced to bark, in very low tones, like a puppy, and this meeting with the same fate as the music he became emboldened and barked louder. Major Jackson, without changing his countenance, turning his head, or raising his voice above an ordinary tone, said, "Mr. C., when you march the section in again, please leave that puppy outside." The laugh was on the young cadet, and the result stated followed.

The following incident illustrates clearly how regardless Major Jackson was of public opinion or personal feeling when in conflict with duty. A young cadet was dismissed through a circumstance that occurred in Major Jackson's class-room, and he became so enraged that he challenged the Major to fight a duel, and sent him word that if he would not fight he would kill him on sight. Major Jackson, actuated solely by conscientious motives, took the necessary precautions to prevent a conflict, and informed the young man, through his friends, that if he were attacked he would defend himself. The attack was not made, notwithstanding the fact that the Major passed back and forth as usual. This cadet, during the Civil War, learned to know Major Jackson better, was under his command, and before the close of the war commanded the "Stonewall Brigade," which was rendered so famous by Jackson; and in later years, when asked his opinion of this great man, said that he was the only man ever born who had never been whipped.

Major Jackson seemed to enjoy the duty of drilling the artillery battery more than any other duty he had to perform, and it was natural that he should, for he had won fame as an artillery officer in the Mexican War.

Near the close of every session of the Institute, Major Jackson was required to drill the battery before the Board of Visitors; and in order to make it more interesting to the public, always present in large crowds, blank cartridges were fired, and the drill had really the semblance of a battery in actual battle. An impressive scene was witnessed at this drill in 1860. It commenced at 5 P. M. Major Jackson had put the battery through its various evolutions, and as the time ap-

*Where Major Jackson trained artillerymen (Virginia Military Institute Parade-Grounds).*

proached for the firing to commence, seemed
more and more interested in his work.   His
old professor of engineering at West Point,
Dennis Mahan, and the commandant of cadets
of that institution, Colonel Hardee, witnessed
the drill.   Ever since the commencement of
the evolutions, a dark cloud had been gather-
ing in the west and the rumbling of thunder
could be heard.   The firing commenced and
all was excitement.   Closer and closer came
the cloud, and the artillery of heaven seemed
replying to the discharges of the battery.
Major  Jackson  had  been  slowly  retreating
before the imaginary foe, firing by half battery.   The  cloud  came  nearer  and  nearer,
unheeded by Jackson.   Suddenly his voice
rang  clear  and  sharp, ''Fire  advancing
by half battery''—the foe were retreating—
''right-half b a t t e r y  advance, commence
firing!''   New positions were rapidly taken,
and the firing was at its height.   Then the
storm broke in all its fury.   Up to that time
the Major had  seemed  oblivious  to  all  save

the drill. The bursting storm brought him to himself and he dismissed the battery, which at once went to shelter. Major Jackson remained where he was, folded his arms and stood like a statue in the driving storm. An umbrella was sent him from a house close by with an invitation to come to cover. He replied, ''No, thank you;'' and there he stood until the storm was over, doubtless thinking of the hard-fought fields of Mexico and the havoc he had there wrought.

In November, 1851, Major Jackson connected himself with the Presbyterian church at Lexington, then in charge of the Rev. Dr. W. S. White. It now seemed his chief desire to do good. He was made a deacon and given a class of young men in the Sunday school. Some of them still live and remember how faithfully he taught them. He also gathered together the African slaves of the town every Sabbath evening for the purpose of teaching them the truths of the Bible. He soon had a school of eighty or a hundred pupils and twelve teachers. This school he kept up from 1855 to 1861, when he left Lexington to enter the army; and until his death it was always a great pleasure to him to hear of his black Sunday school.

Duty became now more than ever the rule of his life—duty to God and duty to man. So great was his regard for the Sabbath that he would not even read a letter, or mail one which he knew would be carried on that day.

The Rev. R. L. Dabney tells us that one Sabbath, when a dear friend, who knew that the Major had received a letter from his lady-love late on Saturday night, asked, as they were walking to church, "Major, surely you have read your letter?" "Certainly not," said he. "What obstinacy!" exclaimed his friend. "Do you not think that your desire to know its contents will distract your mind from divine worship far more than if you had done with reading it?" "No," answered he, quietly, "I shall make the most faithful

effort I can to control my thoughts, and as I
do this from a sense of duty, I shall expect
the divine blessing upon it.''

When a single man, he made it a rule to
accept, if possible, all invitations, saying
that when a friend had taken the trouble to
invite him it was his duty to attend.

Major Gittings, once a cadet, and a rela-
tive of Major Jackson, says: ''Speaking from
a social standpoint, no man ever had a more
delicate regard for the feelings of others than
he, and nothing would embarrass him more
than any *contretemps* that might occur to
cause pain or distress of mind to others.
Hence, he was truly a polite man, and while
his manner was often constrained, and even
awkward, yet he would usually make a
favorable impression, through his desire to·
please.''

When Major Jackson first came to Lexington he was in ill-health, and many things he
did were looked upon as odd, which were
really not so. He had been at a famous

water-cure hospital in the North, and had been ordered to live on stale bread and buttermilk and to wear a wet shirt next to his

*Major Jackson's Home in Lexington.*

body.    He was also advised to go to bed at 9 o'clock.    If that hour found him at a party or lecture, or any other place, in order to obey his physician, he would leave.

The dyspepsia with which he suffered

often caused drowsiness, and he would sometimes go to sleep while talking to a friend
or while sitting in his pew at church.

General Hill says of him: "I have seen
his head bowed down to his very knees
during a good part of the sermon. He
always heard the text of our good pastor,
the Rev. Dr. White, and the first part of
the sermon, but after that all was lost."
Before leaving Lexington, he seemed to have
gained complete control over his muscles,
even while asleep, for no one, in the few
years preceding his departure, ever saw "his
head and his knees in contact," but it was
a common thing to see him sound asleep
while sitting perfectly upright.

Before marriage, Major Jackson had his
room in barracks, but took his meals at a
hotel in Lexington, and it has been said by
some that his eccentricities caused much
comment; more than that, he was laughed at
and insulted by rude, coarse persons. This
could hardly have been true, for an insult

offered to "Old Jack" would certainly have been found out in some way, and if not resented personally, it would have been by the cadets to a man. One who lived in Lexington during four years of Major Jackson's residence there, and more than a quarter of a century after the war, never heard of these insults, and, surely, had they ever been given they would have been talked of, for Jackson's name was on every tongue, and the incidents of his life, from boyhood to death, were almost a constant subject of conversation.

Though Major Jackson was very modest, no man ever relied more fully upon himself. Mentioning one day to a friend that he was going to begin the study of Latin, he received the reply that one who had not studied the forms of that language in youth could never become master of it in later years. To this Jackson replied, "No; if I attempt it, I shall become master of the language. *I can do what I will to do.*"

This stern will-power came to the aid of

his ambition many times. He found it difficult to speak in public, and in order to acquire the art, he joined a literary club called the "Franklin Society." He was always at the meetings, and spoke in his turn; but, at first, his efforts were painful both to himself and to his hearers. His health was poor, his nerves were unstrung, and sometimes he was so confused that he would break down in the middle of a sentence for want of the right word. When this happened, he would quietly sit down, and when his turn in the debate came again would rise and make another attempt. Thus, before the close of the debate, he would succeed in telling what was in his mind. By thus trying time after time, he became a good speaker.

Soon after joining the Presbyterian church, good Dr. White, his pastor, called upon him to pray in public. He prayed in such a halting way that Dr. White told him that he would never again ask him to perform so hard a task. Major Jackson replied that it

was a cross to him to pray in public, but
that he had made up his mind to bear it,
and did not wish to be excused. So he kept
on trying, and soon became a leader in
prayer.

General Hill, speaking of this incident,
says: "I think his conduct in this case was
due to his determination to conquer every
weakness of his nature. He once told me
that when he was a small boy, being sick, a
mustard plaster was placed upon his chest,
and his guardian mounted him upon a horse
to go to a neighbor's house, so that his mind
might be diverted and the plaster kept on.
He said that the pain was so dreadful that
he fainted soon after getting off his horse.
I asked him if he had kept it on in order to
obey his guardian. He answered, 'No, it
was owing to a feeling that I have had from
childhood not to yield to trials and difficulties.'"

The same close friend also writes: "Dr.
Dabney thinks that he was timid, and that

nothing but his iron will made him brave. I think this is a mistake. The muscles of his face would twitch when a battle was about to open, and his hand would tremble so that he could hardly write. His men would see the working of his face and would say, 'Old Jack is making faces at the Yankees.' But all this only showed weak nerves. I think he loved danger for its own sake.''

Like St. Paul, ''he kept his body under,'' and would not let any appetite control him or any weakness overcome him. He used neither coffee, tobacco, nor spirits, and he would go all winter without cloak or overcoat in the mountains of Virginia, giving as a reason that he ''did not wish to give way to cold.''

For a like reason, he never drank spirits of any kind. It is told of him that once during the Civil War, when he was too near the outposts of the foe to have fire, and being greatly chilled, he was advised by his surgeon to take a drink of brandy. He at length agreed to take some, but made such a wry face in swallowing it that some one asked him if it choked him. "No," he replied, "I like it. That is the reason I never use it." Another time, being asked to take a drink of brandy, he said, "No, I thank you; I am more afraid of it than all the Federal bullets."

The immortal Jackson afraid of strong drink! What a lesson to people who have not the courage to say "No," when tempted to do wrong!

In the midst of this busy life as professor, Major Jackson was married, on August 4th, 1853, to Miss Eleanor Junkin, the daughter of the president of Washington College, Lexington, Virginia. This lovely lady lived only fourteen months after her marriage. Major Jackson's grief at her death was so great as to alarm his friends. His health, never good, suffered seriously, and his friends induced him in the summer of 1856 to take a trip to Europe, hoping that "the spell might be broken which bound him to sadness."

His European trip benefited him very materially in health and spirits, and on his return he, with great zeal, resumed his labors in his classes at both the Military Institute and the Sunday School.

He had started on his return trip in ample time to reach the Institute at its opening, September 1st, which he had promised to do; but storms had prevented this and he was behind time.

A lady friend, knowing what a slave he was to his word, asked him if he had not been miserable at the delay. The answer was characteristic of the man. He had done his part, Providence had intervened, and he had not worried in the least. No man ever trusted Providence more implicitly than Jackson, and when he went to God in prayer he knew that his feet would be guided in the right way.

Dr. Dabney tells us that one day, when a friend said that he could not understand how one could "pray without ceasing," Jackson replied that he had, for some time, been in the habit of praying all through the day. "When we take our meals," said he, "there is grace, and when I take a draught of water, I always pause to lift up my heart to God in thanks for the 'water of life'; and when I go to my class-room and await the coming of the cadets, that is my time to pray for them. And so with every other act of the day." Thus we see that Jackson was truly a "praying man."

His pastor, Rev. Dr. White, once said that Major Jackson was the happiest man that he had ever known. This happiness came from his faith in the saving care of God.

We are told that a friend once said to him, "Suppose you should lose your eyesight and then, too, be very ill, and have to depend on those bound to you by no tie, would not this be too much for your faith? Do you think you could be happy then?" He thought a moment and then said, "If it were the will of God to place me on a sick bed, He would enable me to lie there in peace a hundred years."

Such was the faith of this great man! As he grew older his spirit became more saintly until, when called upon to go up higher to meet his Lord, his end seemed more like a passing over than a death.

Major Jackson was married again, on July 15th, 1857, to Mary Anna Morrison, the daughter of Dr. R. H. Morrison, a Presbyterian minister, of North Carolina. This lady is now living, and has quite lately written a life of her husband, in which she gives beautiful glimpses of their home life in Lexington, and also extracts from his letters written to her during the Civil War, of which I must so soon tell you.

Shortly after his second marriage, Major Jackson bought a house and a few acres of land, and soon all of his spare time was spent in working in his garden and fields.

We are told that his little farm of rocky hill-land was soon well fenced and tilled, and that he used to say that the bread grown there by the labor of himself and slaves tasted sweeter than that which was bought.

He liked to have his friends visit him, and

*Mrs. T. J. Jackson in 1899.*

nowhere else was he so easy and happy as with his guests at his own table.

In his home, military sternness left his brow and the law of love took its place.

This story is told of him, which shows how

gentle and tender a soldier may be. "Once a friend, who was taking his little four-year-old girl on a journey without her mother, called on the way to spend the night with Major Jackson. At bed-time, when Mrs. Jackson wished to take the child to her room for the night, the father replied that his little one would give less trouble if he kept her with him. In the still watches of the night, he heard a soft step, and felt a hand laid upon his bed. It was Major Jackson, who, fearing that the little girl would toss off the covering, had come to see that all was safe."

This good and peaceful life at Lexington was short. The black cloud of war was hovering over our land and ere long the storm burst in great fury, sweeping Major Jackson away from his quiet life, his professorial duties, and his loved wife and friends, into the midst of carnage and death, and to deeds that made his fame world-wide and immortal.

Major Jackson had but one more duty to perform as a professor and officer of the Virginia Military Institute. He had been left in charge of the corps of cadets when the superintendent had been called to Richmond. Early on the morning of Sunday, April 21st, 1861, an order was received by Major Jackson from Governor John Letcher, directing him to leave with his command for Richmond at 12:30 P. M. that day. Major Jackson's arrangements were promptly made, and he sent a request to his pastor, good Dr. White, to come to the Institute and hold religious services for the young men prior to their departure. These services were held in front of the barracks. The battalion was drawn up in line of battle, Major Jackson at the head and venerable Dr. White in the front and center. All, with bowed heads, were devoutly listening to the invocations speeding heavenward. The clock in the Institute tower gave the signal for departure, and, without a moment's pause, Jackson took up the line of march and left his beloved pastor praying.

The key-note of his great success as a soldier was prompt obedience to orders and requiring the same of others.

---

Me-mo′ri-al, something designed to keep in remembrance a person, place, or event.

Fac′ul-ty, the body of instructors in a school.

Prof-es-so′ri-al, pertaining to a professor.

Coat-ee′ (cō-tē′), a short military coat.

Con′sci-en′-tious, governed by conscience.

Ŏb′sti-na-cy, stubbornness.

Tell about—

Major Jackson's appointment as professor in the Virginia Military Institute.

His reasons for resigning his position in the army and accepting a professorship.

His life at the Institute.

His method of studying.

His Sunday school for negroes.

His strict observance of the Sabbath.

His home life.

## CHAPTER V.

### A Confederate Colonel.

BEFORE going on with the life of our hero, I must tell you, in a few plain and truthful words, the causes of the Civil War which in 1861 broke out between the States.

You remember that, after the Revolutionary War, the thirteen colonies agreed to form a Union, and adopted a set of laws called the Constitution of the United States.

From the very first, however, the States did not agree; in fact, laws which suited one section did not suit the other, so that there was always some cause for a quarrel.

At last, the question of slavery seemed to give the most trouble. You have been told that African slaves were first brought to Virginia in 1619 by the Dutch, and that afterwards English and Northern traders brought others, until all of the colonies held slaves.

The cold climate of the North did not suit the negroes, who had been used to the hot sun of Africa. So, by degrees, they were sold to Southern planters.

Many influential men North and South wished to see the slaves freed. But, as the slaves increased in the South, Southern men saw that a rapid abolition of slavery would be disastrous to both whites and blacks, because the negroes were not ready for it. As slavery decreased in the North, many Northern people did not realize this. Besides, the North did not wish slave labor to compete with the free labor of the North.

The North insisted that slaves should not be brought into the new States as they came into the Union. The South demanded that a slave-holder should be free to carry his slaves from one State into another.

Many Southern people also believed that the negroes were the happiest and best cared for working people in the world, and that the North was trespassing upon their just rights.

So the quarrel went on until October, 1859, when an event happened in Virginia which greatly increased the hatred of both parties. A man named John Brown laid a plot for freeing the negroes, first in Virginia and then in the whole South.

For two years, he sent men through the South secretly to stir up the negroes and incite them to kill the whites.   He bought long iron pikes for the negroes to fight with, as they did not know how to use fire-arms.

When he thought that all was ready, he entered Harper's Ferry by night, with only eighteen men, and seized the arsenal there, sending out armed men into the country to capture the principal slave-owners and to call upon the slaves to join him.   This was done secretly during the night, and the next morning every white man who left his home was seized, and imprisoned in an engine-house near the arsenal.   Only a few negroes came in, and they were too much scared to aid in the deadly and dastardly work.

As soon as the news of this raid spread over the country, angry men came into town from all sides, and before night John Brown and his men were shut up in the engine-house.

*Harper's Ferry, Virginia.*

Soon a band of marines, under the command of Colonel R. E. Lee, was sent out from Washington by the Government, and as John Brown would not surrender, the soldiers at once stormed the engine-house.

Ten of John Brown's men were killed by the soldiers, and all the rest, including Brown himself, were wounded. Six of the storming party were killed and nine wounded. John Brown and seven of his men were brought to trial at Charles Town, Virginia, and being found guilty of treason, were hanged.

The cadets of the Virginia Military Institute were ordered to Charles Town to protect the officers of the law. Major Jackson commanded a section of light artillery accompanying the battalion, and was present at the death of Brown. He afterwards gave his friends a graphic account of this dreadful scene.

This event cast great gloom over the country. Many persons at the North thought that John Brown had died a martyr to the cause of slavery, while the people at the South saw that they could no longer enjoy in peace and safety the rights granted to them by the Constitution.

Major Jackson was truly Southern in feeling. He believed in the "Rights of States" and also that the South ought to take her stand and resent all efforts to coerce and crush her. He, however, dreaded war and thought it the duty of Christians throughout the land to pray for peace.

A month before South Carolina went out of the Union, Major Jackson called upon his pastor, Dr. White, and said: "It is painful to know how carelessly they speak of war. If the Government insists upon the measures now threatened, there must be war. They seem not to know what its horrors are. Let us have meetings to pray for peace." Dr. White agreed to his request, and the burden of Major Jackson's prayer was that God would preserve the land from war.

After the election of Mr. Lincoln, in November, 1860, to be President of the United States, the Southern States saw no hope of getting their rights and resolved to secede, or withdraw from the Union of the States.

South Carolina took the lead and seceded on the 20th of December, 1860. She was quickly followed by Mississippi, Alabama, Florida, Georgia, Louisiana, and Texas.

On the 9th of January, 1861, these States united and at Montgomery, in Alabama, formed a government called "The Confederate States of America," with Jefferson Davis as President.

Virginia was slow to withdraw from the Union formed by the States; but, when President Lincoln called for seventy-five thousand soldiers to invade the Southern States, she delayed no longer. On April 17th, 1861, she seceded and began to prepare for war.

"In one week," says Dabney, "the whole State was changed into a camp." The sons of Virginia rushed to arms, and soon the city of Richmond was filled with men drilling and preparing to fight.

At daybreak on Sunday morning, April 21st, 1861, an order came to Lexington from the Governor of the State (Governor Letcher)

*View of the Business Portion of Richmond, Va., after the Evacuation Fire of 1865.*

to march the cadets that day to Richmond. As the senior officers were already in Richmond, Major Jackson at once prepared to go forward with his corps.

At eleven o'clock A. M. he went to his home to say good-bye to his wife. They retired to their own room, where he read the 5th chapter of Second Corinthians, which begins with these beautiful words: "For we know, if our earthly house of this tabernacle be dissolved, we have a building of God, an house not made with hands, eternal in the heavens."

He then knelt and prayed for themselves and for their dear country, imploring God that it might be His holy will to avert war and bloodshed. He then said good-bye to his wife and left his dear home, never more to return to it. After a few days, his wife went to live at the home of a friend—his house was closed.

Major Jackson and the cadets marched forward to Staunton, whence they went by train to Richmond, and at once went into camp on the Fair-Grounds.

From Richmond, Major Jackson wrote thus to his wife: "Colonel Lee, of the army, is here and has been made Major-General of the Virginia troops. I regard him a better officer than General Scott."

After a few days, on April 21st, Major Jackson was made colonel of the Virginia forces and ordered to take command at Harper's Ferry, a town on the Potomac river where the United States Government had had a great number of workshops and fire-arms. This important place had already been captured by Virginia troops, and it was necessary to hold it until the arms and machinery could be moved away.

Just here it may be well to give you a word-picture of our hero as he began a career which was to fill the world with his fame.

Jackson was tall and very erect, with large hands and feet. His brow was fair and broad; his eyes were blue placid and clear

*Colonel Thomas J. Jackson.*

when their owner was calm, but dark and flashing when he was aroused. His nose was Roman, his cheeks ruddy, his mouth firm, and his chin covered with a brown beard. His step was long and rapid, and if he was not a graceful rider, he was a fearless

This is a copy of a Portrait I have of my husband which I consider the best likeness extant Mrs. T. J. Jackson

one. In battle, or as he rode along his columns, hat in hand, bowing right and left to his soldiers, whose shouts arose on high, no figure could be nobler than his. Few, even of his intimate friends, were conscious of his military genius, so he burst upon the world as a meteor darts across a star-lit sky.

On his way to Harper's Ferry, he wrote thus to his dear wife:

"WINCHESTER, April 29th, 1861.

"I expect to leave here about two P. M. to-day for Harper's Ferry. I am thankful to say that an ever-kind Providence, who causes 'all things to work together for good to them that love Him,' has given me the post which I prefer above all others. To His name be all the praise. * * * You must not expect to hear from me very often, as I shall have more work than I have ever had in the same time before; but don't be troubled about me, as an ever-kind Heavenly Father will give me all needful aid."

"This letter," says a friend, "gives a true idea of his character. He feels within himself the genius and power which make him long to have a separate command; but he also feels the need of resting upon his Heavenly Father for aid and support."

Colonel Jackson had been ordered by Major-General Lee to organize and drill the men who had gathered at Harper's Ferry and to hold the place as long as possible against the foe.

He went to work with great zeal and, aided by Colonel Maury and Major Preston, soon had the men organized into companies and regiments. As Colonel Jackson was known to have been a brave soldier in the Mexican War, he was readily obeyed by the soldiers in his little army, which soon numbered forty-five hundred men.

But on the 2nd of May, Virginia joined the Southern Confederacy and handed over all of her soldiers to that government, which bound itself in return to defend Virginia and to pay her troops.

General Joseph E. Johnston was sent on the 23rd of May by the Confederate Government to take command at Harper's Ferry and Colonel Jackson at once gave up his trust to General Johnston.

The Virginia regiments at that place—the Second, the Fourth, the Fifth, the Twenty-seventh, and a little after, the Thirty-third,

with Pendleton's battery of light field-guns—
were now organized into a brigade, of which

Jackson was made the com-
mander. This was the bri-
gade which afterwards became
famous as the "Stonewall
Brigade," and which, we shall
see, did much hard fighting,

*Gen. J. E. Johnston.*

and was to the Southern army
what the "Tenth Legion" was to the great
Cæsar.

General Johnston soon found out that he
could not hold Harper's Ferry against the foe
which was now coming up under General
Patterson. He, therefore, burnt the great railroad bridge over the Potomac river at Harper's Ferry and moved away all his guns and
stores; then on Sunday, June 16th, he withdrew his little army to Bunker Hill, a place
about twelve miles from the city of Winchester. There he offered battle to General Patterson, but the latter refused to fight and
withdrew to the north bank of the Potomac.

On June 19th, Colonel Jackson was ordered to march northward and watch the foe, who was again crossing the river. He was also ordered to destroy the engines and cars of the Baltimore and Ohio railroad at Martinsburg.

This he did, though he writes of it in the following words: "It was a sad work; but I had my orders, and my duty was to obey."

Until July 2nd, Colonel Jackson, with his brigade, remained a little north of Martinsburg, having in his front Colonel J. E. B. Stuart with a regiment of cavalry. On that day General Patterson advanced to meet Jackson, who went forward with only one regiment, the Fifth Virginia, a few companies of cavalry, and one light field piece. A sharp skirmish ensued. At last, the foe coming up in large numbers, Jackson fell back to the main body of his troops after having taken forty-five prisoners, and killed and wounded a large number of the enemy. Jackson's loss was only two men killed and ten wounded.

In this battle, which is known as that of Haines's Farm, Colonel Jackson was, no doubt, the only man in the infantry who had ever been under fire, but they all behaved with the greatest coolness and bravery.

Jackson, in this first battle, showed such boldness, and at the same time such care for the lives of his men, that he at once gained a hold upon their esteem.

General Patterson now held Martinsburg; while General Johnston, having come up with the whole army, offered him battle each day. But Patterson had other plans, and soon moved away.

While General Johnston was at Winchester watching his movements, Colonel Jackson received this note:

" RICHMOND, July 3rd, '61.

*My Dear General:*

I have the pleasure of sending you a commission of Brigadier-General in the Provisional Army;

and to feel that you merit it.    May your advancement increase your usefulness to the State.

Very truly,

R. E. LEE."

General Jackson, for so we must now call him, was much pleased at this promotion, and wrote to his wife thus:

" Through the blessing of God, I have now all that I ought to wish in the line of promotion. May His blessing rest on you is my fervent prayer."

---

Ar'se̅-nal, a storehouse for arms and military stores.

Ma-ri̅nes', soldiers doing duty on a ship.

Mär'tyr, one who is put to death for the truth.

Se̅n'ior (sèn-yur), one older in age or office.

Vŏl-ŭn-teer', one who enters into any service of his own free will.

Me̅'teor, a shining body passing through the air.

Cæ'sar (sé-zär), a great Roman general.

Do you remember—

What happened in October 1859?

When Virginia seceded from the Union?

When Major Jackson left Lexington with the
cadets?

Of what place Colonel Jackson first took
command?

About Jackson's first battle?

*General Robert E. Lee.*

## CHAPTER VI.

### A Brigadier–General.

DURING the spring of 1861, the States of North Carolina, Tennessee, and Arkansas, also left the Union and joined the new Confederacy, the capital of which was now Richmond, Virginia.

The great object of the North was to capture Richmond. For this they raised four large armies to invade Virginia. The first was to go by way of Fortress Monroe; the second, by way of Manassas; the third was to march up the Shenandoah Valley; and the fourth was to come from the northwest.

Turn to the map of Virginia on the opposite page and find the places which I have mentioned, and you will understand the plan at once.

Now, the Confederate army was much smaller than the Federal army, because the

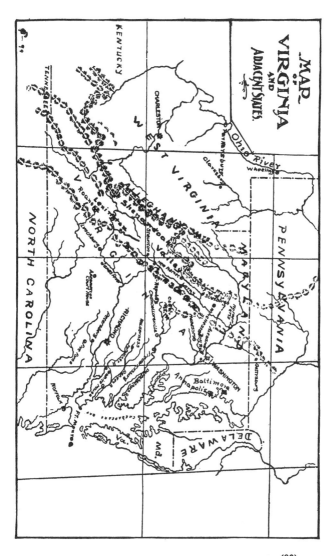

Southern States were thinly settled, while the North contained very many large cities and had the world from which to draw supplies of men as well as munitions of war.

The North also was rich, because it had the treasury of the United States, while the South was poor in both money and arms, and had the outside world closed against her.

So the Confederate leaders had to use great skill in meeting such large armies with so few men.

You remember that in the last chapter I told how General Johnston, at Winchester, with a small force was watching General Patterson. Now, just across the mountains,

*General Beauregard.*

sixty miles southeast, at Manassas, Beauregard (bo-re-gard), another famous Southern general, was facing a large Northern army under General McDowell. This army was thirty-five thousand strong, while the Confederates had only twenty-eight thousand men. General McDowell's army was composed of the best soldiers in the Northern States, and they had splendid fire-arms, artillery, uniforms, and tents—in fact, all that money could buy to make them do good service in the field.

On the other hand, the Confederates were poorly clad and had old muskets and cannon; many of the cavalry had only the shot-guns which they had used for hunting in their boyhood days.

The North fully expected that this fine army would crush the Confederates at one blow, and, when General McDowell was a little slow in marching forward to battle, began to cry, "On to Richmond."

Large crowds of idlers. editors, reporters. members of Congress, government officials, and even ladies went from Washington to the rear of the Federal army in order to witness the defeat of the Confederates.

General Beauregard now sent word to General Johnston to leave Patterson and come across the mountains to his aid. General Johnston at once sent Colonel Stuart with his cavalry to face Patterson, and to try to keep him from finding out that Johnston had left Winchester and had gone to the help of Beauregard.

This order Stuart obeyed so well that Johnston was at Manassas, sixty miles away, before Patterson discovered the ruse.

General Johnston's army set out from Winchester on the forenoon of Thursday, July 18th. The First Virginia Brigade, led by General Jackson, headed the line of march. As they passed through the streets of Winchester, the people asked, with sad faces, if they were going to hand them over to the foe. The soldiers, for reply, said that they knew not where, or for what purpose, they were marching southeast.

But when they had marched about three miles, General Johnston called a halt, and an order was read to them explaining that they were going to Beauregard, who was then on the eve of a great battle with McDowell. The General hoped that his troops would act like men and save their country.

At these words, the men rent the air with their shouts and went forward at a double-quick, waded the Shenandoah river, which was waist deep, crossed the Blue Ridge mountains at Ashby's Gap, and some hours after night paused to rest for awhile at the village of Paris, on the eastern slope of the mountains.

Dr. Dabney tells us that here, while the men slept, Jackson himself kept watch, saying, "Let the poor fellows sleep; I will guard the camp myself." For two hours he paced up and down under the trees, or sat on the fence. At last, an hour before day-break, he gave up his watch to a member of his staff, and rolling himself upon the grass in a fence-corner, was soon fast asleep.

At peep of day, the brigade was up and away, and, by dusk on July 19th, the whole

"*Let the poor fellows sleep; I will guard the camp myself.*"

command, dusty, hungry, and foot-sore, marched into an old pine-field near Manassas, where they spent Saturday in resting for the coming battle.

The Confederate lines stretched for eight miles along the southern bank of Bull Run, which could be forded at several places. At these fords General Beauregard had placed large bodies of men. On July 18th, before Jackson had come up, General McDowell had tried to take these fords, but his troops had been driven back.

He then made a plan to march a part of his forces around the Confederates' left wing at a certain stone bridge, and to get in their rear. Being thus between two large forces, the Confederates would be crushed or forced to surrender.

On Sunday morning, July 21st, General McDowell sent forward a portion of his troops to the stone bridge, which was guarded at that time by the gallant Colonel Evans, with only eleven hundred men. After he had fought desperately for several hours, and just as he was outflanked and sorely beset, Generals Bee and Bartow came up to his aid, and for awhile turned the tide of battle.

At last, however, the Confederates were slowly forced back by larger numbers. At this moment, General Jackson reached the spot with his brigade of two thousand six hundred men. These he quickly placed on the crest of a ridge in the edge of a pine thicket, and before them posted seventeen cannon.

Generals Bee and Bartow and Colonel Evans rallied their broken lines on the right; while on the left were a few regiments of Virginia and Carolina troops. The whole force numbered about six thousand five hundred men. The infantry of his brigade were ordered by Jackson to lie down behind the artillery to escape the fire of the enemy, who were now coming across the valley and up the hill with twenty thousand men and twenty-four cannon. Just then, Generals

Johnston and Beauregard galloped to the front and cheered the men on in every part of the field.

From eleven o'clock A. M. until three o'clock P. M., the artillery shook the earth with its dreadful roar, and thousands of musket-balls whizzed through the air, black with the smoke of battle.

While the artillery fight was going on, General Jackson rode back and forth between the guns and his regiments lying prone upon the ground in the burning sun, and greatly tried by bursting shell and grape-shot. His erect form and blazing eyes brought hope and courage to them in this their first baptism of fire.

At last General Bee, seeing his thin ranks begin to waver, said, "General, they are beating us back." "Then," said Jackson, "we will give them the bayonet." Bee, catching the spirit of Jackson, galloped back to his men, saying, "There is Jackson, standing like a stone wall! Rally behind the Virginians!" A few score of the men rallied around the gallant Bee and charged upon the foe. In a few moments the brave Bee fell dead, with his face to the foe. "From

*" There is Jackson, standing like a Stone Wall ! "*

that time," says Draper, an historian of the North, "the name which Jackson had received in a baptism of fire, displaced that which he had received in a baptism of water, and he was known ever after as 'Stonewall Jackson.'"

Both of Jackson's flanks were now in danger, and he saw that the moment had come to use the bayonet. Wheeling his cannon to right and left, he gave the signal to his men to rise, and cried out to the Second regiment, "Reserve your fire until they come within fifty yards; and then fire and give them the bayonet; and when you charge, yell like furies."

His men sprang to their feet, fired one deadly volley, and then dashed down upon the foe. The latter could not stand this dreadful onset, but turned and fled. A battery which had been captured by the foe was retaken, and the centre of the enemy's line of battle pierced by Jackson's men.

For four hours, Jackson had kept the enemy at bay, but now help was near at hand. Just as the Federals had rallied and again advanced in large numbers, General Kirby Smith, with a body of men which had

just come from the Valley, and Generals Early
and Holmes, with reserve troops, hurried up
and struck the right wing of the Federal
army, while the Confederates in the centre
turned against them their own guns.   This
onset proved too much for the Federals.   They
again fled; and this time, their retreat became a general rout.   The men in terror
cast away their guns, and leaving cannon
and flags, rushed for the nearest fords of Bull
Run.   The Confederate cavalry pursued them,
while Kemper's field battery ploughed them
through and through with shells.   The road
to Washington was one surging mass of human beings struggling to get away from the
dreadful field of death.

General Jackson's troops took no part in
pursuit except to plant a battery and fire at
the fleeing foe, many of whom did not stop
until they were safe across the Long Bridge
at Washington.

Though the Confederates were the victors,
they had lost many brave men.   Generals

Bee and Bartow were killed, and General Kirby Smith was badly wounded. General Jackson had been wounded in his left hand early in the action, but had taken no notice of it. Now that the battle was over, he felt the pain acutely, and went to the field-hospital, which had been placed by the side of a brook beneath the shade of some friendly willow-trees.

When he came up, his friend, Dr. McGuire, said, "General, are you much hurt?" "No," replied he; "I believe it is a trifle." "How goes the day?" asked the Doctor. "Oh!" exclaimed Jackson, "We have beaten them; we have gained a glorious victory." Dr. Dabney says that this was the only time that Jackson was ever heard to express joy at having gained the day.

When the surgeons came around him to dress his wounded hand he said, "No, I can wait; my wound is but a trifle; attend first to those poor fellows." He then sat down upon the grass and waited until the wounds of the badly hurt had been dressed. At first it was thought that his middle finger would have to be cut off, but Dr. McGuire having dressed it very skilfully, it was saved, and his hand at length healed.

It is stated by several friends that General Jackson said, while having his hand dressed, that, with ten thousand fresh troops, he believed that he could go into Washington city. However, as he was not the commanding general, he could not make the attempt, but could only do as he was ordered.

I must not fail to give you a part of a letter which he wrote to his wife the day after the battle, July 22nd:

"Yesterday we fought a great battle and gained a great victory, for which all the glory is due *to God alone*. Though under fire for several hours, I received only one wound, the breaking of the longest finger of the left hand, but the doctor says that it can be saved. My horse was wounded, but not killed. My coat got an ugly wound near the hip. * * * While great credit is due to other parts of our gallant army, God made my brigade more instrumental than any other in repulsing the main attack.

This is for you alone. Say nothing about it. Let another speak praise, not myself."

But the praise of the Stonewall Brigade was not sung by Jackson alone. Both friend and foe unite in saying that if Jackson had not held the hill, which was the key to the Confederate position, until help came, the battle of Manassas (Bull Run) would have been a defeat, and not a victory for the South.

Jackson's eagle eye saw the place to make a stand, and he held it for four hours against all odds.

At one time, while his men were lying upon the ground, they were so harassed by the bursting of shells that some of the officers begged to be permitted to advance. "No," said Jackson, "wait for the signal; *this place must be held.*"

We do not seek to take glory from other heroes of this wonderful battle, many of whom, as Bee and Bartow, bravely gave up their lives in the storm of battle; or, as Smith and Early, made forced marches in order to rescue those so sorely pressed; but we do say that, in one sense, Jackson was the hero of the first battle of Manassas.

In this battle the Confederates captured twenty-eight cannon with five thousand muskets and vast stores of articles useful to their needy army.

The Confederates lost three hundred and sixty-nine killed on the field, and fourteen hundred and eighty-three wounded.

The road to Washington was now open, and there is no doubt that General Jackson thought it best to press on while the enemy was routed and take possession of the city.

But the commanding generals were afraid to risk the attempt with an army which had been drilled only a few weeks and which had so little discipline; and, thus, the moment to strike passed by.

In a few days the North had chosen a

new commander, General McClellan, who set himself to raise new armies to defend Washington and to scourge the South.

Soon after the battle, General Jackson moved his men to a piece of woodland near by, where he employed the time in drilling his troops.    After a time the Confederate lines were pushed forward to within sight of Washington city, but no battle took place, as General McClellan was too wise to risk another engagement so soon after Manassas.

In October, General Jackson was promoted to the rank of Major-General, and was sent to the Shenandoah Valley to take command of the army which had been fighting in West Virginia.

The Stonewall Brigade was left behind with General Johnston.    This was a great trial, both to General Jackson and to the brigade.

When the time came for him to leave for the new field of war, he ordered the brigade to march out under arms, and then rode to their front with his staff. Dr. Dabney says that no cheer arose, but every face was sad.

After speaking a few words of praise and love, he threw his bridle reins on the neck of his horse, and stretching his arms towards them said: "In the Army of the Shenandoah, you were the First Brigade. In the Army of the Potomac, you were the First Brigade. In the Second Corps of the army, you are the First Brigade. You are the First Brigade in the affections of your General; and I hope, by your future deeds and bearing, you will be handed down to posterity as the First Brigade in this, our second War of Independence. Farewell."

He then waved his hand, and left the grounds at a gallop, followed by the cheers of his brave soldiers. This separation, however, was for but a short time. In November following, the First Brigade was ordered to join Jackson at Winchester, and it remained with him until the fatal hour at Chancellorsville, when it lost him forever.

Rüse (rooz), a trick.

Stáff, certain officers attached to an army.

Rout, fleeing in a confused and disorderly manner.

Ĭn'strū-mĕn'tăl, conducive to some end.

Dĭs'ciplĭne, order, rule.

Tell about—

> General Johnston's army ăt Winchester.
>
> Colonel Jackson's first battle in the Civil War.
>
> The march to Manassas.
>
> The first battle of Manassas.
>
> Jackson's farewell to the Stonewall Brigade.

*Jackson's military cap, sword, and buttons.*

## CHAPTER VII.

### A Major–General.

WHEN the year 1862 opened, General Jackson was at Winchester with ten thousand men, Generals Loring and Henry Jackson having come from Western Virginia to join his command.

At the head of Jackson's cavalry was Lieutenant-Colonel Ashby, a gallant, brave,

and watchful officer. At the sound of his well-known shout and the cry of "Ashby," from his men, the Federal soldiers would turn and flee as if from a host. Ever guarding the outposts of the army, he was Jackson's

*Lieut.-Col. Ashby.*

"eyes and ears."

There were now three great armies threatening Jackson, and he well knew that they would crush him if he did not meet each one singly before they could unite.

Jackson's little army was the guard to Johnston's flank. The latter general, with forty thousand men, was still at Manassas facing McClellan, who was at the head of an army of fifty thousand men, and preparing, as soon as spring opened, to "walk over Johnston."

Jackson knew that if his army was defeated, Johnston would have to retreat, and perhaps the whole State would be given up to the foe. The armies were now in winter quarters, and there was not much danger of a move before spring.

In the meantime, Jackson resolved to march against several large forces of Federals which were threatening him from the towns of Romney and Bath, forty miles distant, in Northwestern Virginia.

It was the last of December, however,

before he could collect the men and supplies necessary for the expedition.

At last, on the first day of January, 1862, all was ready. The little army of about nine thousand men set out without knowing whither Jackson was leading, for he had not told even his officers his great plans.

In spite of the winter season, the day was bright and the air soft and balmy. So warm was the weather that the men left their over-coats and blankets to be brought on in the wagons. On the next day, a biting wind began to blow, which was followed by rain and snow.

The men marched all day, and at night the wagons, which had not been able to keep up with the troops, were still far behind. The troops rested that night without rations or blankets, having only camp-fires to keep off the cold.

On the third day, the men were so over-come by cold and hunger that they found it difficult to go forward. Jackson, riding grimly along the way, found his old brigade halted, and asked General Garnett the reason of the delay.

"I have halted," said General Garnett, "to let the men cook rations."

"There is not time for it," replied General Jackson curtly.

"But it is impossible for the men to go farther without them," said Garnett.

"I never found anything impossible with that brigade," said Jackson as he rode on. He was restive and eager to press forward; his plan to surprise the enemy did not admit of delay.

As the army neared the town of Bath, a force of Federals suddenly attacked it from behind trees and fences, but it was soon driven off with the loss of twenty prisoners.

That night the Southern troops went into camp just outside the town, in the midst of a heavy snow storm. The men were without food or blankets, and the wonder is how they lived through the night.

Jackson, however, did not change his plans, though there was great complaint among the men, many of whom straggled back to Winchester.

The next morning, after a hearty breakfast, the order was given to advance upon Bath. The artillery opened fire and the infantry charged the breastworks, but the Federals hastily gave up the town, and fled towards the Potomac river, which they waded that night.

The Southern troops on entering the town found quantities of stores which the Federals had left behind; among them were fine clothes, china, and even dinners, cooked and still smoking, ready to be eaten by the hungry Confederates.

From Bath, Jackson's men passed, with great difficulty and suffering, to a place called Hancock, about three miles distant from Bath, on the north side of the Potomac.

Jackson placed his cannon on the south bank and opened a hot fire on the town, but the commander refused to surrender. As a large force of men came up to reinforce the Federals, Jackson concluded to pass on to Romney.

In the meantime, the railroad bridge over Capon river had been destroyed and the telegraph wires cut by General Loring, so that the commander at Romney could not send to General Banks for help.

The weather had now become terrible. Rain, snow, sleet, and hail beat down upon men still without tents, overcoats, and blankets; for it was impossible for the wagons to come up. The mountain roads were covered with ice and sleet so that horses and men could not keep their footing. Many fell flat, badly hurt, while wagon after wagon slid down the steep banks, and was overturned and broken.

Jackson was everywhere along the line cheering the troops and even helping them along. We are told by Cooke, our great Virginia writer, that, as Jackson was pass-

ing a point in the road where a piece of
artillery had stalled, while a crowd of men
were looking on without helping, he stopped,
dismounted, and, without uttering a word,
put his shoulder to the wheel. The men,
shamed, came forward to take their places,
the horses were whipped up, and the piece
moved on.

After great hardships, the little army at
last reached Romney, on the 14th of January,
to find that the Federals had retreated, leaving behind them large military stores, which
fell into the hands of the Confederates.

Even then, the name of Jackson was a
terror to the foe. With a force much larger
than Jackson's, and when he was more than
a day's march distant, the Federals had fled
and left the greater part of their baggage.

In sixteen days, he had driven the enemy
out of his district, had rendered the railroad
useless to the Federals for more than a hundred miles, and had captured arms enough
to equip an army as large as his own. This

he had done with the loss of four men killed
and twenty-eight wounded.

Leaving General Loring at Romney with
a portion of the army, Jackson hastened
back to Winchester to watch the movements
of General Banks, who was stationed, with a
large army, near Harper's Ferry.

Upon his return, he found the whole country in an uproar over the expedition to Romney through the sleet and snow.    Though
no one could say that Jackson was not full of
courage and devotion to the South, many
said that he was cruel and not fit to be in
command of an army.    Some said that he
was a madman; others, that he was without
common sense.    Another charge against him
was that he was partial to the Stonewall
Brigade, as he had brought it back with him
to the comforts of a town, while he had left
Loring's command in the mountains.    The
soldiers of the brigade were called "Jackson's Pet Lambs," and other like names.

Now, the truth was, that Loring's men

were far more comfortable than those of the Stonewall Brigade; the former being ordered into huts, while the latter were in tents, three miles from Winchester.

Another charge against him was that he would tell his plans to no one. "It was his maxim," says Dabney, "that in war, mystery was the key to success." He argued that no man could tell what bit of news might not be of use to the foe, and therefore, that it was the part of wisdom to conceal everything.

This secrecy irritated his officers, and it must be said that some of them so far forgot their duty as soldiers as to treat General Jackson with disrespect.

Though all of these charges were known to Jackson, he took no notice of them, but was proceeding to connect Romney with Winchester by telegraph wires when, on January 31st, he received this order from Richmond: "Order Loring back to Winchester at once."

The cause of this order was that some of the officers at Romney had sent a petition to Richmond asking to be sent back to Winchester, as the position at Romney was, in. their opinion, too much exposed.

General Jackson recalled the troops from Romney, but he was so angry at the way in which he had been treated by the government, that he at once resigned his command.

This caused great excitement in the army and in the State at large. The people were by no means willing to give up an officer who had shown so much courage and skill, and they begged him to withdraw his resignation. This he refused to do. He said that the government had shown, by the order, that it did not trust him, and that, if he was to be meddled with in that way, he could do no good. At last, however, a sort of an apology being made by the government, he quietly took up his duties again.

In a few days after General Loring left Romney, the Federals again took possession of that town and the country around. So all the efforts of Jackson and the trials of his soldiers were of no avail. This was a great blow to General Jackson, for Winchester was again exposed to the advance of the foe from four directions.

The plan for the invasion of Virginia in 1862 was the same as in 1861. General Fremont was marching from the Northwest; Banks, from Harper's Ferry; McDowell, from Fredericksburg; McClellan faced Johnston at Manassas, and another large army was at Fortress Monroe, ready to march up the Peninsula.

The Northern army was much larger than the year before, but the Southern army was smaller, as the time of many of the men had expired and others had gone home on furlough.

Several brigades were now taken from General Jackson to strengthen other points, and he found himself left, with only six thousand men, to guard the left of Johnston's army and to protect the great Shenandoah Valley.

On the 26th of February, General Banks, with thirty-five thousand men, and General Kelly, with eleven thousand, advanced against Jackson, who was still at Winchester, hoping to hold that place, until help could come from General Johnston. But finding out through Colonel Ashby that he was almost surrounded by the enemy, he left Winchester and fell back slowly to Mt. Jackson, a village on the great turnpike, forty miles from Winchester. Here, he had sent all of his stores and sick soldiers some weeks before; so that, when the Federals entered Winchester, they found not a prisoner or a musket to ''enrich their conquest.''

It was a great trial to Jackson to leave his kind friends in Winchester, but he promised them ''to wait for a better time and come again.'' We shall see how well he kept his promise.

On March 19th, General Johnston wrote
to General Jackson at Mt. Jackson, asking
him to move closer to the enemy and to prevent him, if possible, from sending troops
across to McClellan. Word was brought at
the same time, that fifteen thousand men
were then leaving the army of Banks to aid
in turning the left wing of Johnston's forces,
as he fell back to lines of defense nearer
Richmond.

So Jackson gave orders to his little army,
which now numbered only twenty-seven
hundred men, to march back down the Valley. That night the infantry slept at Strasburg, while Ashby's men drove in the outposts of the Federals at Winchester.

General Banks, thinking that Jackson
would trouble him no more, had left for
Washington, and General Shields was in
command of the army.

General Jackson, on the morning of March
23rd, pushed forward his whole force, and,
when about five miles from Winchester, at a

place called Kernstown, he found Ashby
fighting furiously with the advance of the
foe.    Taking a good position, he at once
gave battle, though he saw that he was
greatly outnumbered.    The battle raged from
about noon until night.    Regiment after
regiment was hurled against Jackson's thin
ranks, but they fought stubbornly and would
have gained the day, had not the ammunition of the Stonewall Brigade given out.
Hearing his fire dying away for want of
ammunition, General Garnett gave orders
for his men to retreat.    When Jackson saw
the lines of his old brigade give back, he
galloped to the spot, and, ordering Garnett
to hold his ground, pushed forward to rally
the men.    Seeing a drummer boy retreating
like the rest, he seized him by the shoulder,
dragged him in full view of the soldiers, and
said in his sternest tones, "Beat the rally!"
The drummer beat the rally, and in the midst
of a storm of balls Jackson saw the lines
reform.

*" Beat the Rally ! "*

But it was too late. The enemy now pressed forward in such numbers that there was nothing left to do but to retreat. This they did in good order, but the Federals held the field of battle where so many dead and wounded men were lying.

In this battle of Kernstown twenty-seven hundred Confederates, with eleven guns. attacked eleven thousand Federals and almost gained the victory. It is said that General Shields had just given orders for his men to retreat when the Stonewall Brigade fell back.

As General Shields followed Jackson up the Valley after the battle, he stopped at a noted country house for the night. General Jackson had also rested there upon his retreat, and from his adjutant the lady of the house had learned the correct number of Jackson's men.

General Shields, at breakfast, entered into a conversation with his hostess, and in a polite way boasted of his great victory. "Ah! General," said the lady, "we can afford such defeats as that, when twenty-seven hundred men hold back eleven thousand for hours and then retreat at leisure! Such defeats are victories." General Shields was surprised to learn the small number of Jackson's forces, and begged the lady to tell him her informant. "Certainly," said the lady, "General Jackson's adjutant, Major Paxton. I have also information that large reinforcements are coming to Jackson and that he will again be ready to meet you." "I have no doubt of that, my dear Madam," smilingly returned the General.

*Major E. F. Paxton.*

That night Jackson's little army rested near Newtown, while Ashby kept watch not far from the field of battle. "Jackson," says Cooke, "got an armful of corn for his horse; and, wrapping his blanket about him, lay down by a fire in a fence corner and went to sleep." Though defeated for the first and last time, he had won the object of the battle. The fifteen thousand men who had started across the mountains to McClellan were recalled to the Valley, and Johnston was able to move safely behind the Rappahannock river, his new line of defense.

At four o'clock on the morning of the 24th, Jackson began to retreat slowly and in good order. The enemy pursued for awhile, but at last fell back to Winchester.

Jackson's army was far from cast down by the defeat at Kernstown. The soldiers felt that they had made a splendid fight against four times their number. And now, too, for the first time, it began to dawn upon them that their general was a great leader. As Jackson passed along the columns, the men would cheer themselves hoarse.

Cooke tells us that one man was heard to ask, as he struggled along, ''Why is Old Jack a better general than Moses?'' ''Because it took Moses forty years to lead the Israelites through the wilderness, and Old Jack would have double-quicked them through it in three days!"

It is said by another writer, that the men would laugh and say that the only rest they had was when they were retreating before the enemy. He always led them by forced marches when going to attack the foe, but never fast enough on a retreat to lose the chances of a fight.

The weather was now mild and balmy, and the men suffered few hardships during their slow retreat. At last they reached the old camp at Mt. Jackson, where Jackson gathered up his wounded and sent them up the Valley.

On the 1st of April, he crossed the north fork of the Shenandoah, and took position on Rude's Hill, five miles below New Market.

General Banks had again come up the Valley, and was pressing upon the rear of Jackson's army.

10

It was left for Colonel Ashby to burn the bridge near Mt. Jackson, after the Southern army had passed over. While Ashby and his men were engaged in this work, the Federal cavalry dashed up and a skirmish ensued, in which Ashby's beautiful snow-white charger was mortally wounded.

General Jackson remained at Rude's Hill until April 17th, when, the waters having subsided so that the Federal army could cross the river, he again took up his line of march through New Market to Harrisonburg. At the last named place he turned east, and, passing the south end of Massanutton mountain, crossed the south branch of the Shenandoah river and posted his troops in the gorge of the Blue Ridge called Swift Run Gap.

The way to Staunton was now open to General Banks, but he was too timid to go forward. Jackson in his rear was worse than Jackson in front of him. So, for two weeks, Jackson held the Gap while Banks occupied

Harrisonburg, and laid waste the country around.

Jackson had now about eight thousand men and thirty guns. His men had returned from hospitals and furloughs and also a number of new recruits had poured in to help in this time of danger. The General employed these weeks of rest in organizing and drilling his men and in mending up his old artillery. In the meantime also, he made bold plans, and with the help of General R. E Lee, who had now been made commander of the "Army of Northern Virginia," proceeded to carry them out.

Now, in order to understand the great genius of our hero, and the bravery and endurance of his men, you must study the map on the next page.

You will see that the Valley of the Shenandoah is bounded on the east by the Blue Ridge mountains, and on the west by the Alleghany. Winchester is situated in the northern part of the Valley, while Staunton

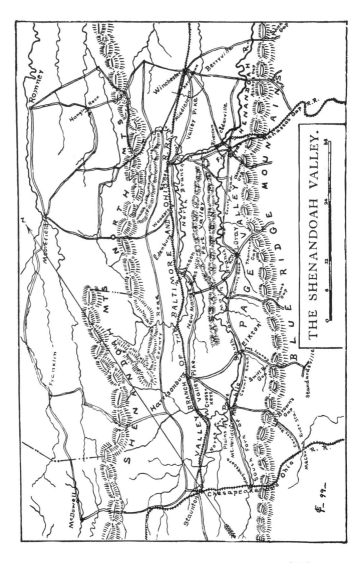

THE SHENANDOAH VALLEY.

is about ninety miles to the south. These two places are connected by a fine turnpike.

Now, near the center of the Valley, rises a beautiful mountain which the Indians called Massanutton, and which still retains that name. This mountain begins near Strasburg and extends about fifty miles towards Staunton, ending abruptly not far from Harrisonburg.

There is only one gap in the Massanutton mountain, and that is opposite the towns of New Market and Luray.

The valley east of the mountain is called the Page Valley, while the entire valley, including the Page Valley, is the Shenandoah Valley.

Some of the children who will read this book live under the shadow and in sight of this lovely mountain, which enabled Jackson to play at "hide and seek" with his foe, and I hope they will understand thoroughly the great movements which I shall relate.

Though Jackson and his little army were

safe in Swift Run Gap, opposite the village of Elkton, for awhile, they could not have remained there long, as three major-generals, with as many large armies, were marching to surround and crush them. Banks was only fifteen miles distant, Milroy was coming by way of Staunton from Western Virginia, and Fremont from the northwest. General McDowell, at Fredericksburg, was also ordered to send twenty thousand men to the Valley, instead of advancing to help McClellan, who was now near Richmond with a large army. You see, Jackson was bravely obeying General Johnston's orders to keep the Federals busy in the Valley and to prevent them from reinforcing McClellan.

Now, there was a small force of Confederates, under General Edward Johnson, on Shenandoah mountain, twenty miles west of Staunton. There was great danger that Milroy with his larger army would overcome Johnson, take Staunton, and march on to

*Generals Jackson, Johnston, and Lee.*

join Banks. Their two armies would then be large enough to crush Jackson.

It was also important to keep Staunton out of the hands of the foe, as it was situated on the Chesapeake and Ohio railway, which carried supplies from the fertile Valley to Richmond.

So General Jackson wrote to General Lee that he would go to the help of Johnson and protect Staunton, if he (Lee) would send a force to hold Banks in check during his absence.

This General Lee did, sending from Richmond General Ewell (ū´-el), a brave officer, with eight thousand men, who marched into Swift Run Gap from the east and took the places which Jackson's men had just left.

It was now Jackson's object to reach Staunton without the knowledge of Banks, so he marched, with great difficulty, through miry roads, down the mountain about eight miles to another gap across the Blue Ridge, called Brown's Gap. When there, he turned

east and marched swiftly across the mountain into Albemarle county, passing through
the village of White Hall to Mechum's River
Station. Thence the troops were carried
swiftly by rail to Staunton, reaching there
on the night of the 4th of May, to the great
joy of the people of Staunton, who thought
that they had been deserted by Jackson in
their time of need.

By Monday the whole army had come up.
They were then joined by General Johnson
and his army. On the 7th, one day having
been spent in preparing for the march, Jackson, with General Johnson's command in
front, marched towards Milroy, who was now
posted on Shenandoah mountain.

Jackson had been joined at Staunton by
the corps of cadets from the Military Institute at Lexington under Col. Scott Shipp.
Many of them were mere boys, but they were
filled with joy at taking their first look at
grim war under Stonewall Jackson, who had
so lately been a professor in that school.

As the Confederate army approached Shenandoah mountain, the Federals retreated to the village of McDowell.

On Thursday, May 8th, Jackson and Johnson, with the command of the latter still in advance, climbed the sides of the mountain overlooking that little village.

That evening, while the generals were waiting for the rest of the army to come up, General Milroy made an attack upon their position.

Though not expecting an attack, Jackson quickly placed his troops for the conflict, the center of the line being held by the Twelfth Georgia regiment with great bravery. It is related that, when ordered at one time to retire behind the crest of the hill to escape the raking fire of the foe, they refused to do so, and kept their position. The next day a tall youth from the Georgia regiment was asked why they did not fall back as ordered. He replied, ''We did not come all the way to Virginia to run before Yankees.''

*The Twelfth Georgia Regiment at McDowell.*

(147)

Just before the close of the battle, General Johnson was wounded in the ankle and compelled to leave the field.

The battle of McDowell raged from half-past four to half-past eight P. M., the shades of night closing the conflict.   Then the Federals gave up the assault and retreated from the field.   "By nine o'clock," says Dr. Dabney, "the roar of the struggle had passed away, and the green battle-field reposed under the starlight as calmly as when it had been occupied only by its peaceful herds of cattle."

It was one o'clock A. M. before General Jackson reached his tent, having waited to see the last wounded man brought off the battle-field, and the last picket posted.   He had eaten nothing since morning, but when his faithful servant, Jim, came with food, he said, "I want none—nothing but sleep"; and in a moment he was fast asleep.

He was in the saddle at peep of day; but, upon climbing the mountain, he saw that the enemy had left during the night. He at once sent this dispatch to Richmond: ''God blessed our arms with victory at McDowell yesterday,'' and then set out in pursuit of the fleeing Federals. He had followed them as far as Franklin, when the woods were set on fire by the Federals to conceal their position.

The dense smoke hung like a pall over the mountain roads, and the heat from the blazing forests was terrible. But still, the long column pressed on until Monday, when General Jackson received an order from General Lee to return to the Valley and pay his respects to General Banks, who was now at Strasburg.

When the latter general had found out that Ewell was holding the Swift Run Gap, and that Jackson had left to go—no one knew whither—he left Harrisonburg and retreated to Strasburg. Jackson was lost, and, not knowing where he might next appear, General Banks thought it more prudent to take a safer position.

Time was now precious to Jackson; so, after halting for a brief rest, during which time the whole army met to render thanks to God for the great victory, he set out on his return march to the Valley.

On the 20th, he was again in New Market, where he was joined by General Ewell.

By a bold plan and a swift march he had saved the army of General Johnson, and prevented Milroy from taking Staunton and joining Banks, and now he was again in pursuit of the latter.

General Banks was fortifying at Strasburg, and seemed to expect an attack in front, so Jackson wisely planned to attack him in the rear.

You remember that I told you that just east of New Market there is a pass, or gap, through the Massanutton mountain. Now Jackson sent a small force of cavalry down the turnpike towards Strasburg to hold it, and conceal the movements of the main army, which he himself led eastward across the mountain into the Page Valley.

Hidden by the friendly mountain, his troops marched quickly and silently to the town of Front Royal, which is at the northern end of the mountain, and which then guarded the flank of Banks' army.

So swift and silent had been the march, that Jackson's men were nearly in sight of the town before anyone knew of their presence.

One mile and a half from the town, the pickets were driven in, and an instant advance was ordered. The Confederate troops rushed to the attack. The Federals, thinking that Jackson was at least one hundred miles away, in the mountains of Western Virginia, were taken completely by surprise. They surrendered by hundreds, giving up quantities of valuable stores, among which were five hundred new revolvers and a wagon load of coffee.

The people of Front Royal were wild with joy at seeing the Confederates again, but the troops were not permitted to stop. On through the town they went at a double-quick, for the Federals had now made a stand outside of the town. But they were speedily put to flight, and the pursuit went on.

In the meantime, the Confederate cavalry came upon a body of Federals near Cedarville, five miles from Front Royal. A charge was at once made upon the Federals by the Confederates, and the whole force was driven back. The Federals then reformed in an orchard, and were again charged upon by the Confederates, and, after a fierce contest, were captured.

As night came on, the weary Southern troops went into camp, for they were quite worn out with marching and fighting.

The next morning, May 24th, the troops were again moving by peep of day. Our hero himself rode forward towards Middletown. When in sight of the turnpike

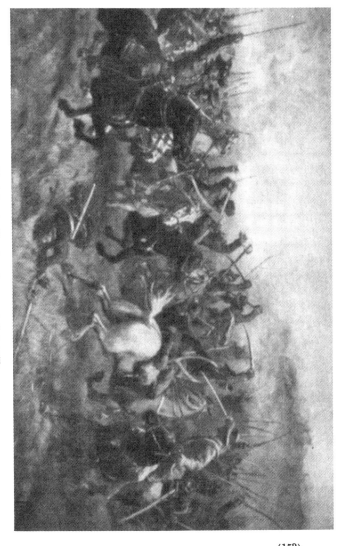

*Confederate Cavalry charge at Cedarville.*

which leads from Strasburg to Winchester, he saw long lines of Federal horsemen in full retreat.

The batteries of Poague and Chew were brought forward and a hot fire opened upon the retreating foe. The latter broke in wild confusion, and soon the turnpike was filled with a mass of struggling and dying horses and men. A few regiments which formed the rear guard fell back to Strasburg, and, leaving their baggage at that place, fled through the western mountains to the Potomac river.

On the turnpike, Ashby with his cavalry followed closely after the fleeing foe, firing upon them with shot and shell.

Cooke says: "Either a shell or a round shot would strike one of the wagons and overturn it, and before those behind could stop their headway, they would thunder down on the remains of the first. Others would tumble in so as to block up the road; and in the midst of it all, Ashby's troopers would swoop down, taking prisoners or cutting down such as resisted."

Ashby himself pressed forward, and at one time, it is said, took as many as thirty prisoners, unaided and alone.

But Ashby's men soon betook themselves to plundering the wagons, which were rich in stores, and thus gave the enemy time to recover from their panic. When near New-town, the enemy turned and fired upon their pursuers.

At dark, however, the firing ceased, and Jackson himself went forward to urge on the pursuit.

The main body of the army had now come up, but no halt was made for food or rest. The "foot cavalry" of the Valley marched all night along the pike lit up by "burning wagons, pontoon bridges, and stores."

Every now and then, they would come upon men ambuscaded along the sides of the pike, and fierce fights would ensue.

About dawn on the 25th of May, Jackson's advance force climbed the lofty hill southwest of Winchester. This hill was already held by the Federals, but they were charged upon by the Stonewall Brigade, and driven back. With a loud shout the Confederates gained the crest of the hill and planted their batteries. Though they had marched all night, they took no rest or food, but at once began the battle of Winchester.

Ewell fought on the right and Taylor on the left. "Jackson," says a writer, "had his war-look on, and rode about the field, regardless of shot and shell, looking as calm as if nothing were going on."

At last, after a fierce fight, the Federals gave way, and Jackson entered Winchester at the heels of the panic-stricken army. The people of the town were beside themselves with delight to see their loved general once more.

Jackson was for the first time excited.

He waved his faded cap around his head and cheered with a right good will.

But the troops still pressed forward, Jackson leading the way. When one of his officers said, "Don't you think you are going into too much danger, General?" his reply was, "Tell the troops to press right on to the Potomac." And they did press onward until the enemy was forced across the Potomac with the loss of many prisoners and valuable stores.

After resting a few days, Jackson advanced towards Harper's Ferry with the view of attacking the Federal force there, but was stopped by the news that two armies, one under General Shields, from the east; the other under General Fremont, from the west, were to meet at Strasburg and thus cut him off from Richmond and capture him.

He at once hastened back to Winchester, where he collected his prisoners and the stores of ammunition and medicine which he had captured. These he sent up the

Valley, and followed rapidly with his whole army.

In the meantime, there was great terror at Washington and in the North. Men wore anxious faces, and were asking each other, "Where is Jackson?" They were afraid that he would turn and capture Washington.

But Jackson had only about fifteen thousand men, and he could not risk the loss of the rich stores which he had gained and the destruction of his noble army, so he put forth all his skill and nerve to save them.

The Confederates now began a race to reach Strasburg before the Federals, the larger part of the army marching from near Harper's Ferry to Strasburg, nearly fifty miles, in about twenty-four hours. Well might they be called the "foot cavalry."

As Jackson marched into Strasburg, General Fremont's advance was almost in sight; and, as the Stonewall Brigade had not yet come up, Jackson sent General Ewell to hold Fremont in check. A fierce battle ensued, but Ewell at last drove back the enemy, and the Stonewall Brigade coming up that evening, the whole army continued to retreat up the Valley.

The race had been won by Jackson, who was, for the present, safe. In a brief space of time, he had flanked the enemy at Front Royal, chased them to Middletown, beaten them at Winchester, and sent them flying across the Potomac. When nearly entrapped by two other columns, he had passed between them, and was now hurrying with his rich stores to the upper Valley. Cooke tells us that he had captured two thousand three hundred prisoners, one hundred cattle, thirty-four thousand pounds of bacon, salt, sugar, coffee, hard bread, and cheese, valuable medical stores, $125,185 worth of other stores, two pieces of artillery, and many small-arms and horses. All this was gained with the loss of about four hundred men.

But, as Jackson retreated up the Valley,

he was again threatened by a great danger. Shields's column marched up the Page Valley with the view of crossing the Massanutton at New Market and striking Jackson in the rear, just as Jackson had done to Banks when he went down to Front Royal. But Jackson was too wary to be taken by surprise.

He sent swift horsemen across the mountain, who burned the bridges over the south branch of the Shenandoah at Columbia Mills and the White House, and then placed signal stations on top of the mountain to inform him of what was going on in the Page Valley.

Fremont was now pressing on his rear, but he moved swiftly up the Valley with the main army, while Ashby kept guard on every side. When Harrisonburg was reached, he again marched east and took his stand near the village of Port Republic.

On the 6th of June, as the gallant Ashby was leading a charge to repel the advance of the Federal forces, he fell, pierced to the heart by a single bullet. His last words were, "Charge, Virginians!" Thus, in the moment of victory, died the brave and noble Ashby. His loss was deeply felt by Jackson, who now needed more than ever, the daring and skill of his "Chief of Cavalry."

As I have told you, Jackson was at Port Republic, a village at the forks of the Shenandoah river. Fremont was at Harrisonburg, fifteen miles to the northwest, and Shields was at Conrad's Store, fifteen miles to the northeast. The space between the three generals formed the sides of a triangle. Just back of Jackson, in the Blue Ridge, was Brown's Gap, through which he could retreat and join Lee before Richmond.

But Jackson had no idea of leaving the Valley without a parting blow. The Shenandoah was very high, so that Shields and Fremont could not unite their forces. Jackson therefore determined to attack Shields first, and, if victorious, then to turn his attention to Fremont. I have forgotten to tell you that Shields was east of the river, and Fremont to the west; while Jackson was between the north and south branches of the Shenandoah, which unite at Port Republic.    There was a bridge over the north branch, between Jackson and Fremont; but over the south branch, between Jackson and Shields, there was only a ford. The north bank was high, while the south was low, and stretched away in broad meadows towards the mountains.

Jackson, leaving the trusty Ewell at Cross

Keys to watch Fremont, who was advancing from Harrisonburg, took possession of the heights overlooking the bridge at Port Republic, and stationed there two brigades and his remaining artillery.    A small

*General R. S. Ewell.*

body of cavalry was sent across South river to find out the position of Shields.

Early on the morning of the 8th of June, the cavalry came galloping back with the news that Shields's army was close at hand. Jackson, who was in the town with some of his staff, at once gave orders for the batteries on the north side to open fire; but before it could be done, the Federal cavalry dashed into the town followed by artillery, which rumbled forward and took position at the southern end of the bridge.

Jackson and his staff were· now cut off from his army, which was on the north bank. We are told by Cooke and others that Jackson, with great presence of mind, rode towards the bridge; and, rising in his stirrups, called sternly to the Federal officer commanding the gun, "Who told you to post that gun there, sir? Bring it over here!" The officer, thinking that Jackson was a Federal general, bowed, "limbered up" the piece, and was preparing to move. In the meantime Jackson and his staff gal-

*General Jackson at Port Republic Bridge.*

(164)

loped across the bridge, and were soon safe on the northern side.

No time was lost by the Confederates. Their artillery opened fire upon the Federals, and Jackson in person led the Thirty-seventh Virginia regiment, drove the foe from the bridge, and captured the gun with the loss of only two men wounded.

In the meantime, Jackson's long wagon-train, which contained his ammunition, was bravely defended on the outskirts of the village by a handful of pickets and a section of artillery until help came.

The fire of the guns on the north bank made it impossible for the Federals to hold the village, so, leaving their other gun, they retreated, and dashed across the ford of the South river by the way they had come.

Hardly had the guns stopped firing at Port Republic, before heavy firing was heard in the direction of Cross Keys, five miles off, between Ewell and Fremont. The latter had twenty thousand men, while Ewell had only about six thousand. The Confederates were posted with great skill upon a ridge, and after fighting from ten A. M. until nightfall, at last drove back the enemy with great loss.

The battle of Cross Keys having been fought, the Confederate troops lay upon their arms, ready to renew the fray the next day; but Jackson had other plans.

He had determined to strike Shields next; so; leaving a guard to watch Fremont, he ordered Ewell to march at break of day to Port Republic.

At midnight he caused a foot-bridge to be thrown across South river so that his infantry might pass over to attack Shields. This bridge was made by placing wagons lengthwise across the swollen stream. The floor of the bridge was formed of long boards laid loosely from one wagon to another. Over this rude, frail structure, the whole body of infantry passed, but not so quickly as its general wished. About midway the stream, for some reason, one wagon was about two feet higher than the next. This made a step, and all the boards on the higher wagon were loose but one. When the column began to move over, several men were thrown, by the loose planks, into the water; so, refusing to trust any but the firm plank, the men went, at this point, in single file. This made the crossing over very tedious; and, instead of being in line to attack Shields at sunrise, it was ten o'clock before the entire army had passed over. Thus, three loose boards cost the Confederates a bloody battle; for they found the Federals drawn up in battle array and ready for the fight. This incident shows how much care should be taken in performing the most trivial duty; as the success of great events is often affected by very slight causes. It is said that Jackson hoped to surprise Shields, whip him in a few hours, and then recross the river to rout Fremont.

But the battle of Port Republic, June 9th,

raged furiously for hours. The Federals fought with great courage, and it was not until evening that they gave way and retreated, panic-stricken, from the field.

The Confederates followed them eight or ten miles down the river, and returned laden with spoils and prisoners.

At ten o'clock A. M., Jackson sent orders for the guard left at Cross Keys under General Trimble and Colonel Patton to march to his aid and to burn the bridge behind them. This they did, and came up in time to join in the fight.

Towards nightfall General Jackson led his weary troops by a side road into the safe recesses of Brown's Gap, in the Blue Ridge.

As they passed the field of battle on their return, they saw the hills on the north side of the river crowded with the troops of Fremont, who had arrived in time to see the rout of Shields.

The river being high, they did not attempt to cross, but began a furious cannonade upon the Confederate surgeons and men who were caring for the wounded and burying the dead.

The next day, scouts brought word to Jackson that Fremont was building a bridge, but soon after, having learned, doubtless, that General Shields's army was entirely routed, he retreated.

On June 12th, the Confederate cavalry under Colonel Munford entered Harrisonburg, Fremont having gone back down the Valley, leaving behind him his sick and wounded, and many valuable stores.

Four hundred and fifty Federals were taken prisoners on the field, while as many more were found in the hospitals. One thousand small-arms and nine field-pieces fell to the victorious Confederates. The Federal loss in the two battles was about two thousand. In the battle of Cross Keys Jackson lost only forty-two killed and two hundred and thirty-one wounded; but in the battle of Port Republic, ninety-one officers and men were killed, and six hundred and eighty-six wounded.

Though Jackson's plans had not been entirely carried out, he was now rid of the two armies of forty thousand men which had been on his front and flanks, and had threatened to crush him.

Within forty days his troops had marched four hundred miles, fought four great battles, and defeated four separate armies, sending to the rear over three thousand prisoners and vast trains of stores and ammunition.

From this time Jackson stood forth as a leader of great genius; the little orphan boy had indeed climbed the heights of fame amid a "blaze of glory."

On the 12th of June, Jackson led his army from its camp, in Brown's Gap, to the plains of Mt. Meridian, a few miles above Port Republic. Here, the wearied men rested for five days, while Colonel Munford, who now commanded the cavalry, kept watch on the turnpike below Harrisonburg.

This is the dispatch which Jackson sent to Richmond:

"NEAR PORT REPUBLIC, June 9th, 1862.

Through God's blessing, the enemy near Port Republic was this day routed, with the loss of six pieces of his artillery.

T. J. JACKSON,
*Major-General, commanding.*"

The Saturday following the battle was set apart by General Jackson as a day of thanksgiving and prayer, and the next day (Sunday) the Lord's Supper was celebrated by the Christian soldiers from all the army. General Jackson was present at this service, and partook of the sacred feast in company with his men.

On the 16th of June, General Jackson ordered Colonel Munford to press down the pike, if possible, as far as New Market, and to make the enemy believe that his whole army was advancing. This Colonel Munford did, and the Federals, believing that Jack-

son was again on the march, retreated to
Strasburg and began to fortify themselves.

In the meanwhile, June 17th, Jackson
had begun a march, but not towards Strasburg. The mighty army of McClellan had
advanced so close to Richmond that at night
the reflection of its camp-fires could be seen
from the city; and General Lee sent for
Jackson to come to his aid as swiftly as
possible.

Great care was taken to make the Federals believe that troops were being sent to
Jackson, so that he could again go down
the Valley, and attack Fremont and Shields
at Strasburg. A division of men was sent
as far as Staunton, and the report was spread
that a large force was on the march to Jackson; but the truth was, that our hero was
already on his way to Richmond, where the
next blow was to be struck.

It was important to keep the Federals in
ignorance of Jackson's movement, so Colonel
Munford was ordered to make a great show
with his men along the turnpike, and to

allow no news to be carried to the foe. The men were told to give this answer to all questions, "I do not know." The historian Cooke tells us this amusing incident, which grew out of the above order: "One of Hood's men left the ranks to go to a cherry-tree near by, when Jackson rode past and saw him. 'Where are you going?' asked the General. 'I don't know,' replied the soldier. 'To what command do you belong?' 'I don't know.' 'Well, what State are you from?' 'I don't know.' 'What is the meaning of all this?' asked Jackson. 'Well,' was the reply, 'Old Stonewall and General Hood issued orders yesterday that we were not to know anything until after the next fight.' Jackson laughed and rode on."

On the 25th of June, the corps reached Ashland, near Richmond.

Jackson had gone on in advance to the headquarters of General Lee, where his post in the coming strife was assigned him.

Flănk, side of an army or fleet.

Rĕ'ĭn-fôrce', to send more soldiers.

Mys'tery, a great secret.

Pĕtĭ'tion (pĕ-tish'-un), a request.

Gĕn'ius (jĕn'-yus), a man of wonderful mind.

Ăd'jutañt, a military officer who assists another.

Describe—

The battle of Kernstown.

The retreat to Swift Run Gap, McDowell, Front Royal, Winchester, Cross Keys, Port Republic.

The march to Richmond.

# CHAPTER VIII.

## A Major–General.

(CONTINUED.)

GENERAL MCCLELLAN was now on the banks of the Chickahominy river, at one point only six miles from Richmond, with the largest and best equipped army that had ever been raised upon American soil.

His position was a strong one, having the Pāmun′key river on one side and the James on the other, with the marshes of the Chickahominy in front as natural barriers to the assaults of the Confederates. Besides, he had thoroughly fortified his line, which swept in a crescent shape from Meadow Bridge road on the right, across the Chickahominy, to the Williamsburg road on the left—a distance of about fifteen miles.

General Lee now determined to send General Jackson to the rear of the enemy to turn their flank, while General A. P. Hill and Longstreet assailed them in front.

On the evening of the 26th of June, General A. P. Hill advanced upon Mechanicsville and attacked the strong position of the Federals. The latter defended themselves bravely, but at last fell back to their works on Beaverdam creek. The victorious Confederates followed, and an artillery fire was kept up until nine o'clock at night. The attack was renewed at dawn the next morning and raged for hours, when, suddenly, the Federals retreated in haste from their strong position, leaving everything in flames.

*Gen. A. P. Hill.*

Jackson had come up, turned their flank, and caused them to retire. Generals Hill and Longstreet followed them until about noon, when they found the Federals again drawn up for battle behind Powhite creek, on a ridge whose slope was fortified by breastworks of trees, and whose crest was crowned with batteries of frowning guns.

The Confederate troops at once advanced, but were repulsed with great loss. Again they charged up the hill, and gained the crest only to be driven back by the storm of shot and shell.

Longstreet was now ordered to make a move on the right towards Gaines's Mill, where the Federals were massed in a strong position. In the meanwhile General Lee ordered General Jackson to advance to the help of Hill. About five o'clock P. M. the sound of guns was heard to the left, and soon Jackson's corps was in the thickest of the fight.

Before them were a swamp, a deep stream, masses of felled timber, and a wood filled with armed men, and cannon belching forth shot and shell. The work was hard, but when Jackson gave the order, his men swept forward with wild cheers and a roar of musketry, while above the clang arose the cry of Jackson! Jackson! Jackson!

The men rushed on through the swamp, across the creek, and up into the wood, and drove the enemy from point to point until they gained the top of the hill.

On the right of the line, Hood's Texas

brigade charged with a yell, leaped ditch and stream, and drove the foe pell-mell before them. In this charge they lost one thousand men, but took fourteen cannon and nearly a regiment of prisoners.

*General J. B. Hood.*

The enemy now retreated in wild disorder all along the line, and the battle of Old Cold Harbor was won by the Confederates. The very name of Jackson had struck terror to the foe!

The next morning, the 29th of June, Jackson was ordered to move on the rear of McClellan's army.

At Savage Station, the Confederates,

under General Magruder, had a fierce fight
with the rear guard of the Federals. At
nightfall the latter again gave way, leaving
behind vast stores and a number of wounded
men. While the battle at Savage Station
had been going on, the main body of the
Federal army passed over the bridge at
White Oak swamp, destroyed it, and were
for awhile safe, for the Confederates could
not pass over the marshy stream under the
fire of the Federals, who were massed on the
opposite bank.

General Jackson opened fire with his
artillery, and the next morning, the 1st of
July, forced the passage of White Oak
swamp, and captured a part of the Federal
artillery.

In the meantime a fierce battle had been
fought at Frasier's farm, by Generals Longstreet and A. P. Hill, with another portion
of McClellan's army. Under cover of night,
the latter drew off, leaving his dead and
wounded, and a large number of prisoners.

General Jackson was now placed in front of the Confederate forces in pursuit of the foe, who was nearing the James river. It was General Lee's plan to cut them off from the river and destroy the whole army, but the Confederates were worn out with much fighting, and General McClellan was allowed to make a stand on Malvern Hill. This strong position he had hastily fortified; and here, as a wild animal at bay, was his whole army, determined to contend for existence.

General Lee ordered an assault, placing Jackson and D. H. Hill on the left and Magruder on the right. Owing to the timber and marshes, the Confederates could use but little artillery, while the Federals, from their greater height, rained a storm of shot and shell from three hundred cannon. The gunboats on the James also threw their monstrous shells above the heads of the Confederates. In spite of all odds, these devoted men (Jackson's) charged across marshes and up the hill, forcing the enemy back; but, after a fierce combat, they fell back with great loss. Again and again they charged, with the same result. At sun-set, Magruder, who with much difficulty had gotten his troops into position, charged on the right with great bravery.

As darkness came on, the Confederates fought with renewed courage. Whole lines of the enemy fell beneath their musket fire, but the guns could not be taken by the Confederates, because no line of men could live within the zone of fire which flamed from the mouths of the blazing cannon.

About ten o'clock P. M. the firing ceased, and the Confederate troops, holding their position, slept upon the battle-field.

When the battle had ended thus, Jackson went slowly to the rear, where his faithful servant, Jim, was waiting for him with food and a pallet made upon the ground. After eating a few morsels, Jackson lay down and fell into a deep sleep. About one o'clock, Generals Hill, Ewell, and Early came to tell him that their commands were cut to pieces, and that when day broke they would not be able to continue the fight. Jackson listened to them in silence, and then said: "McClellan and his army will be gone by daylight." The generals thought him mad, but when morning came, they found that he had foretold aright the flight of McClellan. Malvern Hill was found to be deserted by the foe. They had retreated during the night to Harrison's landing, under cover of their gunboats, and Richmond was for the time safe.

The battle of Malvern Hill was a dearly bought victory for the Confederates. General Jackson lost in the battle three hundred and seventy-seven men killed, and one thousand seven hundred and forty-six wounded, with thirty-nine missing. As soon as possible, the Southern army followed McClellan, but found him too strongly entrenched to attack. So the worn-out men went into camp near by, and rested for the first time in a fortnight.

General Jackson soon grew weary of watching McClellan, and began to plan a bold march into Maryland to threaten Washington city. It was not long before he did move northward. News came that a Federal army of forty thousand men, under General Pope, was coming towards Gordonsville to the help of McClellan. General Jackson was at once ordered to advance to meet him and drive him back.

His corps moved forward, and, on August 9th, fought the battle of Cedar Run. In this fierce battle one of the regiments began to fall back. At that instant Jackson placed himself in front of his men, drew his sword, and cried in a voice of thunder, "Rally, brave men! Jackson will lead you! Follow me!" This turned the tide of battle, and the Federal army broke into full retreat. Just before this battle, some officers enquired of "Jim," the General's servant, if there were any signs of a battle. "Oh, yes, sir," replied he, "the General is a great man for praying night and morning, all times; but when I see him get up in the night and go off and pray, then I know there is going to be something to pay; and I go right straight and pack his haversack, for I know he will call for it in the morning."

General Lee now came up with the greater part of the Southern army, leaving only a small force to watch General McClellan. The plan of the Southern leaders was to rout General Pope and march northward to threaten Washington, thus compelling General McClellan to leave his camp on the James river.

The main body of Lee's army moved nearer to Pope's front, while Jackson's corps moved off to the northwest, and was again "lost." It was marching across the Rappahannock and behind Bull Run mountains, which hid it from the enemy

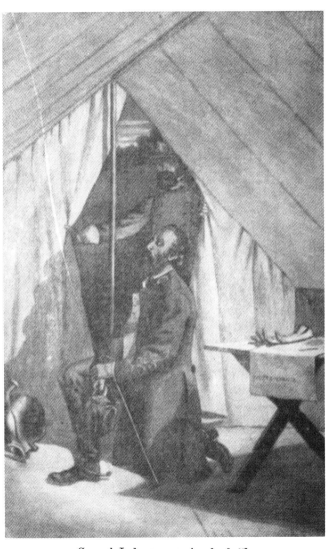

*General Jackson preparing for battle.*

13                                                          (185)

On August 26th it passed through the mountains at Thoroughfare Gap, and took a position between Pope and Washington city.

Jackson at once took Manassas Junction, where three hundred prisoners and immense quantities of stores were captured. The poor, hungry soldiers took what could be carried away, and the rest was burned.

As soon as Pope heard that Jackson was in his rear, he moved to meet him, and ordered McDowell to close in upon him from the direction of Gainesville, saying, "We shall bag the whole crowd." But the wary Jackson was a match for his foes. Taking a good position upon the old battle-field of Manassas, he at once attacked the enemy coming up on the evening of August 28th. When darkness fell upon the blood-drenched plain, the Confederates were the victors. On the next morning the fight was renewed, but Jackson's men were almost exhausted, when Longstreet's corps appeared and soon turned the tide of battle.

It was not long before Pope's army was in full retreat towards Washington, and Jackson was again victor. During a part of the battle a severe storm came up. An aide from General A. P. Hill rode up, and reported that his ammunition was wet, and asked leave to retire. "Give my compliments to General Hill," said Jackson, "and tell him that the Yankee ammunition is as wet as his; to stay where he is." "There was always blood and danger," says a friend, "when Jackson began his sentences with, "Give my compliments."

General Lee now determined to cross the Potomac and threaten Washington, and Jackson led the advance. On September 6th he reached Frederick and remained there several days, resting and refitting his command. When General Lee came up, he at once sent General Jackson to Harper's Ferry (September 10th), to capture the Federal forces at that place. After taking the heights around that town, he proceeded to take the town by storm.

In a short while the garrison of eleven thousand men, with seventy-three cannon, thirteen thousand stand of small-arms and a vast amount of stores, surrendered. Jackson, leaving General Hill to receive the captured prisoners and property, at once set out to return to General Lee, at Sharpsburg, a little village two and one-half miles from the Potomac river. After a weary night-march he reached that place on the morning of the 16th. He found General Lee facing the hosts of McClellan and drawn up for battle. When he had rested his worn-out men for several hours, he took his position on the left, next to the Potomac river. This was the post of danger, for against it, on the 17th, McClellan massed forty-four thousand men.

The corps of Jackson numbered now, after so much fighting and marching, less than seven thousand men, but this little band held the ground throughout the day, and bravely drove back every assault of the enemy.

When night closed the bloody fray, each army held its own position. On the next morning, General Lee awaited another attack, but General McClellan had received so heavy a blow that he would not venture another battle until fresh troops had come up

The 18th was spent by both armies in burying their dead and caring for the wounded. In the evening General Lee, learning that large bodies of fresh troops were reaching McClellan, determined to recross the Potomac. As soon as night came, the troops began to move towards the ford at Shepherdstown. "For hours," says Dr. Dabney, "Jackson was seen seated upon his horse, motionless as a statue, watching the passage until the last man and the last carriage had touched the Southern shore." The battle of Sharpsburg, or Antietam (An tē′tam), as it is sometimes called, was a drawn battle—neither side was victorious, each losing in killed and wounded about twelve thousand men.

The Southern men were so worn out and foot-sore from constant marching, and weak from starvation, that they were really unfit for the battle of Sharpsburg. More than half of Lee's army was left behind along the Virginia roads, and those who, wan and gaunt, fought the battle, were kept up during that bloody day only by their devotion to the Southern cause and leaders. Fortune also had smiled upon McClellan by revealing to him the plans of Lee. An order setting forth Lee's line of march was picked up in D. H. Hill's deserted camp, and taken to McClellan, who then, of course, knew just where to strike Lee.

On the morning of the 19th, a force of Federals crossed the Potomac at Boteler's ford, but were met by A. P. Hill's division of Jackson's corps, and driven back into the river with great loss. On the northern side of the river, seventy large cannon were planted, which rained grape-shot upon the Southern men, but they rushed forward and hurled hundreds of the Federals into the water, and then picked them off with steady aim until the river was black with floating bodies.

While this was going on, a messenger from General Lee found Jackson watching the progress of the fight. His only remark was, "With the blessing of Providence, they will soon be driven back." McClellan made no further attempt to follow Lee.

For some weeks Lee's army lay quietly resting in the lower Valley. But Jackson was never idle. He was now busy in getting clothes and shoes for his men, and filling up the ranks which had been so thinned during the summer. His regiments were at the time filled up by the return of the sick and the foot-sore and by new recruits.

Jackson had now become the idol of his

men. Their pet name for him was "Old Jack." Whenever he rode by they would cheer themselves hoarse; and his devotion to them was just as great. This story is told of him by an eye-witness of the scene: "When Jackson's men were on their famous march to Manassas, at the close of the first day, they found Jackson, who had ridden forward, dismounted, and standing upon a great stone by the road-side. His sun-burned cap was lifted from his brow and his blue eyes gleamed in the rays of the setting sun. His men burst forth into cheers, but he at once sent an officer to request that there be no cheering, as it might betray their presence to the enemy. Instantly the cheering stopped, but as they passed their General their eyes told what their lips could not utter—their love for him. Jackson turned to his staff, his face beaming with delight, and said, 'Who could not conquer with such troops as these?'" Well might he be proud of men who had been marching and fighting for five days, many of them having no rations and living upon green corn found along the way, yet whose courage and devotion knew no bounds!

--------

Crĕs'çent, shaped like the new moon.
Băr'rier, a bar, a defense.
Swamp, soft, low, and spongy ground.
De-vō'-tion, love.
Re-vēal-ing, making known.

Can you describe—

McClellan's position on the Chickahominy river?

The charge of Jackson's men at "Old Cold Harbor"?

The battle of Malvern Hill?

The second battle of Manassas?

The capture of Harper's Ferry?

The battle of Antietam?

# CHAPTER IX.

## A Lieutenant-General.

WHILE our hero was in the lower Valley, on the 11th of October, 1862, the Confederate Government bestowed upon him the rank of Lieutenant-General, next to the highest grade in the service. General Lee's army was now divided into two great corps, one of which was given to Jackson, the other to Longstreet. These generals have been called the "two hands" of Lee.

On the 18th of October, General Jackson's corps was sent forward to destroy the Baltimore and Ohio railroad. This they did in the most complete way. Burning all the bridges and ripping up the cross-ties, they finished their work by setting fire to the ties and throwing the iron rails upon the heaps of blazing logs.

After the work was done, Jackson rode

over the whole distance, thirty miles, to see
that the destruction was complete.

Towards the end of October, Jackson
moved his corps
near the Blue
Ridge mountains
to watch the
movements of
McClellan, who
was again cross-
ing the Potomac
with a vast army
of one hundred
and forty thou-
sand men.

*General James Longstreet.*

But McClellan's movements were so slow
that he was removed from his command,
and General Burnside was put in his place.

The latter general resolved to try a new
way to Richmond, and moved his army
towards Fredericksburg, on the Rappahannock river. General Lee at once marched
to that town to meet him. General Jackson

was called from the Valley to the help of
Lee, and reached that general's camp on the
1st of December.   The Southern army numbered in all about sixty-five thousand men.
Of these, there were in Jackson's corps
twenty-five thousand.

General Lee, with his two corps, was now
upon the heights south of the Rappahannock
river; while General Burnside, with five
corps, held Stafford Heights, north of that
river.   The town of Fredericksburg was
between the two armies.   The winter set in
early, and both armies suffered greatly from
the cold.   The Confederates were for the
most part barefooted, without tents and
warm clothes, and had only rations of fat
meat and corn bread; but these trials did
not lessen their valor.   They dug out trenches
and threw up breastworks, and waited for
the advance of the enemy.

On the 10th of December, General Burnside began to move his men over the river
on pontoon bridges.   One hundred and fifty

big guns on Stafford Heights poured shot and shell upon the town of Fredericksburg, setting it on fire and causing many of the people to leave their homes. By the morning of the 13th, ninety thousand Federals had crossed the river. Longstreet held the Confederate left while Jackson held the right.

The battle began by a fierce attack upon Jackson's right, which onset was bravely met; for the men, fighting fiercely, drove the Federals back to the cover of their big guns. At eleven A. M., the Federals assaulted Longstreet's position, but again and again they were driven back by the Confederates, who did not fire until the foe was close upon them. Charge after charge was made by the Federals, but to no purpose, for the grim Confederates held their own.

When night came, thirteen thousand Federals lay dead or wounded upon the frozen plain, while the Confederates had lost five thousand brave men.

There is no doubt that Jackson ordered a

night attack upon Burnside's beaten army, hoping thereby to turn a defeat into a rout, and to drive them pell-mell into the river, as he had done at Boteler's ford; but his better judgment told him that it was unwise to send his men against the strong works along the river road, under the fierce fire of the cannon on Stafford Heights.

So he recalled the order, and thus lost the chance of a decisive victory; for Burnside did not offer battle again, but on the night of the 16th, in the midst of a great storm of wind and rain, withdrew his forces to their post on Stafford Heights.

Both armies now went into winter quarters. Jackson's corps built huts in the forests, and made themselves as comfortable as possible, while their General accepted for his lodgings a cottage at Moss Neck, the home of Mr. Corbin.

Here he set to work to write out reports to the government of his wonderful battles. This he did with great clearness and regard for the truth, recording briefly the exploits of his little army.

Never had general a more glorious story to relate!

Since the battle of Kernstown, in March, these brave men had fought the big battles of McDowell, Cross Keys, Port Republic, Cold Harbor, Malvern Hill, Cedar Run, Manassas, Harper's Ferry, Antietam, and Fredericksburg—marched hundreds of miles, and captured thousands of prisoners. Never had they quailed in battle; when ammunition had given out they fought with stones, and when there had been no rations, they lived on roots and berries. So rapidly did they march from place to place that they were called the "foot cavalry," and the knowledge that Jackson was "lost," cast terror into the ranks of the foe. Even their best generals could not tell where Jackson would next be found.

"During the battle of Cold Harbor," relates one of Jackson's men, "as we were taking back some prisoners, one of them said: "You think that you are doing great things here, but I tell you we are whipping "Old Jack' in the Valley like smoke." "Well, maybe you are," said I, "being as 'Old Jack' is *here*. You've been fighting his men all day."

Just then, Jackson rode by with his staff. "There's our General," said I; "now, how much are you whipping us in the Valley?" The man looked dazed, and said, "Well, my stars, if that *ain't* 'Old Jack!'"

Indeed, the feats of Jackson had now made him famous. Not only his own people, but strangers from Europe made visits to the camp to see the great general and his men.

During these months of rest, Jackson enjoyed greatly the visits of General Stuart, who made the mess merry with his jokes and gay laughter. He also made the acquaintance of little six-year-old Jane Corbin, who lived near by in the big house.

Every evening when the work of the day

was over, she would run across to see the General, who would always have some little present for her. One evening, having no other gift for her, he ripped off the one band of gold braid from around his new cap, and placed it upon her sunny brow.

This lovely child lived only a few months thereafter. The very day on which General Jackson left Moss Neck in the spring, little Jane was seized with scarlet-fever and died after being ill only one day. General Jackson mourned greatly for his little friend. About the same time he heard of the illness of his own baby daughter, whom he had never seen.

He had never had a furlough since leaving Lexington, and in April, since he could not visit his dear ones, they came to him. He found a quiet home for his wife near by, and great was his pleasure in nursing and caressing his little daughter. He gave her his mother's name—Julia.

14

*General Jackson crowning Jane Corbin.*

During the winter, at Moss Neck, the piety of General Jackson seemed ever to increase. His chief thought was to live for the glory of God. He often worshiped with his men in the log church which they had built in the forest, and toiled early and late for their welfare.

Cooke, the historian, tells us that one day, while talking with a member of his staff about the great battle which he knew would soon take place, he said: "My trust is in God." A brief silence followed these words, and then, rising to his feet, he exclaimed, with flashing eyes, "I wish they would come."

The spirit of battle was upon him, and he longed to go forward to the fray, which proved to be the last, but not least, of his wonderful exploits.

General Burnside had been removed from command of the Federal army after the battle of Fredericksburg, and General Hooker, "Fighting Joe," as he was called, was put in his place. His army now numbered about one hundred and fifty thousand men.

General Lee's army, to the number of forty-five thousand men, lay entrenched upon the southern banks of the Rappahannock river. General Longstreet's corps was now absent in Suffolk county, so Lee had not one-third as many men as Hooker.

Hooker's plan was to divide his army into two parts. The smaller part was to cross the river near Fredericksburg and engage the Confederates in battle, while the larger part would march up the northern bank of the Rappahannock river, and, crossing over, reach the flank of Lee's army, which would thus have the foe in front and also in the rear. At the same time Hooker planned to send a large troop of cavalry to reach and destroy the railroads leading to Richmond, thus cutting General Lee off from the capital.

This was a bold plan, but one that was easily guessed by such soldiers as Lee, Jackson, and Stuart. The last named kept watch, and as soon as a movement was made, reported it to Lee. Lee at once fell back to Chancellorsville, but not until the main army under General Hooker himself had reached "The Wilderness" beyond Chancellorsville, and thrown up strong

*Lee, Jackson, and Stuart at the battle of Fredericksburg.*

earthworks. The left wing of Hooker's army, under General Sedgwick, crossed the river below Fredericksburg on the 29th of April, and was at once met by Jackson, who was ever watchful. Sedgwick, however, did not intend to fight, but merely to keep

General Lee at Fredericksburg while Hooker
was gaining the point on Lee's flank.   General Lee promptly guessed the plan, and
ordered General Jackson to leave only one
division in front of Sedgwick, to proceed at
once in search of Hooker, and to attack and
repulse him.   This order reached Jackson
about eight P. M., and by midnight his
troops were on the march.   Early the next
day they reached the battle-field, where the
troops of General Anderson were already
engaged with the enemy.

Jackson halted his column, and sending
four brigades to the support of Anderson,
drew up the remainder of the corps in line
of battle upon a ridge near by.   The battle
raged fiercely all day, and when night came,
the Confederates had reached Hooker's first
line of entrenchments, in the midst of the
dense forest.

Meanwhile General Lee had come up with
the remainder of the army, and a sharp fight
had taken place in front of Hooker's right

wing. Night put an end to the contest, when, weary and worn, both armies lay down to rest upon the battle-field.

When Lee and Jackson met that night they were joined by General Stuart, who told them that, though General Hooker had strongly fortified his position upon the east, south, and southwest, upon the north and west he had left it open. Jackson's quick mind at once planned to attack Hooker in the rear, just as Hooker had planned to attack Lee.

To the northwest, there were no earth-works, and if Jackson could surprise the Federals he would be almost sure of victory. Stuart was there with his gallant horsemen to cover this movement, and the forests were so dense that Jackson was sure of leading his men silently to the rear of Hooker.

General Lee listened to his arguments, and finally gave consent for his great lieu-tenant to make the trial. He (General Lee) would remain with two divisions in front to engage Hooker, while Jackson would march around and strike him in the rear.

By the aid of his chaplain, Rev. Mr. Lacy, who knew that country well, General Jackson found a road which would lead him to the rear of Hooker's army. By sunrise he was in the saddle at the head of his column. General Stuart was there to cover his line of march, and his troops, knowing at once that their General was making one of his famous flank movements, went forward at a rapid pace. We are told by Dr. McGuire, who was with Jackson, that on the march they were met by General Fitz. Lee, who told Jackson that he would show him the whole of Hooker's army if he would go to the top of a hill near by. They went together, and Jackson carefully viewed through his glasses the Federal command. He was so wrapped up in his plans that on his return he forgot to salute or thank Fitz. Lee, but hurried on to the column, where he ordered one of his aides to go forward and tell General Rodes to cross the plank road and go straight on to the turnpike, and another aide to go to the rear of the column and see that it was kept closed up, and all along the line he kept saying, "Press on, press right on." The fiercest energy seemed to possess him. When he arrived at the plank road he sent this, his last, message to Lee: "The enemy has made a stand at Chancellorsville. I hope as soon as practicable to attack. I trust that an ever kind Providence will bless us with success." At three P. M., having marched fifteen miles, he had reached the old turnpike, and was exactly on the opposite side of the enemy to that held by General Lee.

He had left the Stonewall Brigade, under General Paxton, on the plank road, with orders to block the way to Germanna ford. He found the outposts held by Stuart's vigilant troopers, who had guarded well his advance. As soon as possible he formed his army in three lines—the division of

Rodes in front, that of Colston next, and A. P. Hill's in the rear. Between five and six P. M. the word was given, and the lines marched forward into the forest.

The thickets were so dense that many of the soldiers had the clothes torn from their backs, but on they went, sometimes creeping to get through the thick undergrowth. After a march of two miles they came suddenly upon the right wing of Hooker's army. The men were scattered about, cooking and eating their suppers, wholly unconscious of the approach of the-dreaded Jackson. With a wild yell, the Confederates dashed forward and drove the enemy pell-mell through the forests for three miles. Jackson's only order was "Press forward," and onward rushed his devoted men after the terrified fugitives.

At eight o'clock the line of Rodes was within a mile of Chancellorsville, still in the forest, when General Jackson ordered the fresh troops of A. P. Hill to advance to the front to relieve those of Rodes, who were worn out with marching and fighting.

He knew that Hooker would send forward other troops, so he went to the front himself to get his men in order. As he rode along the line he would say, "Men, get into line! Get into line!" Turning to Colonel Cobb, he sent him to tell General Rodes to take possession of a barricade in front, and then rode away towards the turnpike.

But before the broken ranks of Rodes could gain the barricade Hooker sent forward a large body of fresh troops, and the battle was renewed all along the line.

It was now ten o'clock, and the pale moon sent her silvery rays down into the heart of the dismal Wilderness, whose echoes awoke to the sound of tramping feet, the rattle of musketry, and the groans of the dying. Through moonlight and shadow, with these sounds ringing in his ears, Jackson rode forward to his death.

After riding up the turnpike a short distance, he found the enemy advancing. Turning, he rode back rapidly towards his own line. The Southern men lying hid in the thickets, thinking that Jackson and his staff were a squad of Northern cavalry, opened a rapid fire upon them. So deadly was their aim that nearly every horse in the party was killed. Two officers were killed, others hurt, and General Jackson himself was wounded three times. His left arm was broken just below the shoulder joint, and was also wounded lower down. A third ball had entered the palm of his right hand and broken two bones.

His left hand, so cruelly hurt, dropped by his side, and his horse, no longer controlled by the reins, ran back towards the enemy.

As the horse galloped between two trees, he passed beneath a low bough, which struck his rider in the face, tore off his cap, and threw him violently back in the saddle. He did not fall, however, but grasped the reins with his bleeding right hand, and turned him back into the road. There, the General found the greatest confusion. Horses, mad with pain and fright, were running in every direction, and in the road lay the wounded and dying.

*Where General Jackson fell.*

Captain Wilbourne, one of Jackson's aides, now seized the reins and stopped his horse. Seeing that the General was badly hurt, he lifted him from the saddle, almost fainting from the loss of blood. He was then laid down by the side of the road, his head resting upon Captain Wilbourne's breast, while a messenger went to summon Dr. McGuire, his chief surgeon. Soon General Hill came up, and, pulling off the General's gauntlets, found that his left arm was broken.

As the enemy were not far off, his arm was quickly bandaged with a handkerchief, and he attempted to walk. But after they had gone a few steps a litter was brought, and the General was placed upon it.

The litter was hardly in motion when the fire from the guns of the enemy became terrible. Many men were struck down by it, among whom were General Hill and one of the bearers of the litter.

The litter was placed upon the ground, and the officers lay down by it to escape death.

After awhile the fire changed, and Jackson rose to his feet and walked slowly on, leaning upon two members of his staff. General

Pender, coming up, saw by the moonlight that General Jackson was badly hurt. "Ah! General," said he, "I am sorry to see that

*General Pender.*

you have been wounded. The lines here are so much broken that I fear we will have to fall back."

Though almost fainting, Jackson raised his head, and said : "You must hold your ground, General Pender! You must hold your ground!" This was the last order of Jackson on the field.

The General, being very faint, was again placed on the litter, and the whole party moved through the forest towards the hospital at Wilderness Run.

As they were going slowly through the undergrowth, one of the men caught his foot in a grapevine and fell, letting the litter fall to the ground.

Jackson fell upon his wounded shoulder, and for the first time groaned most piteously.

*General Jackson's last order on the field:*
*" You must hold your ground, General Pender!   You must hold*
*your ground!"*

With great difficulty they made their way until they came to a place in the road where an ambulance was waiting. The General was placed in it, and was soon met by his surgeon, Dr. McGuire, who, having sprung into the ambulance, found the General almost pulseless.

Some spirits was given him, which revived him, and ere long he was laid tenderly in a camp bed at the hospital. Here he fell into a deep sleep. About midnight he was awakened, and told by Dr. McGuire that it was thought best to amputate his arm.

"Do what you think best, Doctor," was the calm reply.

The arm was amputated, and the ball taken out of his right hand by the skillful surgeon, and he again fell into a quiet sleep, which lasted until nine o'clock on Sunday morning.

General Hill being wounded, General Stuart was placed in command of Jackson's corps. He now determined to wait until morning to attack the strong works of Hooker, which were again in front of the Confederates.

The next morning Stuart thundered on the west, and Lee on the east and south. When the Stonewall Brigade went forward, they shouted,

*Gen. J. E. B. Stuart.*

"Charge, and remember Jackson!" "But even as they moved from their position," says Dr. Dabney, "their General, Paxton, the friend and former adjutant of Jackson, was killed where he stood. But his men rushed forward, and, without other leader than the *name* which formed their battle-cry, swept everything before them." At ten A. M., May 3d, Chancellorsville was taken by Lee, and the Federals took refuge behind new barricades nearer to the river.

In the meantime, General Sedgwick, who had been left at Fredericksburg by General Hooker, attacked General Early, and captured a part of his command. General Lee, having Hooker in check, sent help to Early, and on Wednesday, came up himself and drove General Sedgwick back across the river, where Hooker had already retreated on Tuesday night, May 5th.

*General Jubal A. Early.*

When General Jackson awoke on Sunday morning, May 3d, he asked one of his aids to go to Richmond for his wife. He had sent her to that city when the Federals had begun to move across the river. His mind was clear and he stated that if he had had one more hour of daylight, he would have cut off the enemy from the United States ford, and they would have been obliged either to fight their way out or to surrender.

It was now thought best to take him to a more quiet place; so on Monday he was moved to Mr. Chandler's near Guinea's Depot, where every care was taken to make him comfortable. He seemed to take much interest in hearing of the battle on Sunday, and said of the Stonewall Brigade, "They are a noble body of men. The men who live through this war will be proud to say, 'I was one of the Stonewall Brigade.'"

He then went on to say that the name of Stonewall belonged to the men of the Brigade alone, as they had earned it by their steadfast conduct at First Manassas. He spoke

*General R. E. Rodes.*

also of General Rodes, and said that on account of gallant conduct, he deserved to be advanced to the rank of major-general. The death of General Paxton gave him great distress, but he grew calmer when told of the glorious exploits of his old brigade.

He was much pleased at this noble letter from General Lee:

"*General :*

I have just received your note, informing me that you were wounded. I cannot express my regret at the occurrence. Could I have directed events, I should have chosen, for the good of the country, to have been disabled in your stead.

I congratulate you upon the victory which is due to your skill and energy.

Most truly yours,

(Signed)    R. E. LEE, *General.*"

His mind seemed ever dwelling on religious subjects, and he was entirely submissive to the will of God.

On Wednesday, his wounds were doing so well that it was thought possible to take him by railroad to Richmond. On that night, however, while Dr. McGuire was absent from him for awhile, he was taken with a severe pain in his side, which was in fact due to pneumonia, which had now set in.

From that time he grew weaker, and at last it was seen that he could live only a few hours.

Mrs. Jackson arrived on Thursday, and to her he said, "I know you would gladly give your life for me, but I am perfectly resigned." When his weeping wife at last told him that death was near, he whispered, "Very good, very good, it is all right." He then sent

*Julia Jackson at the age of four years.*

messages to many friends, and desired to be buried in Lexington, in the Valley of Virginia.

His little girl was now brought in to receive his last farewell.

Upon seeing her, his face lit up with a bright smile, and he murmured, "Little darling!" He tried to caress her with his poor maimed hand—she smiling in her delight at seeing him again. Thus, she remained by his side upon the bed until it was seen that he was growing very weak.

Then his mind began to wander, and as if again upon the battle-field, he cried out: "Order A. P. Hill to prepare for action!" "Pass the infantry to the front!" "Tell Major Hawks to send forward provisions for the men!" Then his vision changed, and he murmured, "Let us cross over the river, and rest under the shade of the trees."

"The moment had indeed come," says Cooke, "when the great leader was to pass over the dark river which separates two worlds, and rest under the shade of the Tree of Life. From this time, he continued to sink, and at fifteen minutes past three in the afternoon, on Sunday, the 10th of May, he peacefully expired."

Pontoon', a bridge built on boats.

Furlough (fûr'lo), a short leave of absence.

Chăp'lain, a clergyman of the army or navy.

Rātions (or răsh-uns), a certain quantity of food and drink.

Vig'i lant, watchful.

Bărricade', a hastily-made fortification.

Tell about—

The battle of Fredericksburg.

Jackson's life at Moss Neck.

Jackson's march around Hooker.

His death.

## CHAPTER X.

### Upon the Roll of Fame.

Upon hearing the news of Jackson's death, the grief of the South was equalled only by the wish to do him honor.

President Davis sent a special train to bear his remains to Richmond. He also sent, as the gift of the country, the beautiful new flag of the Confederate Congress to be his winding sheet.

Jefferson Davis

When the train reached Richmond, it was met by a vast concourse of weeping people. On Wednesday, the coffin, preceded by military, was borne from the Governor's Mansion to the Capitol through the main streets of the city. The hearse was drawn by four white horses and followed by eight generals as pall-

bearers. Then came his horse, caparisoned
for battle, and led by his body-servant; then
followed his staff, the President, the Governor
of Virginia, the city authorities, and a vast
number of sorrowing people.

*"Fancy," or " Little Sorrel. "*
*General T. J. Jackson's War Horse, 30 Years Old.*

As the procession moved along, cannon
were fired and bells tolled. At last the
Capitol was reached and the body was
borne, amid the tears of the multitude, into
the building where it lay in state all day.

Twenty thousand persons are said to have passed in front of the body to gaze for the last time upon their mighty chief.

It is said that President Davis stood long, gazing at the quiet face, and then in silence left the house.

Old soldiers pressed around the bier with tears streaming down their bronzed faces, while one stooped and kissed the cold lips of his beloved commander.

The next day the remains were borne, attended by a guard of honor, to Lexington, where they were received by General Smith, the corps of cadets, the professors, and many sorrowing citizens. They were borne to the barracks of the Military Institute and placed in the old class-room of the dead general. Every half hour, the cadet battery pealed forth a fitting requiem to the great teacher of artillery tactics. Then "escorted by infantry, cavalry, and artillery, under command of Col. Shipp, and borne to the grave upon a caisson of the cadet battery," he was laid to rest beside the graves of his first wife and child in the beautiful cemetery of Lexington.

The "right hand" of Lee was thus taken away just as the heaviest stroke had fallen upon the enemy. General Lee, the army, the whole South mourned for their fallen hero. There were other generals as brave and true as Jackson, but none who possessed his keen insight into the movements of the enemy, his celerity of action, and the wonderful certainty of victory which made him the idol of his own soldiers and the dread of the foe.

But the renown of Jackson is not confined to the limits of his own land. It has crossed the ocean, and now the plans of his battles in the Valley of the Shenandoah and of Second Manassas and of Chancellorsville are studied by military men, and used by them as models of strategy and tactics. All English-speaking people are justly proud that the greatest military genius of the age belongs to them.

*Jackson's Statue in Capitol Square, Richmond, Va.*

(229)

Not long after the end of the war, his admirers and friends in England presented to the State of Virginia a statue of Jackson in bronze. It was placed in the Capitol Square in Richmond not far from the statue of Washington and the great Virginians of his time.

In the spring of 1891, a beautiful and imposing statue of our hero was erected in Lexington, Virginia, by his old soldiers and friends throughout the South. On July 21st of that year, it was unveiled in the presence of a vast multitude of people.

The anniversary of the First Manassas, when Jackson, in a "baptism of fire," received the new name of "Stonewall," and flashed like a meteor upon the wondering world, was thought a fitting day on which to display to his countrymen his figure in enduring bronze.

For days and nights, the trains bore into the historic town crowds of soldiers and visitors from all parts of the country.

Beautiful arches and mottoes graced the buildings and highways, and the whole was crowned by perfect weather.

At 12 o'clock, the great parade moved from the Virginia Military Institute. General James A. Walker, the only commander of the Stonewall Brigade then living, was chief marshal of the day.

As the procession moved on, band after band of Confederates were seen—battle-scarred veterans in the old Confederate grey, military companies in bright uniforms, famous generals with bronzed faces and grizzled hair, the chaplains of the Confederacy, and visiting camps of veterans from other States.

Following these came the officers of the Virginia Military Institute and Washington and Lee University. Finally came a large concourse of citizens and carriages. Among those in the carriages were General Jubal A. Early, the orator of the day, and his host, General Custis Lee; the sculptor of the statue, Edward V. Valentine; Mrs. General T. J. Jackson and her son-in-law, Mr. Christian, and his children, Julia and Thomas Jackson Christian.

At last, the grand-stand in the University grounds was reached. After prayer and the reading of three Confederate war poems, "Stonewall Jackson's Way," "Slain in Battle," and "Over the River," General Early, clad in Confederate grey, made the address, which gave a simple account of the great battles fought by Jackson. He was greeted with hearty cheers, and tears rolled down the cheeks of many veterans as they again in memory fought and marched with the immortal Jackson.

At the end of the speech the procession again formed and marched to the cemetery where stood the monument.

At the given signal, Mrs. Jackson and her two grandchildren, Julia Jackson Christian, aged five years, and Thomas Jackson Christian, aged three years, mounted the steps of the platform. A single gun sounded, and the two children with united hands pulled the cord and let the veil fall, revealing to admiring thousands the face and form of Jackson.

Cheers and shouts rent the air, while the Rockbridge Artillery fired a salute of fifteen guns from the cannon which they had used at Manassas.

The statue, clad in the uniform of a major-general, stands with the left hand grasping a sheathed sword, upon which the weight of the body seems to rest. The right hand rests upon the thigh and holds a pair of field glasses, which it would seem that the General has just been using.

The figure is eight feet high and stands upon a granite pedestal ten feet tall. Upon the stone are carved only the words, "Jackson, 1824–1863," and "Stonewall."

Under the monument, in a vault, rest the remains of the dead soldier and his

*Jackson Statue at Lexington.*

daughters, Mrs. Christian, and Mary Graham who died in infancy.

The veterans lingered long about their beloved hero. Many times had they followed him on the weary march and through the smoke of battle, and now it seemed as if he were with them again to lead them on to victory.

At last, saluting, they marched in silence away, carrying his image in their memories and the love of him in their hearts.

Perhaps it will interest my readers to have a pen and ink portrait of Mrs. Jackson at that time, as given by a leading journalist of the day. "Mrs. Jackson sat just behind the famous generals. She wore a handsome costume of black silk trimmed with crepe, black gloves, and a crepe bonnet. Her face is a most attractive one. Her black hair, still unmixed with grey, was brushed in graceful waves across her forehead. Her eyes, large and dark, sparkled and filled with tears, as veteran after veteran pressed forward to grasp her hand."

Not long before, her daughter, Mrs. Christian, the baby Julia whom Jackson had loved so well, had died, leaving two children, Julia and Thomas. These children are the only descendants of our beloved General. At this writing, in the year of our Lord 1898, Mrs. Jackson is still living, and to her the hearts of Southern people turn in fond affection, because she was the best beloved of their mighty chief.

But not enough had been done to honor our hero. In 1896, a noble building called the "Jackson Memorial Hall" was completed at the Virginia Military Institute, and dedicated with fitting ceremony to the memory of Jackson. In these halls and beneath the shadow of this building, the cadets of the South for many long years will be trained for war. How fit the place! Near by rest Lee and Stonewall Jackson— mighty soldiers, and Christian warriors!

There the sweeping winds proclaim our heroes' fame, and nightly the glittering stars chant in heavenly chorus: "They shine, they shine with our brightness."

---

Că-is-son, a chest for ammunition.

Capăr'isoned, dressed pompously.

Tăc'tics, the science and art of placing forces for battle.

Rēq'uiem, a hymn sung for the dead.

Vĕte'ran, one who has grown old in service.

Pĕd'-es-tal, the base of a column or statue.

Write in your own words—

    A description of the reception of General Jackson's body in Richmond.

    A description of his monument in Lexington, Virginia.

*General Stuart in 1854, from an ambrotype owned by Mrs. J. E. B. Stuart, which is here reproduced for the first time.*

# LIFE OF

# J. E. B. STUART

BY

MARY L. WILLIAMSON

*Author of Life of Lee, Life of Jackson, and Life of Washington*


EDITED AND ARRANGED FOR SCHOOL USE

BY

E. O. WIGGINS

*English Department, Lynchburg High School, Virginia*

Harrisonburg, Virginia

SPRINKLE PUBLICATIONS

1989

Sprinkle Publications
P. O. Box 1094
Harrisonburg, Virginia 22801

# PREFACE

Some years ago, to fill what appeared to me a need in our literature for children, I made a study of the lives and campaigns of General R. E. Lee and of General Stonewall Jackson and prepared, for very young readers, histories of those great commanders.

In performing these tasks, I became interested in the combats and maneuvers of General Lee's chief of cavalry, Major-General J. E. B. Stuart, who has been justly called "the eyes and ears of Lee." As the years go by, I find no book in print recounting to children his wonderful feats and valorous service, or explaining to them the part played in the battles of Lee and Jackson by the Stuart Cavalry Corps and Horse Artillery whose exploits hold a brilliant place in modern military tactics.

To make good this omission, I have prepared this little life of Stuart, in the hope that it will not only pass on the story of military deeds as captivating as any in history, but warm the hearts of rising generations to lives of courage and devotion.

In the later stages of my work, Miss Evelina O. Wiggins has been associated, contributing various materials, obtaining three pictures and several interesting letters of General Stuart's, and making available Mrs. J. E. B. Stuart's criticism of the manuscript. Miss Wiggins has also rendered the aid of adapting the book to the practical needs of the schoolroom. Her experience and position as a teacher make the latter service highly valuable.

MARY LYNN WILLIAMSON

New Market, Virginia
September 1, 1914

# ACKNOWLEDGMENTS

The publishers wish to acknowledge their obligations to Mrs. H. B. McClellan for permission to use material from her husband's book, *Life and Campaigns of General J. E. B. Stuart;* to General T. T. Munford and to Judge Theodore S. Garnett for information and pictures; to Mr. J. E. B. Stuart and the Confederate Museum, Richmond, Va., for permission to make photographic copies of the personal relics of General Stuart in the Museum; and to Mrs. J. E. B. Stuart for the ambrotype and letters of General Stuart which she allowed to be copied for use in this book and for the invaluable aid of her careful critical reading of the manuscript.

# CONTENTS

LIST OF

# MAPS AND ILLUSTRATIONS

# LIST OF BOOKS

FOR REFERENCE AND TEACHERS' USE

H. B. McClellan: *Life and Campaigns of General J. E. B. Stuart*

Heros Von Borcke: *Memoirs of the War for Confederate Independence*

John S. Mosby: *Campaigns of Stuart's Cavalry*

George M. Neese: *Three Years in the Confederate Horse Artillery*

Theodore S. Garnett: *Major-General J. E. B. Stuart*

G. F. R. Henderson: *Stonewall Jackson and the American Civil War*

Gamaliel Bradford: *Confederate Portraits*

John Esten Cooke: *Surry of Eagle's Nest*

J. William Jones: *Christ in the Camp, or Religion in Lee's Army*

Southern Historical Society Papers,—

Vol. 1, pp. 99-103; Address by Fitzhugh Lee

Vol. 8, pp. 434-'56; Character Sketch by H. B. McClellan

Vol. 37, pp. 210-'31; Stuart at Gettysburg by R. H. McKim

See also other articles on Stuart in the Southern Historical Papers.

# INTRODUCTION

HENRY OF NAVARRE was a famous French king who led his forces to a glorious victory in a civil war. An English writer, Lord Macaulay, wrote a stirring poem in which a French soldier is represented as describing this battle. Here is his picture of the great, beloved king:—

"The King is come to marshal us, in all his armor drest,
And he has bound a snow-white plume upon his gallant crest.
He looked upon his people and a tear was in his eye,
He looked upon the traitors and his glance was stern and high;
Right graciously he smiled on us, as rolled from wing to wing,
Down all our line a deafening shout, 'God save our lord, the King!'

" 'And if my standard bearer fall,—as fall full well he may,
For never saw I promise yet of such a bloody fray—
Press where you see my white plume shine amidst the ranks of war,
And be your oriflamme to-day the helmet of Navarre.'

"A thousand spurs are striking deep, a thousand spears in rest,
A thousand knights are pressing close behind the snow-white crest;
And in they burst and on they rushed, while like a guiding star,
Amidst the thickest carnage blazed the helmet of Navarre."

These lines about the French king of the sixteenth century are often quoted in describing a gallant cavalry leader of our own country. As we read them, we see the Confederate general, "Jeb" Stuart, his cavalry hat looped back on one side with a long black ostrich plume which his troopers always saw in the forefront of the charge. His men would follow that plume anywhere, at any time, and when you read this story of his life, you will not wonder that he inspired their absolute devotion.

You have read about the lives of the peerless commander, General Robert E. Lee, and his great lieutenant, General Stonewall Jackson. In these you have learned something about the movements of the great body of our army, the infantry; but the infantry, even with such able commanders as Lee and Jackson, needed the aid of the cavalry and the artillery. It is with these two latter divisions of the army that we deal in studying the life of General Stuart. As chief of cavalry and commander of the famous Stuart Horse Artillery, he served as eyes and ears to the commanding generals. He kept them informed about the location and movements of the Federals, screened the location of the Confederate troops, felt the way, protected the flank and rear when the army was on

the march, and made quick raids into the
Federal territory or around their army to
secure supplies and information as well as to
mislead them concerning the proposed movements of Confederate forces.    A heavy re-
sponsibility rested on the cavalry, and General
Stuart and his men were engaged in many small
but severe battles and skirmishes in which the
army as a whole did not take part.

*"To horse, to horse! the sabers gleam,*
*High sounds our bugle call,*
*Combined by honor's sacred tie,*
*Our watchword, 'laws and liberty!'*
*Forward to do or die."*

—Sir Walter Scott

# LIFE OF J. E. B. STUART

## CHAPTER I

### YOUTHFUL DAYS

#### 1833-'54

James Ewell Brown Stuart, commonly known as "Jeb" Stuart from the first three initials of his name, was born in Patrick county, Virginia, February 6, 1833. On each side of his family, he could point to a line of ancestors who had served their country well in war and peace and from whom he inherited his high ideals of duty, patriotism, and religion.

He was of Scotch descent and his ancestors belonged to a clan of note in the history of Scotland. From Scotland a member of this clan went to Ireland.

About the year 1726, Jeb Stuart's great-great-grandfather, Archibald Stuart, fled from Londonderry, Ireland, to the wilds of Pennsylvania, in order to escape religious persecution.

Eleven years later, he removed from Pennsylvania to Augusta county, Virginia, where he became a large land-holder. At Tinkling Spring Church, the graves of the immigrant and his wife may still be seen.

Archibald Stuart's second son, Alexander, joined the Continental army and fought with signal bravery during the whole of the War of the Revolution. After the war, he practiced law. He showed his interest in education by becoming one of the founders of Liberty Hall, at Lexington,

RUINS OF LIBERTY HALL ACADEMY, AT LEXINGTON, VA.

Virginia, a school whicn afterwards became Washington College and has now grown into Washington and Lee University.

His youngest son who bore his name, was also a lawyer; he held positions of trust in his native State, Virginia, as well as in Illinois and Missouri where he held the responsible and honored position of a United States judge.

Our general's father, Archibald Stuart, the

son of Judge Stuart, after a brief military
career in the War of 1812, became a successful
lawyer. His wit and eloquence soon won him
distinction, and his district sent him as repre-
sentative to the Congress of the United States
where he served four years.

There is an interesting story told about
General Stuart's mother's grandfather, William
Letcher. He had enraged the Loyalists, or
Tories, on the North Carolina border, by a
defeat that he and a little company of volunteers had inflicted on them in the War of the
Revolution. One day in June, 1780, as Mrs.
Letcher was alone at home with her baby girl,
only six weeks old, a stranger, dressed as a
hunter and carrying a gun in his hand, appeared
at the door and asked for Letcher. While his
wife was explaining that he would be at home
in a short time, he entered and asked the man
to be seated.

The latter, however, raised his gun, saying:
"I demand you in the name of the king."

When Letcher tried to seize the gun, the Tory
fired and the patriot fell mortally wounded, in
the presence of his young wife and babe.

Bethenia Letcher, the tiny fatherless babe,
grew to womanhood and married David Pannill;
and her daughter, Elizabeth Letcher Pannill,

married Archibald Stuart, the father of our
hero.

Mrs. Archibald Stuart inherited from her
grandfather, William Letcher, a large estate in
Patrick county.   The place, commanding fine
views of the Blue Ridge mountains, was called
Laurel Hill, and here in a comfortable old mansion set amid a grove of oak trees, Jeb Stuart
was born and spent the earlier years of his
boyhood.

Mrs. Stuart was a great lover of flowers and
surrounding the house was a beautiful old-
fashioned flower garden, where Jeb, who loved
flowers as much as his mother did, spent many
happy days.   He always loved this boyhood
home and often thought of it during the hard
and stirring years of war.   Once near the close
of the war, he told his brother that he would like
nothing better, when the long struggle was at
an end, than to go back to the old home and live
a quiet, peaceful life.

When Jeb was fourteen years old, he was sent
to school in Wytheville, and in 1848 he entered
Emory and Henry College.   Here, under the
influence of a religious revival, he joined the
Methodist church, but about ten years later
he became a member of the Episcopal church
of which his wife was a member.

Though always gay and high-spirited, Stuart even as a boy possessed a deep religious sentiment which grew in strength as he grew in years and kept his heart pure and his hands clean through the many temptations that beset him in the freedom and conviviality of army life. A promise that he made his mother never to taste strong drink was kept faithfully to his

EMORY AND HENRY COLLEGE ABOUT 1850

death, and none of his soldiers ever heard him use an oath even in the heat of battle. His gallantry, boldness, and continual gayety and good nature, coupled with his high Christian virtues, caused all who came in contact with him not only to love but to respect and admire him.

He left Emory and Henry College in 1850 and entered the United States Military Academy at West Point where he had received an appointment.

At this time, Colonel Robert E. Lee was superintendent at West Point. Young Stuart spent many pleasant hours at the home of the superintendent where he was a great favorite with the ladies of the family. Custis Lee, the eldest son of Colonel Lee, was Stuart's best friend while he was a student at the Academy.

An interesting incident is told about Stuart while he was on a vacation from West Point. Mr. Benjamin B. Minor of Richmond, had a case to be tried at Williamsburg, and when he arrived at the hotel it was so crowded that he was put in an "omnibus" room, so called because it contained three double beds.

Late in the afternoon when the stage drove up, he saw three young cadets step from it and he soon found that they were to share with him the "omnibus" room.

He went to bed early, but put a lamp on the table by the head of his bed and got out his papers to go over his case. After awhile the three cadets came in laughing and singing, and soon they were all three piled into one bed where they continued to laugh and joke in uproarious spirits.

Finally one of them said, "See here, fellows,

we have had our fun long enough and we are disturbing that gentleman over there; let us hush up and go to sleep."

"No need for that, boys," said Mr. Minor, "I have just finished."

Then as he tells us he 'pitched in' and had a good time with them.

The cadet who had shown such thoughtfulness and courtesy was young Jeb Stuart who as Mr. Minor discovered was one of his wife's cousins. He was very much pleased with the boy and invited him to come to Richmond. Stuart accepted the invitation and called several times at the Minor home.

From daguerreotype in Confederate Museum, Richmond, Va.

J. E. B. STUART

When a student at West Point

He explained to Mr. Minor his plan for an invention which was to be called "Stuart's lightning horse-hitcher" and to be used in Indian raids. He excited Mr. Minor's admiration because he had such gallant and genial courtesy and professional pride. He wanted even then to accomplish something useful and important to his country and himself.

General Fitzhugh Lee, who was at West Point with Stuart, and who later served under General Stuart as a trusted commander, tells us that as

a cadet he was remarkable for "strict attendance to military duties, and erect, soldierly bearing, an immediate and almost thankful acceptance of a challenge to fight any cadet who might in any way feel himself aggrieved, and a clear, metallic, ringing voice."

Although the boys called him a "Bible class man" and "Beauty Stuart," it was in good-natured boyish teasing; where he felt it to be intended differently or where his high standards of conduct seemed to be

BADGE OF WEST POINT
GRADUATES

The arms of the United States Academy, suspended by a ribbon of black, gray, and gold from a bar bearing the date of the graduate's class

sneered at, he was well able with his quick temper and superb physical strength to teach the offender a lesson.

As 'Fitz' Lee tells us, Stuart was always

ready to accept a challenge, but he did not fight without good cause, and his father, a fair-minded and intelligent man, approved of his son's course in these fisticuff encounters. Between his father and himself there was the best kind of comradeship and sympathy, and young Stuart was always ready to consult his father before taking any important step in life. The decision as to what he should do when he left West Point, however, was left to him, and just after his graduation he wrote home that he had decided to enter the regular army instead of becoming a lawyer.

"Each profession has its labors and rewards," he wrote, "and in making the selection I shall rely upon Him whose judgment cannot err, for it is not with the man that walketh to direct his steps."

Meanwhile, by his daring and skill in horsemanship, his diligence in his studies, and his ability to command, he had risen rapidly from the position of corporal to that of captain, and then to the rank of cavalry sergeant which is the highest rank in that arm of the service at West Point. He graduated thirteenth in a class of forty-six, and started his brief but brilliant military career well equipped with youth, courage, skill, and a firm reliance on the love and wisdom of God.

## CHAPTER II

# A LIEUTENANT IN THE UNITED STATES CAVALRY

## 1854-'61

MOST of Stuart's time from his graduation at West Point until the outbreak of the War of Secession was spent in military service along the southern and western borders of our country. During this period, there was almost constant warfare between Indians and frontier settlers. Stuart had many interesting adventures in helping to protect the settlers and to drive the Indians back into their own territory. The training that he received at this time helped to develop him into a great cavalry and artillery leader.

The autumn after he left West Point, Stuart was commissioned second lieutenant in a regiment of mounted riflemen on duty in western Texas. He reached Fort Clark in December, just in time to join an expedition against the Apache Indians who had been giving the settlers a great deal of trouble. The small force to which he was attached pushed boldly into the Indian country north of the Rio Grande.

It was not long before the young officer's skill and determination received a severe test. The trail that the expedition followed led to the top of a steep and rugged ridge which to the troopers' astonishment dropped abruptly two thousand feet to an extensive valley. The precipice formed of huge columns of vertical rock, at first seemed impassable, but they soon found a narrow and dangerous Indian trail—the kind that is called a 'mulepath'—winding to the base of the mighty cliff. The

CARRYING THE GUN DOWN THE 'MULEPATH'

officers and advance guard dismounted and led their horses down the steep path that scarcely afforded footing for a man and passed on to choose a bivouac for the night. A little later,

Lieutenant Stuart, with a rear guard of fifty rangers detailed to assist him, reached the top of the ridge, with their single piece of artillery. Stuart worked his way down the trail alone, hoping that when he reached the foot he would find that the major in charge of the expedition had left word that the gun was to be abandoned as it seemed impossible to carry it down the precipice. No such order awaited him, however, and the young officer determined to get the gun down in spite of all difficulties. He noted well the dangers of the way as he regained the top and, having had the mules unhitched and led down by some of the men, he unlimbered the gun and started the captain of the rangers and twenty-five men down with the limber. He himself took charge of the gun and, with the help of the remaining men, lifted it over huge rocks and lowered it by lariat ropes over impassable places until it was finally brought safely to the valley below.

The major had taken it for granted that Stuart would leave the gun at the top of the precipice and was amazed when just at supper time it was brought safely into camp. Such ingenuity, grit, and determination were qualities which promised that the young officer would develop into a skillful and reliable leader.

A few days later, the command encamped for the night in a narrow valley between high ridges. The camp fires were burning brightly and the cooks were preparing supper when a sudden violent gust of wind swept through the valley and scattering the fire set the whole prairie into a moving flame. With such rapidity did the fire sweep over the camp that the men were unable to save anything except their horses, and in a deplorable condition the expedition was forced to return to the camp in Texas.

In May, 1855, Stuart was transferred to the First Regiment of cavalry, with the rank of second lieutenant. In July, this regiment was ordered to Fort Leavenworth, Kansas; and in September, it went on a raid, under the leadership of Colonel E. V. Sumner, against some Indians who had disturbed the white settlers. The savages retreated to their mountain strongholds and the regiment returned to the fort without fighting.

While on this expedition, Stuart learned with deep distress of the death of his wise and affectionate father. It had been only a few weeks before that Mr. Stuart had written to approve his son's marriage to Miss Flora Cooke, daughter of Colonel Philip St. George Cooke who was commandant at Fort Riley. The marriage was celebrated at that place, November 14, 1855.

At this time, there was serious trouble in Kansas between the two political parties that were fighting to decide whether Kansas should become a free or a slave state. Stuart, who had been promoted to the rank of first lieutenant, was stationed at Fort Leavenworth in 1856-'57. Here he was involved in many skirmishes and local raids. It was at this time that he encountered the outlaw "Ossawatomie" Brown of whom we shall hear again a little later.

Stuart passed uninjured through the Kansas contest, and in 1857 entered upon another Indian war against the Cheyenne warriors who were attacking the western settlers. In the chief battle of this campaign, the Indians were routed, but Lieutenant Stuart was wounded while rescuing a brother officer who was attacked by an Indian.

Here is Stuart's own account of the fight as given in a letter to his wife, which she has kindly allowed us to copy:

"Very few of the company horses were fleet enough after the march, besides my own Brave Dan, to keep in reach of the Indians mounted on fresh ponies. . . . . As long as Dan held out I was foremost, but after a chase of five miles he failed and I had to mount a private's horse and continue the pursuit.

"When I overtook the rear of the enemy again, I found Lomax in imminent danger from an Indian who was on foot and in the act of shooting him. I rushed to the rescue, and succeeded in firing at him in time, wounding him in his thigh. He fired at me in return with an Allen's revolver, but missed. My shots were now exhausted, and I called on some men approaching to rush up with their pistols and kill him. They rushed up, but fired without hitting.

"About this time I observed Stanley and McIntyre close by; the former said, 'Wait, I'll fetch him,' and dismounted from his horse so as to aim deliberately, but in dismounting, his pistol accidentally discharged the last load he had. He began, however, to snap the empty barrels at the Indian who was walking deliberately up to him with his revolver pointed.

"I could not stand that, but drawing my saber rushed on the monster, inflicting a severe wound across his head, that I think would have severed any other man's, but simultaneous with *that* he fired his last barrel within a foot of me, the ball taking effect in the breast, but by the mercy of God glancing to the left and lodging so far inside that it cannot be felt. I rejoice to inform you that it is not regarded as at all fatal or dangerous, though I may be confined to my bed for weeks."

After this battle, all of the force pursued the Indians, except a small detachment under Captain Foote, which was left behind to guard the wounded for whom the surgeon established rough hospital quarters on the banks of a beautiful, winding creek. Here Stuart spent nearly a week confined to his cot, and as he wrote his wife at the time, the only books that he had to read during the long, weary days were his *Prayer Book*—which was not neglected —and his *Army Regulations*. A few pages of *Harper's Weekly* that some one happened to have were considered quite a treasure.

At the end of about ten days, some Pawnee guides who had been attached to the expedition brought orders for this little detachment to leave the camp where it was exposed to attacks from the wandering bands of Cheyenne Indians and go back to Fort Kearny a hundred miles away.

Stuart was just able to sit on his horse again, yet we shall see that in spite of his wound he was the life and salvation of the little party.

The Pawnees said they were only four days distant from the fort, but the second day these unreliable guides deserted and the soldiers were lost in a heavy fog, without a compass. They were forced to depend on a Cheyenne prisoner for information. After four days' fruitless and difficult marching through the forest, Stuart, who believed that the guard was willfully misleading them, volunteered to go ahead with a small force, find the fort, and send back help for those who were still suffering too seriously

From McClure's Magazine

INDIANS OF THE PLAINS

from their wounds to keep up on a rapid and uncertain march.

After many dangers and deep anxiety on his part, taking his course by the stars when the fog lifted at night and working his way through it as best he could by day, he finally reached Fort Kearny. The Pawnees had come in three days before, and scouting parties had been searching for Captain Foote's command about which much anxiety was felt. Help was immediately sent them, and as a result of Stuart's indomitable will and able services, the little party was rescued and brought safely to the fort.

From the autumn of 1857 until the summer of 1860, Stuart was stationed at Fort Riley. During these three years, there were few skirmishes with the Indians and Stuart had leisure to perfect the invention of a saber attachment that he had been thinking of ever since his student days at West Point. This invention was bought and patented by the government in October, 1859, while the inventor was on leave of absence in Virginia, visiting his mother and his friends.

It was on the night of the sixteenth of this same October that a band of twenty men, under the leadership of John Brown, seized the United States arsenal at Harper's Ferry. Brown was a fanatic who believed that all slaves should be set free and who had taken an active part in the recent disturbances in Kansas. After seizing the arsenal at Harper's Ferry, he sent out his followers during the night to arrest certain citizens and to call to arms the slaves on the surrounding plantations. About sixty citizens were arrested and imprisoned in the engine house, within the confines of the armory, but the slaves, either through fear or through distrust of Brown and his schemes, refused to obey his summons.

The next morning as soon as news of the seizure of Harper's Ferry spread over the country, armed men came against Brown from all directions. Before night he and his followers took refuge in the engine house, but it was so crowded that he was obliged to release all but ten of his prisoners.

ARSENAL AT HARPER'S FERRY

When the news of Brown's raid was telegraphed to Washington, Lieutenant Stuart, who was at the capital attending to the sale of his patent saber attachment, was requested to bear a secret order to Lieutenant-Colonel Robert E. Lee, his old superintendent at West Point, who was then at his home, Arlington, near Washington city. Stuart learned that Colonel Lee had been ordered to command the marines who were being sent to suppress the insurrection at Harper's Ferry, and he at once offered to act as aid-de-camp. Colonel Lee, who remembered Stuart well as a cadet, immediately accepted his offer of service.

Upon arriving at Harper's Ferry on the night of October 17, they found that John Brown and his men were still in the engine house, defying the citizen soldiers who surrounded the building. Colonel Lee proceeded to surround the engine house with the marines; at daylight, wishing to avoid bloodshed, he sent Lieutenant Stuart to demand the surrender of the fanatical men, promising to protect them from the fury of the citizens until he could give them up to the United States government.

When Lieutenant Stuart advanced to the parley, Brown, who had assumed the name of Smith, opened the door four or five inches only, placed his body against it, and held a loaded carbine in such a position that, as he stated afterward, he might have "wiped Stuart out like a mosquito." Immediately the young officer recognized in the so-called Smith the identical John, or "Ossawatomie," Brown who had caused so much trouble in Kansas. Brown refused Colonel Lee's terms and demanded permission to march out with his men and prisoners and proceed as far as the second toll-gate. Here, he declared, he would free his prisoners and if Colonel Lee wished to pursue he would fight to the bitter end.

Stuart said that these terms could not be accepted and urged him to surrender at once. When Brown refused, Stuart waved his cap, the signal agreed upon, and the marines advanced, battered down the doors, and engaged in a hand-to-hand fight with the insurgents. Ten of Brown's men were killed by the marines and all the rest, including Brown himself, were wounded.

That same day, Lieutenant Stuart, under Colonel Lee's orders, went to a farm about four miles and a half away that Brown had rented and brought back a number of pikes with which Brown had intended to arm the negroes. Colonel Lee was then ordered back to Washington and Stuart went with him. John Brown and seven of his men were tried, were found guilty of treason, and were hanged.

The John Brown Raid cast a great gloom over the country. While many people in the North regarded Brown as a martyr to the cause of emancipation, the southern people were justly indignant at the thought that their lives and property were no longer safe from the plots of the Abolition party which Brown had represented. The bitter feelings aroused by this affair culminated, in 1861, in the bloody War of Secession.

## CHAPTER III

# A COLONEL OF CONFEDERATE CAVALRY

## 1861

THERE seems to have been no doubt in the mind of Lieutenant Stuart as to what he should do in the event of Virginia's withdrawal from the Union. As soon as he heard that the Old Dominion had seceded, he forwarded to the War Department his resignation as an officer in the United States army, and hastening to Richmond, he enlisted in the militia of his native state. Like most other southerners, he preferred poverty and hardships in defense of the South to all the honors and wealth which the United States government could bestow.

On May 10, 1861, Stuart was commissioned as lieutenant colonel of infantry, and was ordered to report to Colonel T. J. Jackson at Harper's Ferry. While he was at Harper's Ferry, Stuart organized several troops of cavalry to assist the infantry and he was soon transferred to this branch of the service.

On May 15, General Joseph E. Johnston was sent by the Confederate government to take command of all the forces at Harper's Ferry; while Colonel Jackson, who had previously been in command of the place, was assigned charge of the Virginia regiments afterwards famous as the "Stonewall Brigade." General Johnston found that he was unable to hold the town against the advancing Federal force; so he destroyed the railway bridge and retired with his guns and stores to Bunker Hill, twelve miles from Winchester, where he offered battle to the Federals. They declined to fight and withdrew to the north bank of the Potomac river.

When the Federals under General Patterson again crossed the river, General Jackson with his brigade was sent forward to support the cavalry under Stuart and to destroy the railway engines and cars at Martinsburg. Jackson then remained with his brigade near Martinsburg, while his front was protected by Colonel Stuart with a regiment of cavalry.

On July 1, General Patterson advanced toward General Jackson, who went forward to meet him, with only the Fifth Regiment, several companies of cavalry, and one piece of artillery. The Confederate general posted his men behind a farm house and barn, and held back Patterson so well that he threw forward an entire division to overpower the small force of Jackson. The

latter then fell back slowly to the main body
of his troops, with the trifling loss of two men
wounded and nine missing.

While supporting Jackson in this first battle
in the Shenandoah valley, known as the battle
of Haines' Farm or Falling Waters, Colonel
Stuart had a remarkable adventure. Riding
alone in advance of his men, he came suddenly
out of a piece of woods at a point where he
could see a force of Federal infantry on the other
side of the fence. Without a moment's hesita-
tion, he rode boldly forward and ordered the
Federal soldiers to pull down the bars.

They obeyed and he immediately rode through
to the other side, and in peremptory tones said,
"Throw down your arms or you are dead men."

The raw troops were so overcome by Stuart's
boldness and commanding tones that they
obeyed at once and then marched as he directed
through the gap in the fence. Before they
recovered from their astonishment, Stuart had
them surrounded by his own force which had
come up in the meantime, thus capturing over
forty men—almost an entire company.

After some marching backward and forward,
General Johnston retired to Winchester; while
General Patterson moved farther south to Smith-
field as if he intended to attack in that direc-

tion. Stuart with his small force was now compelled to watch a front of over fifty miles, in order to report promptly the movements of the Federals, yet he did this so efficiently that later on when General Johnston was ordered west, he wrote to Stuart:

"How can I eat, sleep, or rest in peace, without you upon the outpost?"

General Johnston now received a call for help from General Beauregard who commanded a Confederate army of twenty thousand men at Manassas Junction. Beauregard was confronted by a Federal army of thirty-five thousand men, including nearly all of the United States regulars east of the Rocky Mountains. This army, commanded by General McDowell, was equipped with improved firearms and had fine uniforms, good tents, and everything that money could buy to make good soldiers. The North was very proud of this fine army and fully expected it to crush Beauregard and to sweep on to Richmond.

Beauregard was indeed in danger. He had a smaller army and his infantry was armed, for the most part, with old-fashioned smooth-bore muskets, and his cavalry with sabers and shotguns. One company of cavalry was armed only with the pikes of John Brown, which had been stored at Harper's Ferry. Beauregard stationed his forces in line of battle along the banks of Bull Run from the Stone Bridge to Union Mills, a distance of eight miles. On July 18, the Federals tried to force Blackburn's Ford on Bull Run, but were repulsed with heavy loss. Beauregard, knowing that the attack would be renewed the next day, sent a message to Johnston at Winchester, sixty miles away.

"If you are going to help me, now is the time," was Beauregard's message.

Two days before, Stuart had been transferred to the cavalry, with a commission as colonel, and he entered at once upon his arduous labors. At first he had in his command only twenty-one officers and three hundred and thirteen men, raw to military discipline and poorly armed with the guns they had used in hunting, but all were fine horsemen and good shots.

General Johnston, leaving Stuart with a little band of troopers to conceal his movements, immediately commenced his march from Winchester to Manassas. So skillfully did Colonel Stuart do his work that General Patterson was not aware of General Johnston's departure until Sunday, July 21, when the great battle of Manassas was fought. Owing to a collision which had blocked the railway, some of the infantry did not reach Manassas until near the close of the battle, but the cavalry and the artillery marched all the way and arrived in time to render effective service during the entire battle.

It was at Manassas that General Jackson won his name of "Stonewall" because of the wonderful stand that his brigade made, just when it seemed that the Federals were about to overcome the Confederates. But we are concerned particularly with the movements of the cavalry which rendered fine service, protecting each flank of the army. Colonel Stuart, with only two companies of cavalry, protected the left flank from assault after assault. At one time Stuart boldly charged the Federal right and drove back a company of Zouaves resplendent in their blue and scarlet uniforms and white turbans.

General Early, who arrived on the field about three o'clock in the afternoon and assisted in holding the left flank, said, "But for Stuart's presence there, I am of the opinion that my brigade would have arrived too late to be of any use. Stuart did as much toward saving the First Manassas as any subordinate who participated in it."

General Jackson, in his report of the battle, said: "Apprehensive lest my flanks be turned, I sent orders to Colonels Stuart and Radford of the cavalry to secure them. Colonel Stuart and that part of his command with him deserve great praise for the promptness with which they moved to my left and secured my flank from the enemy, and by driving them back."

Thus we see at the very crisis of the battle, Stuart with only a small force aided largely in gaining the great victory. When he saw the Federals fleeing from all parts of the field, he pursued them for twelve miles, taking many prisoners and securing much booty.

After the battle of First Manassas, the main armies were inactive for many months; but the Confederate cavalry was kept busy in frequent skirmishes with the Federal pickets and in raids toward the Potomac river. Stuart took possession of Munson's Hill, near Washington, and for several weeks sent out his pickets within sight of the dome of the Capitol.

In a letter from General F. E. Paxton, of the Stonewall Brigade, we find this interesting mention of Colonel Stuart and his life at the outpost: "Yesterday I was down the road about ten miles, and, from a hill in the possession of our troops, had a good view of the dome of the Capitol, some five or six miles distant. The city was not visible, because of the woods coming between. I saw the sentinel of the enemy in the field below me, and about half a mile off and not far on this side, our own sentinels. They fire sometimes at each other. Mrs. Stuart, wife of the colonel

PICKETED CAVALRY HORSE

who has charge of our outpost, visits him occasionally—having a room with friends a few miles inside the outpost. Whilst there looking at the Capitol, I saw two of his little children playing as carelessly as if they were at home. A dangerous place, you will think, for women and children.''

Mrs. Stuart, however, was a soldier's daughter

and a soldier's wife, and she took advantage of every opportunity to be with her husband at his headquarters. During the beginning of the war, before the engagements with the Federals became frequent, she was often able to be with her husband or to board at some home near which he was stationed. Although he was a favorite with women, there was no woman who, in General Stuart's eyes, could compare with his wife, and he was never happier than when with her and his children. When the general's duties compelled him to be away from her, two days seldom passed that Mrs. Stuart did not hear from him by letter or telegram.

On September 11, Stuart's forces encountered a raiding party which was forced to retire with a loss of two killed and thirteen wounded, while Stuart lost neither man nor horse.

During the summer, Stuart had been ordered to report to General James Longstreet who commanded the advance of the Confederate army.

General Longstreet in a letter to President Davis said of Stuart: "He is a rare man, wonderfully endowed by nature with the qualities necessary for an officer of light cavalry. Calm, firm, acute, active, and enterprising, I

know no one more competent than he to estimate events at their true value.  If you add a
brigade of cavalry to this army, you will find
no better brigadier general to command it."

CHAPTER IV

# A BRIGADIER GENERAL:
## THE PENINSULAR CAMPAIGN AND THE CHICKAHOMINY RAID

### 1861-'62

ON SEPTEMBER 24, 1861, Stuart received his promotion as brigadier general. His brigade included four Virginia regiments, one North

STUART'S GAUNTLETS

From originals in Confederate Museum, Richmond, Va.

Carolina regiment, and the Jeff Davis Legion of Cavalry. These regiments were composed of high-spirited, brave young men who could ride dashingly and shoot with the skill of backwoodsmen, but who were for the most part untrained in military affairs. Stuart, however, was an untiring drillmaster and by his personal efforts he developed his brigade into a command of capable and devoted soldiers.

The young general was not yet twenty-nine years old. He was of medium height, had winning blue eyes, long silken bronze beard and mustache, and a musical voice. He usually wore gauntlets, high cavalry boots, a broad-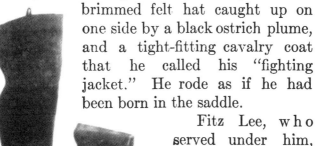brimmed felt hat caught up on one side by a black ostrich plume, and a tight-fitting cavalry coat that he called his "fighting jacket." He rode as if he had been born in the saddle.

Fitz Lee, w h o served under him, said: "His st r o n g figure, his big brown beard, his piercing, laughing blue eyes, the drooping hat and black feather, the

STUART'S CAVALRY BOOTS
From originals in Confederate Museum, Richmond, Va.

'fighting jacket' as he termed it, the tall cavalry boots, formed one of the most jubilant and striking pictures in the war."

Later on, John Esten Cooke described Stuart thus: "His 'fighting jacket' shone with dazzling buttons, and was covered with gold braid; his hat was looped up with a golden star and decorated with a black ostrich plume; his fine buff gauntlets reached to the elbow; around his waist was tied a splendid yellow sash and his spurs were of pure gold."

One who formed an opinion of him from a casual glance might have thought that he was merely a gay young fop, fond of handsome and even showy dress. But his friends and his enemies knew better. Gay and even boyish as he was when off duty, loving music and good cheer, his men knew that the instant the bugles called him he would become the calm, daring, farsighted commander, leading them to glorious deeds. No leader of the southern army was more feared by the Federal troops or more admired by the commanders of the Federal cavalry—Sheridan, Pleasanton, Buford, and others—than Stuart whom they nicknamed "the Yellow Jacket." He seemed to fly from place to place, guarding the Confederate line and charging the Federals at the most unexpected times and places; gayly dressed as that brilliant-colored insect, he was as sharp and sudden in attack.

Possessing the daring courage that is necessary for a great cavalry leader, he was so wary and farsighted that he won the respect of conservative leaders as well as the confidence of his men. And in victory or defeat he was the soul of good cheer. His mellow musical voice could be heard above the din of battle singing,

> "If you want to have a good time
> Jine the cavalry."

Once General Longstreet laughingly ordered General Stuart to leave camp, saying he made the cavalrymen's life seem so attractive that all the infantrymen wanted to desert and "jine the cavalry."

On December 20, 1861, while the army was in winter quarters at Manassas, Stuart was placed in command of about 1,500 infantry, a battery of artillery, and a small body of cavalry, for the purpose of covering the movements of General J. E. Johnston's wagon train which had been sent to procure forage for the Confederate troops. It was most important that this wagon train should be protected and the pickets had advanced to Dranesville with the cavalry following closely, when a Federal force of nearly 4,000 men, supported by two other brigades, attacked the pickets. The pickets were driven back, and the Federal artillery and infantry occupied the town, where they posted themselves in a favorable position.

Stuart, when informed that the Federals held the town, sent at once to recall the wagons and advanced as quickly as possible with the rest of his force to engage the Federals while the wagons were gaining a place of safety. The Federals had a much larger force of infantry and had a good position for their artillery; so

Stuart, after two hours of unequal combat, was forced to retire with heavy loss in killed and wounded. The wagons, however, were saved from capture; and the next morning when Stuart returned to renew the attack, he found that the Federals had retired.

In this battle of Dranesville, the Confederate loss was nearly 200 and that of the Federals was only 68. This was the first serious check that Stuart had received, but he had displayed so much prudence and skill in extricating the wagons and his small force from the sudden danger that he retained the entire confidence of his men.

Writing about this battle to his wife, Stuart said, "The enemy's force was at least four times larger than mine. Never was I in greater personal danger. Horses and men fell about me like tenpins, but thanks to God neither I nor my horse was touched."

In the meanwhile, the Federal commander, General McClellan, had been organizing his forces and by March, 1862, he had under him in front of Washington a large army splendidly armed and equipped. General Johnston had too small an army to engage the Federal hosts; and so late in March he fell back from Manassas and encamped on the south side of the Rappahannock river.

General McClellan moved his large army to Fortress Monroe, and it was then seen that he intended to advance to Richmond by way of the Peninsula,—that is, the portion of tidewater Virginia lying between the James and York rivers.

The brave Confederate general, Magruder, stationed at Yorktown, was joined by General Johnston with his whole army. They saw, however, that it would be impossible to hold that position against McClellan, and so the Confederates gave up the town and retired toward Richmond.

The cavalry under Stuart skillfully guarded the rear of the army and concealed its movements from the Federals. At Williamsburg a stubborn and brilliant battle was fought, in which Johnston's rear guard repelled the Federals. After the battle, the cavalry and the Stuart Horse Artillery protected the rear of the Confederate army as it withdrew toward Richmond and screened the infantry as it took position along the southern bank of the Chickahominy river.

McClellan placed his army on the north bank of the same river, and on May 31 and June 1, he threw a large force across the river and engaged the army of Johnston in the battle of

Seven Pines. This battle was only a partial victory for the Confederates, and as the river was bordered by wide marshes and dense woods, neither side could make use of cavalry in the conflict. General Stuart, however, was actively engaged in giving personal assistance to General Longstreet on the field.

In his report of the battle, General Longstreet said: "Brigadier J. E. B. Stuart, in the absence of any opportunity to use his cavalry, was of material service by his presence with me on the field."

In this battle of Seven Pines, General Johnston was severely wounded and gave place to General R. E. Lee, who was thus put in command of the army defending Richmond and of all of the other Confederate forces in Virginia. McClellan's magnificent army, now numbering 115,000 men, stretched from Meadow Bridge on the right to the Williamsburg Road on the left, having in front the marshes of the Chickahominy as natural barriers. By entrenching his army behind positions which he secured from time to time, he advanced until at one point he was only five miles from Richmond and could see the spires of the churches and hear the bells ringing for services.

General Lee had a much smaller army with

which to repel this large entrenched army and he withdrew to the south side of the Chickahominy. It was very important to him to learn the position and strength of the Union forces, so that he might be able to attack them at the weakest point. In order to gain this information, he resolved to send General Stuart with 1,200 cavalry to make a raid toward the White House on the Pamunkey river, which was the base of supplies for the Federal troops. General Lee wrote to General Stuart, giving definite instructions about this scouting expedition.

The letter said: "You are desired to make a scout movement, to the rear of the enemy now posted on the Chickahominy river, with a view of gaining intelligence of his operations, communications, etc., of driving in his foraging parties, and securing such grain and cattle for ourselves as you can make arrangements to have driven in.

"Another object is to destroy his wagon trains said to be daily passing from the Piping-Tree road to his camp on the Chickahominy. The utmost vigilance on your part will be necessary to prevent any surprise to yourself, and the greatest caution must be practiced in keeping well in your front and flanks reliable scouts to give you information.

"You will return as soon as the object of your expedition is accomplished, and you must bear in mind while endeavoring to execute the general purpose of your mission, not to hazard unnecessarily your command. Be content to accomplish all the good you can, without feeling it necessary to obtain all that might be desired."

Such a raid demanded great daring and skill, coupled with cool judgment, and General Lee knew that these qualities were possessed by the man to whom he entrusted this responsible and dangerous undertaking. As we are to see, Stuart carried out his instructions in an able and brilliant manner and accomplished even more than was hoped by General Lee.

In the first place, Stuart chose for the enterprise men and horses picked to stand the strain of rapid movement. Colonel Fitzhugh Lee, Colonel W. H. F. Lee, and Colonel W. T. Martin were in command of the cavalry and Colonel James Breathed commanded the one battery of artillery.

Early on the morning of June 12, Stuart and his chosen troopers started on the famous "Chickahominy Raid," or "Pamunkey Expedition" as it is sometimes called. In order to mask his real purpose, Stuart marched directly northward twenty-two miles. At sun-

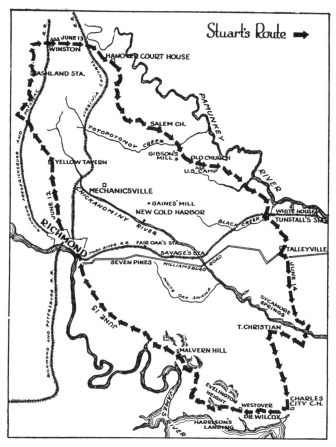

MAP OF THE CHICKAHOMINY RAID

rise the next morning, the little band of horsemen mounted and turned abruptly eastward
toward Hanover Courthouse. They found the

town in possession of a body of Federal cavalry that retired as the Confederate troopers advanced. The Confederates then passed on without serious trouble as far as Totopotomy Creek. Here, however, Stuart's advance guard was attacked by a company of Federal troopers. Finding themselves outnumbered and almost surrounded, these troopers retired to the main body of Federal troops commanded by Captain Royall, who at once drew up his forces to receive the attack. Stuart immediately ordered a squadron to charge with sabers, in columns of fours. Captain Latané, a gallant young officer who was that day commanding the squadron, met Captain Royall in a hand-to-hand encounter. Royall was seriously wounded by a thrust from Latané's saber. Latané fell dead, pierced by a bullet from Royall's pistol. The Federals fled in dismay, but soon rallied and returned to the charge, only to be again repulsed, whereupon they retired to the Union lines.

Fitz Lee learned from some of the prisoners that the Federal camp was not far away and, having obtained from Stuart permission to pursue the Union troops, he pushed on to Old Church, repelled the cavalry, and destroyed the camp.

General Stuart had now carried out the chief order given by General Lee,—that is, he had

From a painting by W. D. Washington

ridden to the rear of McClellan's army and had
discovered that the Federal right wing did not
extend toward the railway and Hanover Courthouse—but it was a vexing problem how to
bring this valuable information to his commanding general. The route the young officer
had just passed was doubtless by this time
swarming with Federals. The best way to return
to Richmond would probably be to ride quickly
around the entire Federal army and cross the
Chickahominy river to the left of McClellan,
before troops were sent to cut him off. Without
halting or consulting with any of his officers,
Stuart decided that there was less risk in
following this circuitous route, especially as he
had with him for a guide Lieutenant James
Christian whose home was on the Chickahominy
and who said that the command could safely
cross a private ford on his farm.

The Federals were under the impression that
there was a very large force of Confederates on
the raid; and so they were collecting infantry
and cavalry at Totopotomy Bridge to cut off
the return of the raiders. Stuart, however,
passed on toward Tunstall's Station, on the
York River Railroad, four miles from the
White House which was the principal supply
station of the Federal army.

He now proceeded to carry out the second part of Lee's instructions,—namely, to destroy whatever supplies he might find on the way. As he passed on, numbers of wagons fell into his hands. He sent two squadrons to Putney's Ferry and burned two large transports and numbers of wagons laden with supplies. Approaching Tunstall's Station, one of the supply depots of the Federals, he sent forward a body of picked men to cut the telegraph wires and obstruct the railroad. Before they could perform the latter task, a train approached bearing soldiers and supplies to McClellan's army. The Confederates fired on it, but instead of stopping the brave engineer stood at his post and carried the train by at full speed. He was struck by a shot and fell dying at his post, while the Confederates gave a cheer for his courage in risking his life to save his charge from their hands.

Vast quantities of Federal stores were destroyed by the Confederates whose men and horses reveled in an unusual supply of good rations and provender. It was now nearly dark and Stuart's position was exceedingly dangerous. Behind him were regiments of cavalry in hot pursuit. Not more than four or five miles distant were the entrenchments of McClellan, whence in a short time troops could be sent by

rail to cut off his progress to the James river.
Before him was the Chickahominy, now a
raging torrent from the spring rains. His chief
guides through this maze of swamps and forest
roads were Private Richard Frayser and Lieu-

From a war-time photograph

THE CHICKAHOMINY RIVER

tenant Christian whose homes were near and
who knew every part of the country through
which they were passing. Stuart had the advantage also of knowing from his scouts just
where the enemy was located.

Having formed his plans, swiftness and boldness were his watchwords. After he had destroyed the Federal supplies at Tunstall's Station and burned the railroad bridge over Black Creek, he set out about dark for Talleysville, four miles distant, where he halted for three hours and a half, in order to allow men and horses to rest and scattered troopers to come up.

Colonel John S. Mosby, later one of Stuart's chief scouts, was at that time his aide. In describing the raid, Mosby said that one who had never taken part in such an expedition could form no idea of the careless gayety of the men that night. When they had set out the day before, they did not know where they were going. Now they were aware they were riding around McClellan and the boldness of the movement fired their imaginations, quickened their pulses, and roused their courage to any deed of daring. Therefore, in the midst of danger, they sang and laughed and feasted; and at midnight when the bugle sounded "Boots and Saddles," every horseman was ready for whatever might come.

At daybreak on June 14, the Confederates reached the ford on Sycamore Springs, Christian's farm,—a ford no longer for the river swollen by the heavy rains had overflowed its banks and become a raging torrent. Colonel Lee and a few men swam their horses across the stream and back again; but it was evident that the weaker horses and the artillery could not cross at that point. The Confederates then cut down trees tall enough to span the stream, and attempted to build a rough bridge, but the trees were swept down the rapid current as soon as they touched the water.

Stuart rode up and sat on his horse, calmly stroking his long silken beard as he watched his cavalrymen's bootless efforts. Every other face betrayed keen anxiety. Learning there was the remains of an old bridge a few miles below, he moved the command thither with all speed. A deserted warehouse was near the old bridge, and a large force of men was set at work to tear down the house in order to secure material to rebuild the bridge. While the work was going on, Stuart laughed and jested with his officers.

The men worked with such swiftness that within three hours the bridge was ready for the cavalry and artillery to pass over; and at one o'clock that afternoon, the whole command had crossed. During those hours of anxiety, Fitz Lee, in command of the rear guard, had driven off several parties of Federal cavalry. After all the Confederates gained the southern shore—Fitz Lee being the last man to cross—, the bridge was burned to prevent pursuit. The men were exultant and happy at having crossed the river, but they were by no means out of danger, being thirty-five miles from Richmond and still far within the lines of McClellan. Stuart, who knew that every moment was precious to General Lee, hastened on at sunset with only one courier and his trusty guide Frayser and arrived at Richmond about sunrise on the morning of June 15. The men rested several hours and then were led by Colonel Fitz Lee safely back to their own camp where they were greeted with enthusiastic cheers by their comrades.

As soon as General Stuart reached Richmond, he sent Frayser to inform Mrs. Stuart of his safe return, while he himself rode to General Lee's headquarters with his wonderful report.

He had been sent to find out the position of the right wing of McClellan's army. He had not only located that, but he had destroyed a large amount of United States property, brought off one hundred and sixty-five prisoners and two hundred and sixty horses and mules. With only twelve hundred men, he had ridden around

the great Federal army—a distance of about
ninety mil⸱ₛ in about fifty-six hours—with the
loss of only one man, the lamented young
Latané. By that dashing ride, Stuart gained
for himself world-wide fame and an honorable
place among the great cavalry leaders of all
time. The Chickahominy Raid was one of the
most brilliant cavalry achievements in history,
and it inspired the Confederates with fresh
courage and excited Federal dread of the bold
cavalrymen who attempted and accomplished
seemingly impossible things.

The information gained was invaluable for it
made it possible for General Lee to send Jackson
against the right flank of McClellan and to
defeat the Federals at Cold Harbor.

In the Seven Days' Battle around Richmond,
which began on June 26, Stuart at first guarded
the left of Jackson's march. In the battle of
Gaines's Mill, he found a suitable position for
the artillery. He sent forward two guns under
Pelham, a gallant young gunner from Alabama,
who kept up an unequal combat for hours
with two Federal batteries. When the Federal
lines had been forced at Gaines's Mill and
Cold Harbor, Stuart advanced three miles to
the left; but finding no trace of the Federals, he
returned that night to Cold Harbor. On June

28, he proceeded toward the White House on the Pamunkey river, which the Federals had abandoned and burned. They had also set fire to many valuable stores and munitions of war. The illustration on this page is from a war-time photograph, showing the railroad bridge across the Pamunkey river which was destroyed

From a war-time photograph

RUINS OF RAILROAD BRIDGE ACROSS PAMUNKEY RIVER

in order to render the road useless to the Confederates. When McClellan changed his base from the White House to James river, he had two trains loaded with food and ammunition run at full speed off the embankment in the left foreground into the river, in order to keep these stores from falling into the hands of the southern troops.

An interesting account of this campaign is given by Heros Von Borcke. Von Borcke was a noble young Prussian officer who gave his services as a volunteer to the Confederacy, just as LaFayette had given his services to the Colonies in the War of the Revolution; Von Borcke served the South so loyally that near the close of the war the Confederate Congress drew up a resolution of thanks for his services in just the same form that the Colonies had thanked LaFayette.

Von Borcke was one of Stuart's aides and he distinguished himself by his gallantry during the Chickahominy raid. He tells us that when the Confederates arrived at the White House they found burning pyramids built of barrels of eggs, bacon and hams, and barrels of sugar. There were also boxes of oranges and lemons and other luxuries. Many of these luxuries were rescued by the Confederates, and when Von Borcke reached the plantation, shortly after it had been taken, he found General Stuart seated under a tree drinking a big glass of iced lemonade, an unusual treat for a Confederate soldier. All of Stuart's troops had such a feast as was seldom enjoyed during the war, and large quantities of supplies and equipments were forwarded to the Confederate quartermaster at Richmond.

The Federal gunboat, *Marblehead*, was still in sight on the river. The soldiers at that period had an almost superstitious fear of the bombs thrown by the big guns of the gunboats, which made an awful whizzing noise and burst into many fragments. Stuart decided that he would teach his troopers a lesson and show them how little harm the dreaded shells did at short range. He selected seventy-five men whom he armed with carbines and placed under command of Colonel W. H. F. Lee who led them down to the landing. They fired at the boat and skirmishers were sent ashore from the boat to meet them. A brisk skirmish followed, during which Stuart brought up one gun of Pelham's battery. This threw shells upon the decks of the *Marblehead*, while the screeching bombs of the big guns of the boat went over the heads of Pelham's battery, far away into the depths of the swamps. The skirmishers hurried back to the *Marblehead*, and it steamed away down the river, pursued as far as possible by shells from Pelham's plucky little howitzer.

Stuart sent General Lee the important news that McClellan was seeking a base upon the

James river, and then stayed the remainder of the day at the White House, where he found enough undestroyed provisions to satisfy the hunger of the men and horses of his command.

After severe engagements with the Confederates at Savage Station and Frayser's Farm, the Union forces were forced to retreat, closely followed by Jackson and Stuart. On the evening of July 1, was fought the bloody battle of Malvern Hill, after which McClellan retreated by night down the James to Harrison's Landing where he was protected by the gunboats.

Early on the morning of July 2, Stuart started in pursuit and found the Federals in position at Westover. The next day he took possession of Evelington Heights, a tableland overlooking McClellan's encampment and protecting his line of retreat. Here Stuart expected to be supported by Longstreet and Jackson, and he opened fire with Pelham's howitzer.

The Federal infantry and artillery at once moved forward to storm the heights. Jackson and Longstreet were delayed by terrific storms, and Stuart unsupported held his position until two o'clock in the afternoon when his ammunition gave out. He then retired and joined the main body of the infantry, which did not arrive until after the Federals had taken possession of Evelington Heights and were fortifying it strongly.

The two armies now had a breathing spell of about one month. McClellan's defeated hosts remained in their protected position at Harrison's Landing until the middle of August, when they were recalled to join General Pope at Manassas. General Lee's army was withdrawn nearer to Richmond which was saved from immediate danger.

## CHAPTER V

# A MAJOR GENERAL:
# CAMP LIFE AND THE SECOND BATTLE
# OF MANASSAS

## 1862

As a reward for his faithful and efficient services in the Peninsular Campaign, Stuart received his commission as major general of cavalry on July 25, 1862. His forces were now organized into two brigades, with Brigadier-General Wade Hampton in command of the first and Brigadier-General Fitzhugh Lee in command of the second. During the month following the defeat of McClellan, these two brigades were placed by turns on picket duty on the Charles City road to guard Richmond and in the camp of instruction at Hanover Courthouse.

While conducting this camp of instruction where he drilled his men in the cavalry tactics that were later to win them such honor, Stuart and his staff were often pleasantly entertained at neighboring plantations. Mrs. Stuart with her two little children, Flora, five years of age, and "Jimmy," aged two, was able to be near the general once more. The time passed pleasantly, enlivened by cavalry drills, visits from the young officers to the ladies of the vicinity, serenades and dances, and visits from the ladies to the general's headquarters.

One Sunday evening as the general and most of his staff were visiting at Dundee, the plantation near which their camp was situated, a stable in the yard caught fire and the visitors proved themselves as good firemen as they were soldiers. The young Prussian officer, Von Borcke, an unusually large and heavily-built man, was so energetic in his efforts, that after the fire was out, the general, who was always fond of a joke, insisted that he had seen the young officer rush from the burning building with a mule under one arm and two little pigs under the other.

Stuart was soon called away from this pleasant life to make an inspection of all the Confederate cavalry forces. It was evident that General Lee's army would soon be engaged against a new Federal commander, General Pope, who was concentrating a large army on the Rapidan river. General Jackson, who had been sent to hold General Pope in check, had his headquarters at Gordonsville.

Major Von Borcke tells us that the cars carrying the Confederate troops to Gordonsville were so crowded that General Stuart rode on the tender of the engine, rather than take a seat away from one of the soldiers. It was a hot night in July and there was a dense smoke from the engine, but it was so dark that it was not until they reached Gordonsville that the general discovered that both Von Borcke and himself were so black with soot that their best friends would not have recognized them. Indeed, it took a great deal of soap and water to make them presentable once more.

Stuart reached Jackson's headquarters on August 10, the day after the Federal advance guard had been defeated in the battle of Cedar Run. At Jackson's request, Stuart took command of a reconnaissance to find out the position and strength of the enemy. Upon hearing his report, Jackson decided to remain for the present on the defensive.

In the meantime, General Lee, who was watching General McClellan's army still encamped at Harrison's Landing, received information that the latter had been ordered to withdraw his forces and join General Pope at Manassas.

Leaving a small force in front of Richmond, Lee hastened to join Jackson so that they could engage Pope before his already large army was reenforced by McClellan. The cavalry was kept very busy at this time as it was necessary to defend the Central Road, now the Chesapeake and Ohio, from Federal raids.

On the night of August 17, Stuart himself barely escaped capture. He wrote an interesting account of this adventure to his wife, and Mrs. Stuart has kindly allowed us to use the letter in this book. Here it is:

Rapidan Valley, August 19, 1862.

My Dear Wife—I had a very narrow escape yesterday morning. I had made arrangement for Lee's Brigade to move across from Davenport's bridge to Raccoon ford where I was to meet it, but Lee went by Louisa Court House. His dispatch informing me of the fact did not reach me, consequently I went down the Plank road to the place of rendezvous.

Hearing nothing of him, I stopped for the night and sent Major Fitzhugh with a guide across to meet General Lee. At sunrise yesterday a large body of cavalry from the very direction from which Lee was expected, approached crossing the Plank road just below me and going directly towards Raccoon ford. Of course I thought it was Lee—as no Yankees had been seen about for a month, *but* as a measure of prudence I sent down two men to ascertain. They had not gone 100 yards before they were fired on and pursued rapidly by a squadron.

I was in the yard bareheaded, my hat being in the porch. I just had time to mount my horse and clear the

being in the porch. I just had
time to mount my horse & clear
the back-fence, having no time
to get my hat or anything else.
I lost my haversack, blanket,
talma. cloak, & _hat_, with
that _palmetto_ _star_ —
too bad wasn't it?
   I am all right again how-
-ever, & am greeted, on all
sides with congratulations
and "where's your _hat_!"
I intend to make the
yankees pay for that hat.
   Poor FitzHugh was not
so fortunate, he was cap-
-tured four miles off us
& der similar circumstances,
with his fine grey. He will

back fence, having no time to get my hat or anything else. I lost my haversack, blanket, talma, cloak, and *hat*, with that *palmetto star*—too bad, wasn't it? I am all right again, however, and I am greeted, on all sides with congratulations and *"where's your hat!"* I intend to make the Yankees pay for that hat.

Poor Fitzhugh was not so fortunate. He was captured four miles off under similar circumstances, with his fine grey. He will be exchanged in ten days, however. Von Borcke and Dabney were with me (five altogether) and their escape was equally miraculous. Dundee is the best place for you at present. We will have hot work I think to-morrow. My cavalry has an important part to play.

Love to all, my two sweethearts included.

God bless you.

J. E. B. STUART.

A few days later, as you will hear, General Stuart collected payment for his lost hat from General Pope himself. But before this took place, the Confederate cavalry was engaged in several skirmishes with the Federals. There was a severe encounter at Brandy Station on August 20 when sixty-five prisoners were captured. The regiments which had fought under Ashby, a gallant young officer who had been killed in the Valley, were now added to Stuart's division as Robertson's Brigade. At Brandy Station, these troopers fought under

Stuart for the first time and he was much pleased at their dash and bravery.

While Lee, who had now joined Jackson, was waiting a favorable opportunity to attack the Federals, Stuart begged permission to pass to the rear of Pope's army and cut his line of communication at Catlett's Station where there was a large depot of supplies. General Lee gave his consent, and on the morning of August 22, General Stuart crossed the Rappahannock at Waterloo Bridge, to make a second raid to the rear of the Federal army.

By nightfall the Confederates reached Auburn near Catlett's Station, where they captured the Federal pickets. Just as they reached the station, however, a violent storm arose; and amid the wind and the rain and the darkness, it seemed impossible to find their way. Fortunately, they captured a negro who knew Stuart and who offered to show them the way to Pope's headquarters. They accepted his guidance and soon the Confederate cavalry surprised the unsuspecting enemy, attacked the camp, and captured a number of officers belonging to Pope's staff, as well as his horses, baggage, a large sum of money, and his dispatch book which contained copies of the letters he had written to the government, telling the location and

Catlett Station where Stuart made a raid and captured Popes baggage; AₜₐₐR Ward

**CATLETT'S STATION**

From a war-time sketch by Harper's Artist

[75]

plans of his army. But for the fact that General Pope was out on a tour of inspection, he himself would have been captured.

In the meantime, two of Stuart's regiments had gained another part of the camp, and an attempt was made to destroy the railroad bridge over Cedar Run. But on account of the heavy rain it was impossible to fire it, and, in the dense darkness, it was equally hard to cut asunder the heavy timbers with the few axes which they found. Therefore, with more than three hundred prisoners and valuable spoils, Stuart retired before daybreak and regained in safety the Confederate lines.

Major Von Borcke gives an interesting incident of their return march. As the troops— wet, cold, and hungry—passed through Warrenton, coffee was served them by a number of young girls. One of the girls recognized among the prisoners General Pope's quartermaster. He had boasted several days before, when at her father's house, that he would enter Richmond within a month. She had promptly bet him a bottle of wine that he would not be able to do it, but as he was now a prisoner he would be obliged to enter the city even earlier than he had hoped. She, therefore, asked General Stuart's permission to offer the quartermaster a bottle of wine from his own captured supplies. The general readily granted her request, and the Yankee prisoner entered good-naturedly into the jest, saying that he would always be willing to drink the health of so charming a person.

In retaliation for the loss of his hat and cloak, General Stuart sent General Pope's uniform to Richmond where for some days it hung in one of the shop windows, to the delight of the populace who especially disliked Pope on account of his bombast and cruelty. He had boasted that he had come from the West where his soldiers always saw the backs of their enemies, and he had authorized his soldiers to take whatever they wished from the citizens of Virginia, whom he held responsible for damage done by raiding parties of the Confederate army.

Two weeks later, General Stuart wrote his wife that Parson Landstreet, a member of his staff who had been captured by the Federals, brought him a message from General Pope. Pope said that he would send back Stuart's hat if Stuart would return his coat.

"But," wrote Stuart, "I have got to see my hat first."

It was against General Pope that the second Battle of Manassas was fought, August 28, 29, and 30, 1862. General Stuart and his cavalry in the maneuvers preceding the battle, screened the flank march of Jackson's troops to Grovetown, by which movement they placed themselves between the Federal rear and Washington. It took two days for Jackson's "foot cavalry" to make this march, and so perfectly did Stuart do his work that as late as August 28, Pope did not know to what place Jackson had marched from Manassas.

In the three days' battle that followed, the cavalry was ever on the flank of the army, observing the Federals and guarding against attacks. On the morning of August 29, after a sharp skirmish, Stuart met Lee and Longstreet and opened the way for them to advance to the support of Jackson whose forces on the right wing were engaged in unequal and critical combat. Later on the same day, Stuart saw that the Federals were massing in front of Jackson, and with a small detachment of cavalry aided by Pelham and his guns, he gallantly held large forces in check and protected Jackson's captured wagon train of supplies. On the afternoon of August 30, the cavalry did most effectual service, following the retreating Federals and protecting the exposed Confederate flank against heavy cavalry attacks. During the engagements, the Confederate infantry could not have held its position but for the assistance of the cavalry under the able direction of Stuart.

In these battles, Pope had forces largely superior in number and equipment to Lee's, but Pope's losses in killed and wounded were much the heavier. Finally he was forced to retreat toward Washington, leaving in the hands of the Confederates many prisoners as well as captured artillery, arms, and a large amount of stores. The North seemed panic-stricken, as Washington was now directly exposed to the attacks of the Confederates.

CHAPTER VI

# THE MARYLAND CAMPAIGN

## 1862

GENERAL LEE knew, however, that he did not have men enough to take by assault the strong fortifications around Washington, and he, therefore, planned to cross over into Maryland before the Federal army had recovered from its defeat, when its commanders were least expect-him. In order that he might completely mislead them and make it appear that he was beginning a general attack on Washington, he ordered Stuart and his troops to advance toward that city.

In their advance, they engaged in several sharp skirmishes with the Federals, finally driving them from Fairfax Courthouse, where, amid the cheers of the inhabitants, Major Von Borcke planted the beloved Confederate flag on a little common in the center of the village.

The people of this section had been under Federal control for several months and their joy at seeing Stuart and his troops was unbounded. They flocked to the roadside to get a glimpse of the great cavalry leader.

One lady, who had lost two sons in battle, came forward as the troops passed her home and asked permission to kiss the general's battle flag. She held by the hand her only surviving son, a lad of fifteen years, and declared herself ready if it were needed to give his life too for her country.

On September 5, General Stuart and his forces crossed the Potomac. Four days later, General Lee moved his entire army across the river, encamped at Frederick, Maryland, and sent General Jackson to capture the strongly fortified Federal arsenal at Harper's Ferry.

Major Von Borcke, from whose *Memoirs of the Confederate War for Independence* we shall borrow several interesting incidents of this Maryland campaign, tells us that the crossing of the cavalry at White's Ford was one of the most picturesque scenes of the war. The river is very wide at this point, and its steep banks, rising to the height of sixty feet, are overshadowed by large trees that trail from their branches a perfect network of graceful and luxuriant vines. A sandy island about midstream broke the passage of the horsemen and artillery, and as a column of a thousand troops passed

MAJOR HEROS VON BORCKE

over, the rays of the setting sun made the
water look like burnished gold. The hearts of
the soldiers crossing the river thrilled at the
sound of the familiar and inspiring strains of
"Maryland, my Maryland," which greeted them
from the northern bank.

The enthusiasm of the Maryland people at
Poolesville, where Stuart first stopped, was
boundless. Two young merchants of the village
suddenly resolved to enlist in the cavalry and
they put up all their goods at auction. The
soldiers with the eagerness and carelessness of
children cleared out both establishments in
less than an hour. Many other recruits were
made in this village, all the young men seeming
to feel the inspiration of General Stuart's
favorite song,

> "If you want to have a good time
> Jine the cavalry."

At Urbana, a pretty little village on the road
to Frederick, where General Stuart with one
division of his forces camped for several days,
a most exciting ball was held on the evening
of September 8. There were many charming
families living in the neighborhood, and General
Stuart and his staff decided to give a dance at an
old, unused academy located on a hill just
outside of the town. The young ladies of the

neighborhood willingly lent their help, and evening found the halls of the academy lighted by tallow candles and draped with garlands of roses and with battle flags borrowed from the regiments of the brigades. Music was furnished by the band of a Mississippi regiment. The ball, which had opened to the rousing strains of "Dixie," was at its height, when a young orderly rushed in and to the accompaniment of distant shots reported that the Federals had driven in the pickets and were attacking the camp.

Wild confusion prevailed. The officers got rapidly to horse and anxious mammas collected their daughters. Upon reaching the scene of action, General Stuart found that the danger had been overestimated and the Federals were already beginning to retreat. In a short while, they had been driven back; and by one o'clock, the staff officers had brought the young ladies back to the academy and the ball had a second and more auspicious opening. Dancing continued until dawn, when some soldiers wounded in the skirmish were brought in, and the ball room was soon converted into a hospital and the fair dancers into willing if inexperienced nurses.

The next day, General Fitz Lee's brigade was engaged in a skirmish, and the day following

Colonel Munford, who was commanding Robertson's Brigade, had a sharp encounter with Federals at Sugar Loaf Mountain. By Sept. 11, the Federal cavalry was attacking in such force that General Stuart saw that it was necessary to order a retreat toward Frederick. General Fitz Lee commanded the advance; Colonel Munford protected the rear, which as it approached Urbana had a sharp skirmish with the closely-following Federal cavalry. General Stuart and his staff, however, did not tear themselves away from their friends in this hospitable little village until the Union troops were within half a mile of the place and several shells had exploded in the street. From Urbana the cavalry went to Frederick. Many years after the war was over, Mrs. Stuart received a letter from a New York physician, who at the time of the Maryland campaign had just won his title and a position on the staff of one of the Union hospitals in Frederick.

He told about meeting General Stuart and then said, "I wish to bear testimony to the fact that not only myself, but all the friends of the Union cause in Frederick, so far as I could learn, were kindly treated by both officers and private soldiers. I do not remember of a single instance where private property was molested, nor was any taunt, indignity, or insult offered to any person. Whittier's 'Barbara Frietchie,' which has attracted so much attention,—even that is fiction."

At Frederick, Stuart found that General Lee had already retreated across South Mountain and taken a position at Sharpsburg on Antietam Creek, while Jackson was investing Harper's Ferry. Look at the map on page 95 and you will see that southwest of Frederick rises a small spur of the Blue Ridge, called Catoctin Mountain on the other side of which is a broad, fertile valley extending for about six miles to the base of South Mountain. On the opposite side of South Mountain is Sharpsburg, and across the same mountain to the south is Harper's Ferry which Jackson had been ordered to capture before he marched north to join Lee and Longstreet at Sharpsburg.

Now you can see that until Harper's Ferry fell it was necessary that the cavalry should hinder the advance of the Federal army under McClellan until Jackson could join Lee. This was especially difficult, because an order from General Lee to General D. H. Hill, explaining fully the commanding general's plans and the location of all his forces, had fallen into the hands of General McClellan and he was ad-

vancing a tremendous army toward Sharpsburg as rapidly as possible.

As General McClellan's forces advanced,
General Stuart retreated slowly, contesting
every inch of ground. His retreat across
Catoctin Mountain was through Braddock's
Gap, along the same road where eighty-seven
years before, the young patriot, George Washington, had accompanied General Braddock
on the fatal expedition against Fort Duquesne.
In this gap, Stuart had a sharp encounter with
the Federals. He and Major Von Borcke who
was commanding a gun on the height above the
pass, narrowly escaped being captured by
Federal skirmishers who, under cover of the
dense forest, had worked their way around
behind the gun.

Another sharp encounter took place on
Kittochtan creek at Middletown, half way
across the valley, where General Stuart delayed
the retreat of his forces so long that they barely
escaped capture and reached the foot of South
Mountain just in time to protect the two
principal passes,—Turner's Gap which led
directly through Boonsboro to Sharpsburg, and
Crampton's Gap which led through Pleasant
Valley to Harper's Ferry.

It was necessary to hold these gaps and delay

the enemy until Jackson could capture Harper's Ferry and unite his division with the remainder of the army under General Lee. A heavy part of this work fell on the cavalry and the artillery. The retreat of Generals Longstreet and Hill, who had held Turner's Gap until the afternoon of Sept. 14, was covered by General Fitz Lee's brigade which held the Federals in check at every possible point. There was a sharp encounter at Boonsboro, where, in charging, General W. H. F. Lee was ridden down by his own men and narrowly escaped capture.

At Crampton's Gap, which led through Pleasant Valley to Harper's Ferry, Colonel Munford gallantly checked the Federal advance until the evening of Sept. 14, when the troops sent to assist him broke and retreated in bad order through Pleasant Valley. General Stuart had been at Harper's Ferry conferring with General McLaws; when they heard of the engagement at Crampton's Gap, both generals rode quickly forward to meet the routed and panic-stricken troops which they rallied and formed into line of battle. The position that they held the next morning was so strong that the advancing Federals hesitated to attack; just as the first shots were being exchanged, the news of the surrender of Harper's Ferry caused the attacking party to begin a hasty retreat along the road that they had come.

General Stuart at once reported to General Jackson, who requested him to convey the news to General Lee at Sharpsburg. But even now Lee was in great peril. He had with him, on the evening of Sept. 14 when the gaps were stormed, only about 20,000 men; and McClellan's army of more than 87,000 was advancing rapidly to attack him. Lee had now either to recross the Potomac or to fight a battle north of that river.

He decided to make a stand, and on the night of Sept. 14, drew his army across Antietam creek and took a strong position on a range of hills east of the Hagerstown turnpike. Here he waited for Jackson who, by a forced march, came up in time to take position on the left wing on the morning of September 16. Even when reenforced by Jackson, Lee had a much smaller force than McClellan.

On the evening of Sept. 16, McClellan attacked Jackson's wing at the left of Lee's army, but was repulsed. At early dawn the next day, the attack was renewed and the combat raged all day. When night ended the bloody contest, the Confederates not only held their position, but had advanced their lines on a part of the field. During the entire battle, Stuart with his horse artillery and a small cavalry escort had guarded the open hilly space between Jackson's left and the Potomac river.

General Jackson in his report of this battle said: "This officer (General Stuart) rendered valuable service throughout the day. His bold use of artillery secured for us an important position which, had the enemy possessed, might have commanded our left."

The next day, Lee waited for McClellan to attack, but no movement came from the hostile camp. Finding out through Stuart's scouts that large bodies of fresh troops were being sent to McClellan, Lee withdrew that night to the south side of the Potomac, and by eleven o'clock the next morning, he was again ready to give battle should the Federals pursue. He had brought off nearly everything of value, leaving behind only several disabled cannon and some of his wounded.

While Fitz Lee's and Munford's troops were left to protect the retreat of the army, Stuart with a small force had gone up the Potomac to Williamsport, hoping to divert the attention of the Federals from the main body of the army and so enable it to cross the river unhindered. This movement was successful, for large Federal forces were sent against him, yet he maintained his position without reenforcements until the night of September 20, when he recrossed the Potomac in safety.

During this short campaign, several interesting incidents occurred. On one occasion, when the Federals were advancing toward Williamsport, a young lady of the town obtained permission to fire a cannon that was about to be discharged. After this, the soldiers always called that cannon "the girl of Williamsport."

Another time, Major Von Borcke tells us that he accompanied the general on one of his favorite, yet dangerous reconnoitering expeditions outside of the Confederate lines. They tried to keep themselves concealed by the dense undergrowth, but they must have been observed by the pickets, for in a short while Major Von Borcke heard the "little clicking sound that a saber scabbard often makes in knocking against a tree," and, looking quickly around, he saw a long line of Federal cavalry. A few whispered words to the general were enough; he and his aide put spurs to their horses and once more justified their reputations as expert horsemen, for they were soon hidden by the friendly trees, while their pursuers were firing wildly in vain search for the escaped prey.

There were no serious engagements for the

next few weeks and General Lee's army enjoyed a well deserved rest. The cavalry watched the movements of the Federals and protected the camps from alarms. The cavalry headquarters were delightfully situated near Charlestown on the plantation of Mr. A. S. Dandridge. Because of its beautiful grove of huge oak trees, this plantation was called The Bower. A comfortable old brick mansion crowned the summit of a sloping hill on the sides of which the tents of the camp were located under oak trees. At the foot of the hill wound the sparkling little Opequan river. Here provisions were plentiful once more, and the soldiers enjoyed fishing and hunting the small game,—squirrels, rabbits, and partridges,—that abounded in the nearby woods.

General Stuart had attached to his staff a remarkable young banjo player, Bob Sweeny, who, with the assistance of two fiddlers and Stuart's mulatto servant Bob who rattled the bones unusually well, furnished music around the camp fire for the men and served also on serenades and at dances given to the officers at the hospitable Dandridge mansion.

General Stuart was very fond of dancing, and when some of the young officers of his staff were occasionally too tired and sleepy to want to join in the fun, he would have them awakened and ordered to attend. Yet they complained that when they did come the general would always get the prettiest girl for his own partner.

But in spite of his joyous, fun-loving disposition, General Stuart was always ready when duty called him. In his book, *Christ in the Camp*, the Rev. J. William Jones says, "Stuart was an humble and earnest Christian who took Christ as his personal Saviour, lived a stainless life, and died a triumphant death."

He tells us that General Stuart often came to get his advice in planning services for the soldiers. Once when General Stuart wanted Dr. Jones to recommend a chaplain for the cavalry outposts, the general said, "I do not want a man who is not able to endure hardness as a good soldier. The man who can not endure the hardships and privations of our rough riding and hard service and be in place when needed would be of no earthly use to us and is not wanted at my headquarters."

## CHAPTER VII

# THE CHAMBERSBURG RAID

## 1862

On October 8, after a final dance and serenade to the ladies at The Bower, Stuart started out to join the forces that he had ordered to assemble at Darkesville, from which point he was to lead them on the famous "Chambersburg Raid."

The purpose of this raid, which had been ordered by General Lee, was to march into Pennsylvania and Maryland and to secure information concerning the location of McClellan's army, and also to secure provisions and horses for the Confederate forces.

Not a soldier of the 1,800 picked cavalrymen from the brigades of Hampton, Fitz Lee, and Robertson or the gunners under Pelham, knew whither they were going or for what purpose. Most of them, however, had been with Stuart on his Chickahominy Raid, and all were content to follow wherever he led.

In his address to his men at the beginning of

the expedition, Stuart said that the enterprise on
which they were about to start demanded cool-

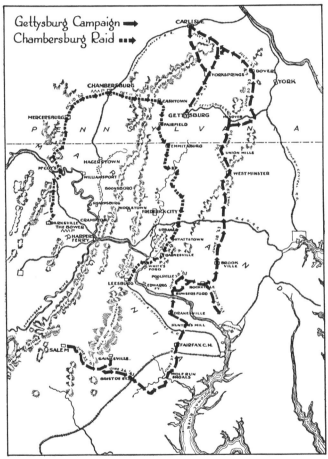

MAP SHOWING THE ROUTES OF STUART'S CAVALRY IN GETTYSBURG
CAMPAIGN AND CHAMBERSBURG RAID

ness, decision, and bravery, implicit obedience and the strictest order and sobriety in the camp and on the bivouac, but that with the hearty coöperation of his officers and men he had no doubt of a success which would reflect credit on them in the highest degree.

The men in fine spirits reached the Potomac after dark. The next morning, they crossed the river at McCoy's Ford, west of McClellan's army which was posted north of the Potomac between Shepherdstown and Harper's Ferry. A heavy fog hung over the river valley and hid them from the Federal infantry which had just passed by.

A signal station on Fairview Heights was taken by twenty men detailed for the purpose and then the column passed on toward Mercersburg. By this time, the Federal pickets were aware of the raid; but as there was no large force of cavalry at hand, its progress was unchecked. On and on the little band of horsemen rode until at nightfall they reached Chambersburg in Pennsylvania. As Maryland was regarded as a southern State, nothing belonging to its citizens had been disturbed; but when Pennsylvania was reached, soldiers detached from the commands for that purpose, seized all suitable horses, giving each owner a receipt, so that he could call upon the United States government for payment,—thus forcing the administration at Washington cither to help equip the Confederate army or to make its own citizens suffer. Stuart, with his usual gallantry, gave orders that the men should not take the horses of ladies whom they might meet along the highway.

As the command approached Chambersburg on the night of October 10, a cold drizzling rain set in. Two pieces of artillery were posted so as to command the town, and Lieutenant Thomas Lee with nine men was sent into the town to demand its surrender. No resistance was made and the troops were at once marched into the town and drawn up on the public square. Strict discipline was observed and only Federal property was used or destroyed.

During the night, the rain came down in torrents on the weary, hungry Confederates. Surrounded by increasing dangers, Stuart with his staff neither rested nor slept. By that time, cavalry and infantry were on his track and every ford of the Potomac was strongly guarded. At any time, the heavy rains might cause the river to rise and cut off retreat. His only hope was to move boldly and swiftly to a crossing before the water could descend from the mountains and flood the streams. Stuart decided,

however, not to return the way he had come, as
large forces of Federal cavalry, like hornets,
would be awaiting him there. He resolved to
make another ride around McClellan's army
and to cross at White's Ford some distance to

STUART'S SWORD
From Original in Confederate Museum,
Richmond, Va.

the east, so close to the Federals that
they would not be looking for him
there. The very boldness of the
plan was its best guarantee of success and the next morning the general started his men on their dangerous march around the enemy

Colonel A. K. McClure of the
Philadelphia *Times*, then a colonel
in the Federal army and a resident
of Chambersburg, gives the following account of Stuart as he was
preparing to leave Chambersburg:
"General Stuart sat on his horse in
the center of the town, surrounded
by his staff, and his command was
coming in from the country in large
squads, leading their old horses and
riding the new ones which they had
found in the stables hereabout. General Stuart
is of medium stature, has a keen eye, and wore
immense sandy whiskers and mustache. His de-
meanor to our people is that of a humane

soldier. In several instances his soldiers began to take property from stores, but they were arrested by Stuart's provost guard.'

This evidence as to the discipline of Stuart's men comes from a Federal officer, and shows fully the control that the general exercised over his command.

The wounded in the Chambersburg hospital were paroled, the telegraph wires were cut, and the ordnance storehouse was blown up by brave Captain M. C. Butler of South Carolina, who now commanded the rear guard. He notified the people near the ordnance storehouse that he

STUART'S PISTOL
From Original in Confederate
Museum, Richmond, Va.

was about to set fire to it and then applied a slow fuse. There was a loud explosion and then the flames burst forth. Satisfied that his work was

STUART'S CARBINE
From Original in Confederate Museum, Richmond, Va.

well done, Colonel Butler and his escort set out at a trot to rejoin the command.

On the outskirts of the town, there came galloping up from the rear a young soldier in gray, riding a big black horse. He wore no hat and one boot was gone. He was covered with mud and was soaking wet, for he had come into town with the rear guard about midnight in the darkness and pouring rain. The command had halted for a few hours in a quiet side street and had set out at break of day as the advance guard.

The young soldier's foot had been hurt, so he dismounted and pulled off his boot, in order to ease the pain. He then concluded to lie down for a while and perhaps take a nap, for he was very tired. Tying the bridle rein to his foot, he lay down in the pouring rain and went to sleep. When he awoke, it was broad daylight and he was all alone. In the darkness of the cloudy dawn, his comrades had left him sleeping. His big black horse was still tied to his foot, but his hat, his haversack, and one of his boots were gone. Rising quickly, he mounted his horse and was trying to decide which way to go when an old lady raised a window near by and called out, "Sonny, your folks have gone that way." With a lighter heart he thanked her, and set off at a gallop along the Gettysburg road to which she had pointed. As he sped along, the

people called out, "Go it, Johnny! Goodby,
Johnny! Hurry, Johnny!" All seemed to be
in a good humor over the speedy departure of
the Confederates. It was not many minutes
before he reached the rear of Butler's detachment, and was safe.

Soon after the break of day, the advance
column under General Fitz Lee started towards
Gettysburg, but at Cashtown the column turned
south toward Emmitsburg in Maryland. When
Stuart arrived at the latter place, the people
received him with great joy and the young
ladies of the town threw flowers at the troops.
But in spite of this hearty welcome, the Confederates could not linger, for they learned that a
party of Federals in search of them, had passed
only a short time before.

Going in a steady trot without halting, Stuart
passed on to the woods of Frederick, and
captured a courier with a dispatch from the
commander of the party sent out to find him.
From this dispatch, he learned the arrangements
which had been made to capture him, and
learned also that the Federals did not know just
where he was.

In the meantime, the Federal cavalry was
hurrying to overtake him, but Stuart, aware of
his extreme danger, aimed straight for the

Potomac. His tired men and horses marched all night, and by dawn on October 13, they reached Hyattstown where a few wagons were captured. On the march, Stuart had learned that a division of five thousand men was guarding the fords in front of him. Knowing that delay would increase his peril, he hastened on in the direction of Poolesville where a body of Federal cavalry was located.

When within two miles of that town, guided by Captain White who was familiar with the region, he turned abruptly through some woods which concealed his movements and gained the road leading to the river about two miles distant. Hardly had the Confederates entered this road when the advance squadron met the head of the Federal column coming from Poolesville. General Stuart, who was at the head of the squadron, ordered a charge and drove the Federals back upon the main body half a mile away. Thinking that Stuart was aiming to cross the strongly-guarded ford at the mouth of the Monocacy river, the Federals, instead of seizing this favorable opportunity to make an advance and crush the Confederate cavalry, waited for their infantry to come up.

In the meanwhile, General Fitz Lee's sharpshooters leaped from their horses and went

forward while one of Pelham's guns was brought
up. Under cover of its fire and screened from
view by the ridge upon which it was placed,
General Lee's command moved on by a farm
road to White's Ford.

When General Lee reached White's Ford, he
found a force of two hundred Federal infantry
so strongly posted on the steep bank overlooking the ford that a crossing seemed impossible. Infantry in front and cavalry in the
rear! Would it be possible to escape from the
snare by which they were surrounded? Nothing
but boldness and swiftness could save them.
General Lee sent a courier to General Stuart
who was on the Poolesville road with Pelham's
guns and the skirmishers keeping back Federal
troopers until the rear guard should come up.

"I do not believe that the ford can be crossed,"
said General Lee.

Stuart replied, "I am occupied in the rear, but
the ford must be crossed at all hazards."

General Lee, therefore, prepared to attack the
Federal infantry in its strong position on the
bluff. One part of his force was to assail it in
front and on the left flank, while a strong body
of cavalry endeavored to cross and hold the
ford. Lee hoped to be able to get one gun placed
on the opposite bank and then to fire on the
Federal rear.

While making his hurried preparations, it occurred to General Lee to try a game of "bluff." Under flag of truce, he sent a note to the Federal commander, saying that General Stuart's whole command was in his front and needless bloodshed would be avoided if he would surrender. Fifteen minutes was allowed him to consider this demand.

After fifteen minutes' anxious waiting and no reply, General Fitz Lee opened with his artillery and was preparing to advance his horsemen, when it was seen that the Federals, with flags flying and band playing, were retreating in perfect order down the river.

A wild cheer broke from the Confederates as some of their men rushed across the ford to place a piece of artillery at the top of the steep bank on the Virginia side of the Potomac. Another gun was hurried forward and placed so as to sweep the tow-path and the approaches to the ford, while the long line of cavalrymen and captured horses passed rapidly across to safety. Once more Stuart had slipped through the hands of his enemy.

In the meanwhile, Pelham held the Federals in check until all but the rear guard under Colonel Butler had passed. Then he began to withdraw, making his last stand on the Maryland side of the ford, where he fired up and down the river at the Federal cavalry now advancing in both directions.  But the rear guard was still far behind.  Major McClellan tells us that General Stuart had sent back four couriers to hurry up Colonel Butler; still he did not come.  In this dilemma, Captain  Blackford volunteered to find him.

Stuart paused a moment and then extending his hand said, "All right! and if we do not meet again, good-by, old fellow."

Blackford galloped off and found Butler with his own regiment and the North Carolina detachment and one gun, engaged in delaying the advance of the enemy in the Poolesville road.  Blackford rode rapidly toward him and shouted, "General Stuart says, 'Withdraw at a gallop, or you will be cut off.' "

"But," replied Butler, with great coolness, "I don't think I can bring off that gun.  The horses can't move it."

"Leave the gun and save your men!" replied Blackford.

"Well, we'll see what can be done," said Butler, and then he ordered the drivers to make one more effort.  That time they were successful.  The weary horses pulled the wheels out of the mudhole and the gun went rattling down the road, followed by the tardy but gallant rear guard. The Federal cavalry and artillery were following and infantry was approaching in two directions; but the rear guard slipped through the net, dashed rapidly across the ford, and soon was safe in Virginia.

The joy of the men and their commander at the success of their expedition was unbounded. The Federals were near enough to hear the Confederate cheers that greeted General Stuart as he rode along his lines on the Virginia side.

In the official report of the expedition, Stuart claimed no personal credit, but closed the report by saying, "Believing that the hand of God was clearly manifested in the deliverance of my command from danger and the crowning success attending it, I ascribe to him the praise, the honor, and the glory."

The march of the Confederate cavalry from Chambersburg is one of the most remarkable in history. In thirty-six hours, the Confederates rode ninety miles, going completely around the Union army. They carried off hundreds of horses, and recrossed the Potomac in the presence of vastly superior forces of the Federals. Only one man was wounded and two stragglers were captured.

General Stuart himself, however, suffered a

GENERAL STUART IN 1862      [107]
From an original negative by Cooke, the only negative from life that is extant

heavy personal loss, for his servant Bob who rattled the bones so well, got separated from the column, with two of the general's favorite horses, Skylark and Lady Margaret. He wrote his wife that he hoped that they had fallen into the hands of the good secessionists at Emmitsburg, for he could not bear to think of the Federals having his favorite horses.

The horses of the Federal cavalry had been so worn out in pursuit of the wily Stuart that remounts were necessary before the cavalry could again advance into Virginia. The whole North was astonished and indignant that Stuart had again ridden completely around the Union army and had again made his escape.

To the South, Stuart was a peerless hero and he was welcomed with great acclamation. A lady of Baltimore, as a token of her appreciation of his gallantry, sent him a pair of gold spurs. He was very proud of these and in his intimate letters after this, he sometimes signed himself, "K. G. S.", or "Knight of the Golden Spurs."

## CHAPTER VIII

# THE CAVALRY AT CULPEPER AND FREDERICKSBURG

## 1862-'63

THE BRIEF space of two days was all the time given to the men and horses of Stuart's command to rest and enjoy life at The Bower, before they were again called out to active service. General McClellan had sent two large forces of infantry and cavalry across the river to find out whether General Lee's army was still in the Valley or whether it had moved east of the Blue Ridge mountains. After several skirmishes with Stuart's cavalry, these troops retired, convinced that Lee was still in the Valley.

On October 26, McClellan crossed the Potomac and the weather continuing fine, he advanced his entire army to begin an autumn campaign against Lee. A week later, his forces began to advance toward Washington, a little village northwest of Culpeper and near the headwaters of the Rappahannock. This position was desirable because it would give an easy route toward Richmond. General Lee, however, sent Longstreet at once with some of the cavalry to head off the Federals at Culpeper, while Jackson was to remain in the Valley and threaten their rear.

MAJOR JOHN PELHAM

In the meantime, Stuart bade a final farewell to his pleasant camp quarters and his friends at the Dandridge mansion. His force fell slowly back toward Culpeper, contesting every inch of ground against the overwhelming numbers of the Federal cavalry. Sharp encounters took place at Union, Middleburg, and Upperville, in which the artillery under Pelham did wonderfully daring and effective work. In these encounters, the Federals lost nearly twice as many men as did the Confederates, but it was impossible for Stuart's small forces to hold any permanent ground against the greatly superior numbers now marching against him.

At Ashby's Gap, General Stuart came near being cut off from his own forces. He had commanded Colonel Rosser to hold this gap while he, accompanied by a few members of his staff, rode across the mountain for a conference with General Jackson. When Stuart returned the next day, after a hard ride over a little-used mountain trail, what was his surprise on reaching a point just above what had been his own camp, to find the place literally swarming with blue-coats.

Rosser had found it necessary to withdraw before the superior numbers of the Federals and his couriers who went to inform Stuart of this fact had missed the general who had returned by a short cut across the mountain. He and his men were indeed in a serious predicament, and had they not found a mountaineer, who knew the trails on the other side of the mountain, there is no telling when or where General Stuart would have joined his command. He was guided safely to Barber's Cross Roads where his forces had retreated and he made the simple and faithful mountaineer happy with a fifty-dollar note.

On November 10, there was an engagement

at Barber's Cross Roads, and the Confederate cavalry was forced to retreat through Orleans and across the Rappahannock at Waterloo Bridge. That night Stuart received the news of the death of his dear little daughter, Flora. For some time he had known of her serious illness, and the doctor had written that he must come home if he wished to see her, but he knew that his country needed him to hold the Federal cavalry in check.

When the second urgent call reached him on the field of battle near Union, he wrote Mrs. Stuart: "I was at no loss to decide that it was my duty to you and to Flora to remain here. I am entrusted with the conduct of affairs, the issue of which will affect you, her, and the mothers and children of our whole country much more seriously than we can believe.

"If my darling's case is hopeless, there are ten chances to one that I will get to Lynchburg too late; if she is convalescent, why should my presence be necessary? She was sick nine days before I knew it. Let us trust in the good God who has blessed us so much, that He will spare our child to us, but if it should please Him to take her from us, let us bear it with Christian fortitude and resignation."

Major Von Borcke, who opened the telegram

telling of the child's death, says that when the general read it he was completely overcome, but that he bore his loss most bravely, especially when Mrs. Stuart came to visit him a few days later at Culpeper.

He never forgot his "little darling" and often talked of her to Von Borcke, who says very prettily: "Light blue flowers recalled her eyes to him; in the glancing sunbeams he caught the golden tinge of her hair, and whenever he saw a child with such eyes and hair he could not help tenderly embracing it. He thought of her on his deathbed, and drawing me to him he whispered, 'My dear friend, I shall soon be with my little Flora again.'"

Yet such a father could put aside his own feelings when he felt that his country needed him. Duty to God and his country were his watchwords, and this high and unselfish sense of duty and patriotism was the foundation of his greatness both as a man and a soldier.

The cavalry fell back from Waterloo Bridge to join Longstreet at Culpeper, but every day it was engaged in sharp skirmishes with the Federal cavalry. In one of these engagements, General Stuart had an amusing experience that narrowly escaped being a serious one. Major Von Borcke tells us that while his cavalry was being forced back under a very heavy fire, Stuart in endeavoring to make it hold its position, uselessly but according to his custom, exposed his own person on horseback by riding out of the wood into an open field where he and his aide were excellent targets for their enemies. Von Borcke remonstrated, but the general, who could not bear to have the day go against him, curtly said to his young aide, "If it is too hot for you, you can retire."

Of course, Von Borcke remained in his position at the general's side, but he did shelter himself from the rain of bullets, behind a convenient tree. From this position, a few moments later he saw Stuart raise his hand quickly to his beloved mustache, one half of which had been neatly cut away by a whistling bullet.

As a result of their heavy and continuous marching, the horses of Stuart's troops were in bad condition, many of them having sore tongues and a disease known as "grease heel"; in spite of this and the absence of many men who had gone home to procure fresh horses, the services now rendered by the cavalry were invaluable. General Lee said in his report of this campaign that the vigilance, activity, and courage of the cavalry were conspicuous, and to its assistance was due in a great measure the success of some of the army's most important operations.

While General Lee was awaiting the movements of the Federal army, an event happened which changed the entire aspect of military affairs. General McClellan was removed from command and General Burnside was put in his place. General McClellan had been too slow and cautious to suit the authorities at Washington; so, much to the delight of the Confederate government, this able general was removed just as his campaign had begun.

General Burnside remained at Warrenton ten days in order to reorganize his army into three divisions. Then he began to move his forces toward Fredericksburg on the Rappahannock river. This movement was at once observed by Stuart and reported to General Lee who immediately began to move troops toward Fredericksburg. When Burnside's forces reached the northern bank of the river, they found the town in Lee's possession and the heights to the south of it crowned by his artillery.

General Lee now ordered General Jackson to come from the Valley to join him. While waiting for this reenforcement, he began to construct earthworks for his artillery and to dig rifle-pits for his infantry on the range of hills extending in a semicircle for five miles south of the river. Here with Hampton guarding the left wing of the army and Stuart the right, the Confederates camped in comparative quiet until early in December.

During this period, there were several heavy snowstorms which the soldiers enjoyed like so many schoolboys. Major Von Borcke tells of a snow battle when several hundred men of McLaws' division charged across a snow-covered plain half a mile wide, on the quarters of Hood's division. Suddenly Hood's whole division, led by its officers with colors flying, advanced against the attacking party which was driven back some distance. Then receiving reenforcements from their own division, the men rallied and threw up entrenchments behind which they made a stand. The air was white with flying snowballs, and the contest waxed hottest just at at Stuart's headquarters where he stood on a box and cheered the contestants. Hood's men finally drove their opponents from the snow entrenchments, and would have routed them utterly, had not Anderson's division come up to assist their fleeing comrades. With these reenforcements, McLaws' men suddenly turned and drove Hood's division back home. From these sham battles, the army turned soon to real warfare.

General Burnside had posted guns on Stafford Heights opposite Fredericksburg and on December 10, he shelled the town. Then his splendid army of 116,000 men crossed the river on pontoon bridges, and on the morning of December 13, it stormed Lee's position. The battle raged all day, but the Federals were repulsed at all points and when night closed, the Confederates were still holding their position.

This battle of Fredericksburg offered little opportunity for cavalry charges, but General Fitz Lee kept watch over the fords on the Confederate left, while General W. H. F. Lee was posted on the right. Stuart also remained on the right as it was the weakest part of the line, and was in constant conference with Lee and Jackson.

As the Federals made their first advance against the troops of Jackson at Hamilton's Crossing near the extreme right, Major Pelham of the Stuart Horse Artillery in an exposed position opened a cross fire with one gun and caused them to halt for over an hour. Five Federal batteries opened upon him, but he continued to fire until withdrawn by Stuart.

Both General Lee and General Jackson were on the extreme right and witnessed the wonderful work done by Major Pelham's gun. Both of them in their reports of this battle mentioned the genius and bravery of the young Alabamian.

General Jackson asked General Stuart, "Have you another Pelham, general? If so, I wish that you would give him to me."

General Lee expected the battle to be renewed the next morning, but Burnside remained quiet, and, on the night of December 15, in a violent storm of wind and rain, he withdrew to the opposite bank.

It soon became evident that Burnside had no intention of renewing the combat, but was preparing to pass the winter on the Stafford hills on the northern side of the river. General Lee's army, therefore, went into winter quarters along the south bank of the Rappahannock. The infantry and artillery built snug log huts, and began, in spite of the want of good rations and warm clothes, to enjoy the rest from marching and fighting.

The cavalry, however, had no rest, for upon its vigilance depended the safety of the army. It observed the Federal movements, watched the fords of the river, and made continual raids to the rear of Burnside's army.

On December 20, General Stuart set out with 1,800 men under the command of his tried and true generals, Hampton, Fitz Lee, and W. H. F. Lee, on what is known as the "Dumfries Raid." They were to pass by different routes to the rear of Burnside's army, to cut his line of communication with Washington city, and to destroy all wagons and stores that they could not bring off.

From a war-time photograph

CONFEDERATES DESTROYING RAILROAD

Stuart led his forces between various army-posts that guarded the rear of Burnside's army, avoiding the strongest and attacking others which he knew to be weak or ignorant of his approach. He at last marched north to Burke's

Station, where his keen sense of humor caused him to play a joke on the authorities at Washington.

He surprised the telegraph operator at the instrument, just as he was receiving a message from headquarters at the capital, telling of measures which were being taken to capture Stuart's command. Having thus gained important information, Stuart put one of his own men in the operator's place and sent a message to Meigs, the quartermaster general at Washington.

"I am much satisfied with the transport of mules lately sent, which I have taken possession of, and request that you send me a fresh supply.

J. E. B. STUART."

This message produced great consternation in Washington, where the people were as afraid of Stuart and his cavalry as they were of the whole Confederate army.

After thus revealing his whereabouts, Stuart marched quickly back to Culpeper Courthouse, which he reached on December 30, having lost on the raid, one killed, thirteen wounded, and fourteen missing. About twenty wagons and some stores had been captured. This was the fourth raid that Stuart had made around or to the rear of the Federals, without capture or serious loss.

The Rev. Dr. Dabney in his *Life of Stonewall Jackson* tells us that during this winter, General Jackson had for his headquarters a hunting lodge near Moss Neck. Here he was often

From a war-time photograph

FEDERALS REPAIRING RAILROAD WHICH CONFEDERATES HAD DESTROYED

visited by General Stuart on his rounds of official duty. These visits were always welcome to Jackson who admired and loved the young cavalry leader and they were the signal of fun for the young men of the staff. While Stuart poured out "quips and cranks," often at Jackson's expense, the latter sat by, silent and blushing, but enjoying the jests with a quiet laugh.

The walls of the lodge were ornamented with pictures which gave Stuart many a topic for jokes. Pretending to believe that they had been selected by Jackson himself, he would point now to the portrait of a famous race horse and now to the print of a dog noted for his hunting feats, and remark that they showed queer taste for a devout Presbyterian. Once Jackson, with a smile, replied that perhaps in his youth he had been fonder of race horses than his friends suspected.

One day, in the midst of a gay conversation, dinner was announced and the two generals with their aides passed to the mess table. The center of the table was graced by a print of butter upon which was impressed the image of a rooster. It had been presented to Jackson by a lady of the neighborhood and had been placed upon the table in honor of Stuart.

As the eyes of the gay young general fell upon it, they sparkled with glee and he exclaimed, "See there, gentlemen! We have the crowning evidence of our host's sporting tastes. He even puts his favorite gamecock upon his butter!"

The dinner, of course, began with merry

laughter in which General Jackson joined with much zest.

In patriotism, in bravery, and in military skill, says Dr. Dabney, these two men were kindred spirits, but Stuart's cheerfulness and humor were the opposites of Jackson's serious and diffident temper.

Though bitter cold weather had now set in, General Burnside resolved to make an effort to turn the right of General Lee's army and drive him from his winter quarters at Fredericksburg. This attempt, however, was unsuccessful, and General Burnside's failure at Fredericksburg caused him to be replaced by General Joseph Hooker, called "Fighting Joe Hooker.'

Hooker reorganized the army into corps; and made one corps of the cavalry, with tried and skillful officers. He also provided the cavalry with the best horses and equipments that money could procure. He realized that the Federal cavalry had never been fit to contend success-fully with Stuart and the forces under his com-mand, and so now did all in his power to strengthen this branch of the Federal service. By the early spring, Hooker had his army com-pletely reorganized and ready to begin a cam-paign against General Lee.

## CHAPTER IX

# CHANCELLORSVILLE

## 1863

IN THE meanwhile, General Lee's soldiers across the Rappahannock river suffered greatly for want of proper food and clothing during the long cold winter. The appeals of their beloved commander to the Confederate government were not heeded; but the soldiers endured their privations with great fortitude and when spring arrived, they were ready for the coming great battle with the army of "Fighting Joe Hooker."

On March 17, St. Patrick's Day, there was a cavalry engagement at Kelly's Ford, near Culpeper, where General Fitz Lee won a remarkable victory over a large force of Federal cavalry under Brigadier-General Averell. Lee, who was stationed at Culpeper, had only about 800 men to meet more than 2,000 Federals, but he disposed his forces with such skill and fought so stubbornly that Averell, in spite of the fact that he had a large force in reserve, was unable to break Lee's thin lines and retreated across the river.

General Stuart happened to be at Culpeper, attending a court martial, when this engagement occurred. He saw how skillfully Lee was handling the situation and unselfishly refused to assume command, wishing his able brigadier general to win all the glory of repulsing such a large force.

In this battle, John Pelham, Stuart's young chief of artillery of whom we have so often spoken, was killed. He had accompanied Stuart to Culpeper, merely on a visit of pleasure, but when he heard the call of Confederate artillery, even though it was not his own guns, he immediately went forward to take part in the engagement. Borrowing a horse from Bob Sweeny, he hurried to the battle ground. He rushed into the thickest of the fray, to rally a regiment that was beginning to waver.

Just as he shouted, "Forward, boys! forward to victory and glory!" he was mortally wounded by a fragment of a shell.

The whole South mourned the death of this young hero. James R. Randall, the author of "Maryland, My Maryland," said of him:

> "Gentlest and bravest in the battle brunt,
>     The Champion of the Truth,
>   He bore the banner to the very front
>     Of our immortal youth."

His body was carried to Richmond and lay in state in the Capitol, until it could be borne under proper military escort to his native state, Alabama. Stuart, who loved Pelham like a son, went to Richmond to be present at the funeral.

When he wrote Mrs. Stuart of the young hero's death, he said, "His record is complete and it is spotless and noble. His character pure and his disposition as sweet and innocent as our child." The general had a strong personal affection for the young men of his staff and the death of Pelham was as great a grief to Stuart as it was a loss to the army.

Stuart's men and horses were greatly weakened by the heavy and almost constant skirmishes, picket duty, and raids in which they had been engaged since the fall. On the other hand, the Federal cavalry, just reorganized into one splendid corps under the command of Major-General George Stoneman, was in better condition than ever before. General Hooker depended upon this large and finely-equipped force to open a campaign which would prove fatal to General Lee's army.

General Stoneman was ordered to cross the Rappahannock river at one of the fords in Culpeper county and, after dispersing the small force of Confederate cavalry in that vicinity, to proceed toward Richmond, destroying the Central Railroad, capturing all supply stations, and doing all possible damage along the Pamunkey river. He was then to proceed to the Richmond and Fredericksburg Railroad, and by breaking up that road and burning certain bridges, to cut General Lee's army off from Richmond. As soon as Stoneman started on his raid, the "Grand Army," as it was called, under General Hooker himself, was to move to Chancellorsville about ten miles southwest of Fredericksburg. Thus General Lee was to be forced to come out of his entrenched position and to give battle on ground of Hooker's own choosing.

Several bodies of Federal cavalry tried to cross at various fords on the Rappahannock and Rapidan rivers, but were repulsed by small bodies of watchful Confederate pickets. The rivers were now rising rapidly from the usual spring rains, and the Rappahannock became so swollen that the advance of Stoneman was checked for two weeks. Many of Stuart's troopers were absent for various reasons and he had only about two thousand men with whom to guard the fords and to cover a front of more than fifty miles.

On the afternoon of April 24, three corps of

Federal infantry appeared at Kelly's Ford. A strong party crossed in boats and drove the pickets from the ford. They then laid a pontoon bridge; and during the night, the Twelfth Army Corps passed to the southern shore. The next morning, Stuart learned that the entire Grand Army was on the move. He telegraphed this

From a war-time photograph

A PONTOON BRIDGE
Made by laying timbers on wooden or canvas boats

information to General Lee who ordered Stuart at once to swing around the Federal divisions that had crossed the river and join him at Fredericksburg. General W. H. F. Lee with only two regiments—a small force but all that could be spared—was sent to protect the Central Railroad from Stoneman's cavalry.

Stuart, skirmishing day and night with the Federal cavalry, marched rapidly to the help of Lee. As the cavalry passed at night through the dark forest lighted only by the faint rays of a crescent moon, they had frequent alarms and several encounters with small forces of the Federal cavalry already posted in the woods.

At one time, Stuart, accompanied by only a few officers of his staff, was riding some distance ahead of his brigade, and met such a large Federal force that he was compelled to take flight. Later, when riding at the head of a regiment that he had called up as an advance guard, he suddenly encountered several regiments of hostile cavalry drawn up across a field in line of battle. Stuart's small force became panic-stricken. All efforts of the general to rally his men were in vain and he was compelled a second time to retreat hastily. It seemed for a time that he would be cut off from his forces, but Colonel Munford came up with his regiment, charged gallantly, captured most of the attacking Federals, and left the road again open. Several such skirmishes occurred and the troops were rendered almost panic-stricken by these unlooked-for attacks. In the darkness, they often fired on each other instead of on their foe, and they feared an ambush at each turn of the road. Altogether, it was a march of doubt and danger, but they finally reached Lee's army without serious loss.

Chancellorsville, to which place the main army of General Hooker was being moved, was not a town, but merely a large farmhouse surrounded by the usual outbuildings. Toward Fredericksburg ten miles distant, the country was somewhat open; but in every other direction it was covered with tall pines and with dense thickets of scrub oaks and many other kinds of trees and flowering plants. This forest, called "the Wilderness," was about twenty miles long and fifteen broad. It was traversed by two good roads, the Plank road and the old Turnpike; it was along these roads, the possession of which would, of course, be hotly contested by the Federal troops, that General Lee would have to send his forces to attack General Hooker in his strong position at Chancellorsville.

But on the night of the first of May, just after the first skirmishing had occurred along these two roads, Stuart brought information that changed the situation decidedly. He rode up about eleven o'clock to an old fallen tree where

Lee and Jackson were talking over the plans for the next day, and reported that while Hooker had fortified his position at Chancellorsville on the east, the south, and the southwest, upon the north and the west he had no defences. At the same time, information had been secured concerning an old road by which a circuit could be made around Hooker's army. Jackson at once conceived the idea of making a forced march by this road so as to attack Hooker in the rear on the next day. Lee agreed, as on this plan seemed to depend their one chance of success.

The next morning, General Lee with about 14,000 men remained in front of the Federals on the Plank and Turnpike roads, while Jackson with three divisions marched fifteen miles through the forest and about three o'clock in the afternoon reached the rear of Hooker's army on the west. General Fitz Lee with the First Virginia cavalry led the advance while the other regiments of cavalry protected the right of Jackson's line of march. Colonel Munford, commander of one of these regiments, was familiar with this part of the country and rendered valuable service as a guide to Jackson.

As Jackson's command marched first directly south by the Furnace road, Federal scouts, who were spying from the tops of tall pine trees, thought that Lee's army was in full retreat. They carried this report to Hooker who sent forward two divisions to attack the marching column. By that time, Jackson had turned to the west and, completely screened by trees and undergrowth, was marching rapidly along the old road. The rear of his column, however, was attacked near Catherine Furnace. This attack was soon checked by McLaws, whom Lee sent forward from his small force, and by two regiments sent back by Jackson when he heard the firing in his rear.

While the infantry was swinging along the forest road, the cavalry had reached the Plank road, near Chancellorsville, and was awaiting General Jackson. Fitz Lee, impatient at the delay, rode toward the Federal line, and found to his surprise that it was near at hand and in full view from his post of observation. The Federals did not dream that the Confederates could reach the road at this point and so had no guards stationed there.

Afterwards Fitz Lee thus described the scene: "Below and but a few hundred yards distant, ran the Federal line of battle. There was the line of defense and long lines of stacked arms in the rear. Two cannons were visible in the part of the line seen. The soldiers were in groups in the rear, laughing, chatting, smoking; probably engaged, here and there, in a game of cards and other amusements indulged in when feeling safe and awaiting orders. In the rear were other persons driving up and butchering beeves."

Realizing the importance of his discovery, Lee rode back to meet Jackson and guided him to the same place of observation. Jackson immediately placed his troops in position on the turnpike and ordered them to advance and attack the unsuspecting enemy. As long as the dense growth and rough ground permitted, Stuart and his cavalry guarded the left flank. After a rapid march through the tangled thickets, the men rushed forward with wild cheers and dashed upon the unsuspecting Federals as they were cooking their suppers. The panic-stricken Federal soldiers rushed back upon their center, and as the terror spread, after them went horses, wagons, cannon, men— speeding to recross the Rappahannock. The officers tried in vain to stop the fleeing men. For a while, the panic was so great that the desstruction of Hooker's army seemed certain.

After pursuing the Federals for two hours until they were within half a mile of Hooker's headquarters at the Chancellor house, the Confederates stopped in the darkness to reform. Just at this critical moment, General Hooker succeeded in bringing up reenforcements and posted fresh artillery in the edge of the woods on Hazel Grove, a small hill in front of General Jackson's assaulting column.   Still, however, the soldiers in gray advanced.  General A. P. Hill's division was now ordered to the front to take charge of the pursuit.  While he was engaged in forming his lines, General Jackson with several aides and couriers rode down the Plank road nearly to the defenses around Chancellorsville.  As they were returning, they were fired upon by some of their own men who had been posted in the thickets and who, in the moonlight, mistook Jackson and his escort for Federal cavalry.

General Jackson was wounded and was borne from the field.  A little later, General Hill also was wounded.  Jackson then sent for Stuart who had been ordered to hold the road to Ely's Ford, one of the Federal lines of retreat.

As soon as Stuart received the sad news that Jackson had been wounded, he placed Fitz Lee in command of the force holding the road and hastened into the heart of the Wilderness.  It was midnight when he arrived at the front and according to Jackson's orders assumed command of the victorious but wearied corps.

GENERAL STONEWALL JACKSON
From an original negative by Cooke, the last photograph made of General Jackson

[ 135 ]

Stuart, not knowing Jackson's plans for completing the movement, sent an aide to Jackson to request instructions.

General Jackson replied, "Tell General Stuart to act upon his own judgment and do what he thinks best. I have implicit trust in him."

Such a message from his loved chieftain must have meant much to the young general who found himself suddenly confronted with such a serious situation, and the next day he proved that Jackson had not trusted him in vain.

First of all, it was necessary that Stuart, who had been absent from the front sometime, should have a clear idea of the position of his men and of the Federals. He, therefore, at once called a meeting of the infantry commanders. As a result of this consultation, it was decided to defer until the next morning the attack upon the strong fortifications around Chancellorsville. The rest of the night was spent by the officers in preparations for the coming assault; the men lay upon their arms and took a brief rest.

When morning dawned, the guns of Lee, who was working his way along the two main roads to join Jackson, thundered on the east and the south, and those of Stuart answered on the west. In both wings of Lee's army, the battle raged furiously. After many assaults, Hazel Grove where the Federal artillery and infantry were posted in force, was taken by Stuart. Then arose a mighty struggle for the clearing around the Chancellor house. Stuart ordered thirty pieces of artillery to be posted so as to sweep the clearing with canister and grapeshot. Under this fire, his own men advanced, Stuart himself leading two of the charges. One of his officers said that he "looked like a very god of battle." As he rode forward at the head of his forces, he sang at the top of his clear voice which could be heard above the din of battle,

> "Old Joe Hooker,
> Won't you come out of the wilderness?"

At the third assault, the works were carried and connection was made with General Lee's force. By ten o'clock, the Chancellor house and the woods around it, full of wounded men, were on fire from the bursting shells. The Confederate flag floated proudly in the clearing around the house and the Confederate army was again united, while Hooker's forces in full retreat were swept back into the woods north of Chancellorsville.

A great southern historian and military critic, General Alexander, says "the promptness and boldness with which Stuart assumed command, and led the ranks of Jackson, thinned by their hard day's march and fighting to not more than 20,000 men, against Hooker's 80,000 soldiers was one of the most brilliant deeds of the war."

While the battle of Chancellorsville was in progress, Stoneman, the Federal cavalry leader, had crossed the Rappahannock and was marching toward Richmond. General W. H. F. Lee followed him with two regiments and so hindered his line of march that the Federal general, in spite of his excellent cavalry, was forced to retire with few spoils and little glory. Stoneman was soon after relieved of his command, and Pleasanton was put in his place as major general of the Federal cavalry.

CHAPTER X

# THE BATTLE OF BRANDY STATION

## 1863

Soon after the battle of Chancellorsville, Lee's army was reenforced by the return of Longstreet's corps, which had been for some time at Suffolk, Va., and the cavalry was increased by the addition of new regiments from North Carolina and the Shenandoah Valley. Lee's total forces were now about 80,000 and his men, encouraged by their recent victory, were in good fighting trim. Lee decided to carry the scene of war once more into northern territory. He hoped to form a line of battle near the Susquehanna river in the fertile fields of Pennsylvania, where he could force the Federals to fight on ground of his own choosing. The next weeks were spent in preparation for this northward movement.

On June 6, there was a cavalry review on the open plain between Culpeper Courthouse and Brandy Station. Great preparations had been made for this review. Each trooper had burnished his weapons and trappings and rubbed down his much-enduring charger, in order that they might make the best appearance possible. Visitors, especially many ladies, from all the country round attended the magnificent spectacle.

Stuart and his entire staff took their position on a little grassy knoll. Eight thousand troopers and sixteen pieces of horse artillery passed before him in columns of squadrons,—first at a walk, then at a gallop—while the guns of a battery on a hill opposite the reviewing stand fired at regular intervals.

An eyewitness of the scene tells us that Stuart "was superbly mounted. The trappings on his proud, prancing horse all looked bright and new and his sidearms gleamed in the morning sun like burnished silver. A long black ostrich plume waved gracefully from a drab slouch hat cocked up on one side and held by a clasp which also stayed the plume."

The same authority, Gunner Neese, tells an amusing story about himself during this review. He says that, as acting first sergeant of his battery, he was riding at the head of the horse artillery, mounted on a mule with ears about a foot long. Just before the artillery arrived at the reviewing stand, the searching eye of General Stuart, who was very fastidious in all things, spied the waving ears of the mule and he quickly dispatched an aide to tell the captain to order the mule and his rider off the field. Neese says that he was not greatly surprised at the order, but that the mule was.

For sometime General Hooker had wanted to know what was going on behind the dense screen of cavalry that Stuart had collected at Culpeper, for it was evident that General Lee was planning an important movement. Just two days after the big review, Hooker sent to find out, and for once the Federal cavalry took Stuart by surprise. General Pleasanton marched cautiously to the north bank of the Rappahannock, at Beverly's Ford, with three divisions of cavalry and five brigades of infantry. No fires were allowed in the Federal camp, and every precaution was taken to prevent the Confederate pickets on the south bank from discovering the presence of the large force.

Stuart's brigades, under Fitz Lee, Robertson, W. H. F. Lee, and Jones, were encamped near the fords of the Rappahannock in readiness to cross the river the next morning and protect the flank of Lee's army which was already beginning its northward movement. Four batteries of horse artillery were encamped in the edge of the woods, in advance of Jones's brigade, near St.

James Church. This church was about two hundred yards to the west of the direct road to Beverly's Ford and was about two miles from the ford.

Stuart himself camped on Fleetwood Hill, half a mile east of Brandy Station and four miles from Beverly's Ford. As an early start was ordered for the next morning, all of Stuart's camp equipage was packed in wagons in readiness for the move. Pickets were placed at all fords and the weary men slept, unaware of the lurking enemy.

At dawn on June 9, General Pleasanton divided his command into two columns and sent one, under Brigadier-General Gregg, to cross the river at Kelly's Ford, four miles below the railroad bridge, and to gain the road to Culpeper Courthouse. The other column, under General Buford, was ordered to cross at Beverly's Ford and proceed toward Brandy Station. This advance was gallantly disputed by the Confederate pickets at the ford, but being greatly outnumbered they were retiring slowly toward St. James Church when Major Flournoy with about one hundred men charged down the road upon the advancing regiments. The colonel who was leading the Federal charge was killed and the troops were driven back.

But the skirmishes of the picket force and the charge of Major Flournoy had given General Jones time to draw up his men in line of battle and to withdraw the artillery from its exposed position. General Jones then charged to the support of Major Flournoy. This charge was repelled by the Federals, and Jones retired to

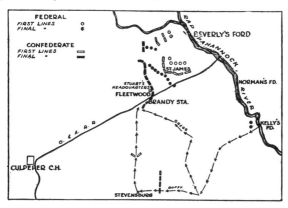

MAP OF BATTLE OF BRANDY STATION

his line of battle at St. James Church where he was soon joined by the brigades of Hampton and W. H. F. Lee.

From ten o'clock in the morning, the battle raged furiously. The Confederates advanced, but were met by Federal troops that charged gallantly across an open field up to the very muzzles of the cannon which were sending forth shell and canister into their midst. They advanced, however, too far beyond their guns and, being attacked on both flanks, they retreated with heavy loss.

Stuart, who had hastened to the front to dispute the march of Buford, was suddenly threatened by more serious danger in the rear. The gallant Colonel Butler had been left with a regiment of South Carolina cavalry to guard Brandy Station, two miles in the rear of St. James Church and just half a mile from Fleetwood Hill where Stuart's headquarters had been located for several weeks. While on duty at Brandy Station, Colonel Butler was informed by a scout that a body of Federal cavalry was moving toward Stevensburg. This was a part of the column that had been sent to Kelly's Ford early in the morning. General Gregg had driven in the Confederate pickets at the ford, and although General Robertson moved at once to the help of his pickets, he was too late to prevent General Gregg from sending a considerable force toward Stevensburg which was on the direct road to Culpeper Courthouse where General Lee was encamped. General Gregg himself, with the remainder of his force, marched on toward Brandy Station.

Colonel Butler knew that it was most important to keep the Federals from finding out

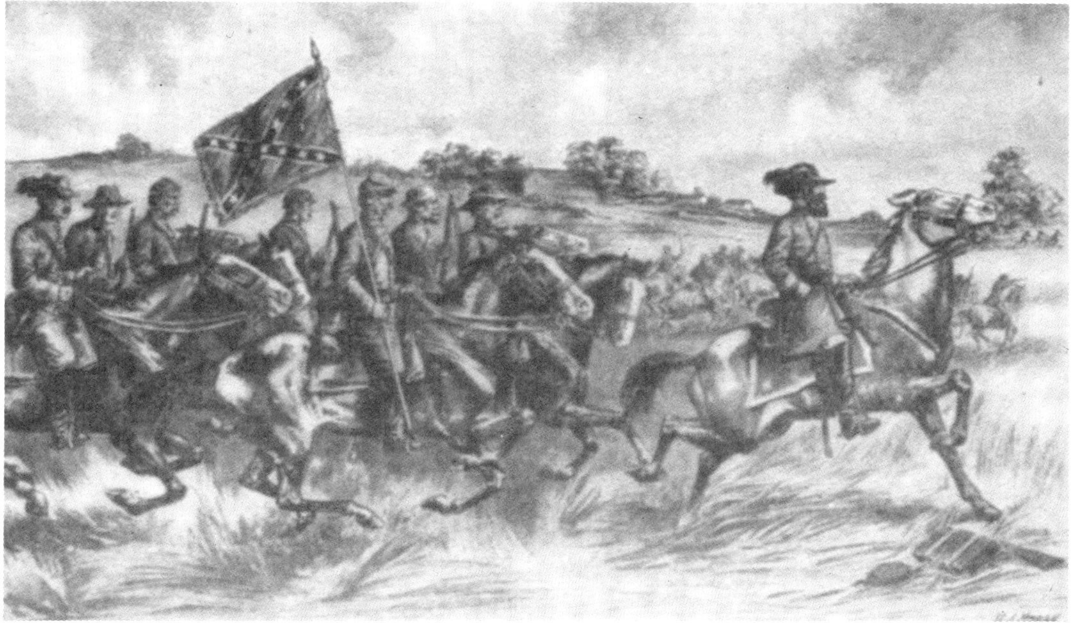

THE BATTLE OF BRANDY STATION

that Lee's army was at Culpeper, and as soon
as he heard that they were marching along the
Stevensburg road, he advanced without orders
down that road. After a fierce fight, he stopped
the advance of the Federals who turned back to
join Gregg at Brandy Station.

In the meantime, General Gregg had marched
to the station where, Colonel Butler being
absent, he met no opposing force. From this
point, he immediately passed on to Fleetwood
Hill which that morning had been vacated by
General Stuart as headquarters. Stuart had
left there Major H. B. McClellan and several
couriers, with orders for all brigades and regiments to communicate with him at that place.
These staff officers saw Gregg's large forces
approaching and knew that they must hold the
hill at any cost, as it was the key to Stuart's
whole position.

In Major McClellan's *Life of Stuart* he gives
us a very vivid and accurate account of the combats which raged up and down and over the
crest of Fleetwood Hill. He says that every
vestige of the camp had been removed and
there remained upon the hill only McClellan and
the couriers. A six-pound howitzer, which for
want of ammunition had been sent back from the
fight going on at St. James Church, was halted

at the foot of the hill and later proved their salvation. As soon as the young major saw the long Federal columns approaching, he dispatched a courier to General Stuart with information of this movement. For fear that some accident might befall the first courier, he sent a second, praying for help lest the entire force be enclosed between the divisions of Buford and Gregg.

Finding some round shot and imperfect shells in the limber chest, Major McClellan ordered the howitzer to be brought up the hill and a slow fire to be opened upon the rapidly-advancing Federals. The fire caused surprise and a halt. It seemed to indicate the presence of a considerable force.

General Gregg, therefore, made preparations for a serious attack upon the hill, and opened fire with three rifled guns. But Major McClellan and the men with their one gun, held the hill until help came. Reenforcements promptly sent by General Stuart arrived just as the lieutenant in charge of the gun had fired his last cartridge and the Federal cavalry was advancing "in magnificent order of columns of squadrons, with flags and guidons flying."

There now followed a number of combats which for dash and bravery have rarely been equaled. First the Confederates, then the Federals, seemed to have possession of the hill. Stuart himself soon arrived, bringing Hampton and Jones from the other firing line to help hold this important position. Back and forth swept the blue and the gray, each fighting stubbornly and well. For a brief space of time, the New Jersey cavalry held the hill. Soon they were repulsed by a charge led by the Virginia cavalry. There was a fierce contest at the foot of the hill over three Federal guns. The Confederates charged and took the guns, but were driven back by overwhelming numbers and forced to cut their way out. About this time, Hampton came up with his four regiments formed in columns of squadrons with a battery of four guns. As they advanced at a gallop, they saw the crest of Fleetwood Hill covered with Federal cavalry. Passing the eastern side of the hill, they struck the column just beyond the railroad and there followed a fierce hand-to-hand fight. When the smoke and dust of the conflict lifted, it was seen that Hampton had won. The Federals were retiring. At the same time, a charge had been made straight up the hill on the northeast side by Georgia and South Carolina cavalry. A saber charge was made and the hill was cleared of the opposing troops. As soon as the Confederates gained the summit of the hill, three batteries were placed in position there.

Fleetwood Hill was now in the possession of the Confederates, but the Federals still held Brandy Station. Stuart at once brought up a regiment which charged on both sides of the road to the station, drove out the Federals and pursued them for some distance.

While the battle was raging at Fleetwood Hill, W. H. F. Lee with a small force held the Confederate lines near St. James Church. There was a lull in the fighting while Buford was retiring some of his cavalry and bringing up fresh troops, and so Stuart was able to withdraw both Hampton and Jones, in order to repel the attack on Fleetwood Hill.

As soon as the Federals were driven from Brandy Station, Stuart formed a new line of battle between the church and the station, where he received a heavy Federal onset. This battle was waged with varied success, but at last Gregg joined Buford and late in the evening the Federals retired across the river,—defeated in spite of their superior numbers.

The losses in the battle of Brandy Station were heavy on both sides. The Federal loss was nearly 1,000 officers and men, while the Confederate loss was over 500. The Federals were forced to leave in the hands of the Confederates three cannon, six flags, and nearly 500 prisoners. Pleasanton was really driven back by Stuart and the cavalry, but he claimed that as he had found out that there was a force of infantry at Culpeper Courthouse, which was the information he had been sent to obtain, he retired as soon as possible after he had been joined by Gregg.

Gunner Neese tells us that several times during the day he saw General Stuart, when the battle raged fiercest, dash with his staff across the field and pass from point to point along the line, perfectly heedless of the surrounding danger. During the engagement, Neese fired his faithful gun one hundred and sixty times. Just before the battle closed in the evening he saw the fire flash from the cascabel of his gun and found that it was disabled forever—burnt out entirely at the breech.

We have described this battle at length because it is considered one of the greatest cavalry combats of the nineteenth century.

## CHAPTER XI

# THE GETTYSBURG CAMPAIGN

## 1863

STUART did not attempt to follow Pleasanton, because Lee's plan for the invasion of the North would not allow the useless sacrifice of men and horses. Indeed, all of the cavalry was needed to screen his army as it marched through the Blue Ridge gaps into the Valley, from which point it was to cross the Potomac into Maryland.

While Longstreet's corps, which was the last to move from Culpeper, was advancing to the Valley, Stuart and his cavalry had a hard time trying to protect Ashby's and Snicker's gaps, through which Longstreet's forces would have to pass. The battles of Aldie, Middleburg, and Upperville, severe cavalry engagements in which Stuart's forces were slowly forced back to the foot of the Blue Ridge, were all fought to protect these gaps until Longstreet could pass through them on his northward march.

On June 22, General Pleasanton, who had forced General Stuart back from Upperville to

Ashby's Gap, withdrew, and Stuart moved forward to Rector's Cross Roads, where he could better watch the Federal movements. On that same day, General Ewell, who commanded the advance division of General Lee's army, crossed the Potomac. By June 27, Lee's entire army had reached Chambersburg, Pennsylvania.

In the meantime, Stuart was in Virginia watching the Federals, in order to report to Lee the moment that Hooker began to move. He wrote General Lee that he thought he could move with some of his cavalry around General Hooker's rear into Maryland, thus throwing himself between the Federals and Washington, and so probably delay Hooker's northward movement. General Lee wanted General Stuart and his cavalry to join General Early and guard his flank as he marched toward York, Pennsylvania; he thought that Stuart could reach him in this way just as easily as by crossing at Shepherdstown where the rest of the army crossed. Therefore, he gave Stuart permission to cross at one of the lower fords, telling him to annoy the Federals in the rear and collect all possible supplies for the army.

Major Von Borcke, the young Prussian officer, had been severely wounded and Major Mc-

Clellan was now Stuart's adjutant general. He tells us that on the night before General Stuart started, a cold drizzling rain was falling, but the general insisted on sleeping on the ground under a tree, because he said his men were exposed to the rain and he would not fare better than they. He could have had more comfortable quarters on the porch of a deserted house near by, where McClellan, by the light of a tallow "dip," was receiving and writing dispatches. When General Lee's letter, containing instructions for Stuart's march, came, McClellan carried it to the general, who quietly read it, and then turned to go to sleep on his hard, cold bed.

It was by such an example as this, as well as by his bravery in battle, that Stuart won the undying love of his soldiers. I am going to quote for you a beautiful tribute paid him by Mosby, his chief scout, who guided Stuart past the Federal lines on the first part of this expedition.

Mosby says that when he went to the general for instructions before starting, "he was in his usual gay humor. I never saw him at any time in any other. Always buoyant in spirits, he inspired with his own high hopes all who came in contact with him  I felt the deepest affection for him. My chief ambition was to serve him. He was the rare combination of the Puritan and the knight-errant,—he felt intensely the joy of battle and he loved the praise of fair women and brave men.

"I served under him from the beginning of the war until he closed his life, like Sidney, leading a squadron on the field of honor. Yet I do not remember that he ever gave me an order. There was always so much sympathy between us and I felt so much affection for him that he had only to express a wish, that was an order for me."

In making their plans, neither Lee nor Stuart had counted on an immediate northward movement of the Federal army. Yet when Stuart with three brigades passed eastward through a gap in Bull Run Mountain, he found Hooker's army already moving northward. He at once sent General Lee a dispatch conveying this valuable information, but the courier bearing it never reached headquarters, and so Lee did not know of this important movement until Hooker's whole army had crossed the Potomac and moved toward Frederick, Maryland.

It was now impossible for Stuart to cross the river where he had intended, and it would take too much time to retrace his steps and cross at Shepherdstown, so he determined on the bold move of crossing at Rowser's Ford, or Seneca, only thirteen miles from Washington city. At this point, the water was very deep and swift, and the artillery had difficulty in crossing, but time was too precious for them to seek a better ford.

The caissons and limber chests were emptied and dragged through the water, and the ammunition was carried over in the hands of troopers. By three o'clock on the morning of June 28, Stuart's command was on the Maryland side of the river, but the whole Federal army now lay between the cavalry and General Lee. Stuart would have to march around this army before he could obey Lee's order to join Early at York.

But General Lee had also told Stuart to collect all the supplies that he could get for the use of the army. He now had an opportunity to carry out these instructions, for he met and captured a long line of Federal supply wagons.

Fitz Lee's brigade tore up the track of the Baltimore and Ohio Railroad, burned the bridge, and cut the telegraph wires, thus destroying the line of communication between Washington city and General Meade who had taken Hooker's place as commander of the Federal forces. At one time, Stuart's troopers were so near Washington that they could see the dome of the Capitol, and the whole North was in a panic lest the dreaded Stuart should attack the city. General Stuart, however, was hastening northward in order to join General Early at York.

His long train of captured wagons seriously hindered the rapid movement of his horsemen, but he was unwilling to abandon these supplies that he knew were so greatly needed by Lee's army.

If, however, he could have foreseen the events of the next few days he would have burned the wagons and hurried by forced marches to join General Lee who had to fight the first two days' battle at Gettysburg without the valuable aid of Stuart and his cavalry. But Stuart acted in the light of what he knew and did what seemed best at the time, holding on to his valuable prize in spite of the fact that it delayed his march to York nearly two days.

On the morning of June 30, Stuart had a sharp encounter with cavalry, at Hanover, Pennsylvania, and at one time it seemed that he would have to give up his captured wagons. He already had them parked, so that they could easily be burned if he was compelled to leave them, but Hampton's and Fitz Lee's brigades, which had been guarding the wagons in the rear, came up and the Federals were dislodged.

Stuart remained at Hanover until night, in order to hold the Federals in check, while the wagon trains were sent toward York under the protection of Fitz Lee's brigade.

Major McClellan tells us that this night's march was terrible to both the troopers and the drivers of the wagons. The men were hungry and exhausted, and so were the mules. Every time a wagon stopped, it caused a halt along the whole line, and as the drivers were constantly falling asleep, these halts occurred very frequently. It required the utmost vigilance on the part of every officer on Stuart's staff to keep the train in motion.

When Fitz Lee reached the road leading from York to Gettysburg, he learned that Early had already marched westward. When Stuart arrived at this point, he sent out couriers to find Early and locate the other Confederate forces. He then pushed immediately on to Carlisle where he hoped to obtain provisions for his weary and hungry troops, but when he reached Carlisle, he found it already in possession of the Federals.

Smith, the Federal general in command, was summoned to surrender, but he replied, "If you want the city, come and take it."

Stuart was preparing to storm the city when he received orders from General Lee to move at once toward Gettysburg

For eight days and nights, Stuart's men had been almost continually on the march and had been surrounded by superior cavalry forces, but he reached Gettysburg on the evening of the second of July, in time to take part in the third day's battle.   He delivered to the quartermaster one hundred and twenty-five captured wagons and teams.   He would willingly have sacrificed this valuable prize could he have been on hand two days earlier to assist his beloved chief in the battle that had been unexpectedly forced at this point, but in which he held his ground during two days of stubborn fighting.

General Lee's plan for the third day's battle was to have General Longstreet's corps storm the Federal center in its strongly-fortified position upon Cemetery Ridge.   Stuart's cavalry was to march unobserved to the Federal rear. Here it was to attack, thus protecting the Confederate left flank and drawing attention away from the forces which were to storm Cemetery Ridge.

About noon on the third of July, Stuart led two brigades along the York turnpike and took position on Cross Ridge in the rear of the Federal line of battle.   Hampton and Fitz Lee were ordered to follow as soon as they were supplied with amunition.

On the slope of Cross Ridge stood a stone dairy, and farther down in the valley was a barn belonging to a farmer named Rummel. Concealing his men in the woods on the top of the hill, Stuart pushed forward a gun and fired a number of shots, probably to notify General Lee that he had gained a good position on the

From a war-time photograph
THE TOLL OF WAR
Dead Confederate sharpshooters on the battlefield of Gettysburg

left flank. He then sent word for Hampton and Fitz Lee to hasten, as he wished to attack the Federal rear. While waiting for them, he sent some dismounted cavalry to hold the Rummel barn and a fence to the right of it.

Before Fitz Lee and Hampton came up, Stuart saw that he had stirred up a hornet's nest.

The Federal cavalry had discovered his movements and were ready for him. A battery of six
guns opened fire upon his gun and soon disabled
it. Then a strong line of sharpshooters advanced
and a fierce fight took place near the barn. On
the left, the Confederate sharpshooters drove
the Federals for some distance across the field.
Just then a large force of Federal cavalry appeared and drove back the Confederate dismounted men almost to the Rummel barn.
There the Federals were met and driven back
by the Confederates, but the Federals were
reenforced and returned. Hampton advanced to
the charge, and the battle surged back and
forth over the open field in a hand-to-hand fight
with pistols and sabers, until nearly all of
Hampton's and Fitz Lee's regiments were engaged.

At last the Federals retired to the line held at
the beginning of the fight and the Confederates
held the Rummel barn. There followed an
artillery duel which lasted until night. Then
Stuart withdrew to the York turnpike, leaving
a regiment of cavalry picketed around the barn
which was full of wounded Confederates.

Stuart encamped that night on the York road.
Early the next morning, he withdrew in the rain
and rejoined the main army on the heights west

of Gettysburg. The Confederates under Pickett had stormed the Federal heights opposite and had taken the guns, but as Hood, who was to support the charge was detained by the Federal cavalry, they could not hold their position, and finally had to retreat with the loss of many lives. The Federals did not pursue the Confederates, but remained the whole of the next day upon their entrenched heights.

Being now nearly out of ammunition and supplies for his men, General Lee ordered a retreat on the night of July 4. He had a difficult task to perform. But happily his army had not been routed nor had the men lost confidence in him. As long as he was leading, they were willing to go anywhere and to endure anything.

He had now before him a long march, and he was encumbered with four thousand prisoners and a wagon train fifteen miles long. It would take great skill and courage to conduct his army safely back into Virginia.

In this extremity, he relied on his cavalry for aid. Both men and horses were by this time reduced in numbers and were worn out by hunger and fatigue. They, however, took promptly the position assigned by General Lee and guarded the army and its trains from the attacks of the Federal cavalry. General Stuart's command guarded both wings of the army,— Stuart himself being on one side and Fitz Lee on the other. They, of course, were pursued by the Federal cavalry, and before they reached the fords of the Potomac, both Stuart and Fitz Lee had been engaged in several skirmishes.

The wagon train reached Williamsport on July 6, and found the river too much swollen to cross. The wagons were massed in a narrow space near the river and were guarded by a small force. Here they were attacked by General Buford. This engagement is called "the Teamsters' Battle," because the teamsters assisted the troopers so well in holding the Federals in check. Together they succeeded in resisting the attack of Buford until the arrival of Stuart who had been engaged in driving the Federal cavalry from Hagerstown. A little later, Fitz Lee came thundering down the Greencastle road. Buford then retired without having taken or destroyed the trains so important to Lee.

On July 7, when the infantry and artillery arrived at Hagerstown from which Stuart had driven the Federal cavalry the day before, General Lee was not able to cross the Potomac. He, therefore, selected a strong position and fortified it while waiting for the waters

to fall.   From July 8 to 12, Stuart protected
the front of Lee's army, fighting a number of
battles.   Then, all the Federal forces having
come up, Stuart retired to the main body of
the army and General Lee prepared for battle.
But Meade, who was very cautious, thought
Lee's position too strong to attack.

Major McClellan, General Stuart's adjutant
general, says in his *Life of Stuart* that those
days will be remembered by the cavalry
leader's staff as days of great hardship.   The
country had been swept bare of provisions and
nothing could be purchased.   Scanty rations had
been issued to the men, but none to the officers.
For four or five days, they received all the food
that they had from a young lady in Hagerstown, whose father, a Southerner, loved the
Confederacy.   After a day of incessant fighting,
Stuart and his officers reached the house of this
friend about nine o'clock at night.   While food
was being prepared, Stuart fell asleep on the
sofa in the parlor.   When supper was announced,
he refused to rise.   Knowing that he had eaten
nothing for twenty-four hours, Major Mc-
Clellan took him by the arm and compelled him
to take his place at the table.   He ate sparingly
and without relish.

Thinking that the supper did not suit him,

their kind hostess inquired: "General, perhaps you would like to have a hard-boiled egg?"

"Yes," he replied, "I'll take four or five."

This singular reply caused a good deal of astonishment, but nothing was said at the time. The eggs were brought in; Stuart broke one and ate it, and rose from the table.

When they returned to the parlor, Major McClellan sat down at the piano and commenced singing,

> "If you want to have a good time
> Jine the cavalry."

The circumstances hardly made the song appropriate, but the chorus roused the general and he joined in it with a right good will. During all that time, he had been unconscious of his surroundings, and when told of his seeming rudeness to his hostess he hastened to make apologies.

This little incident shows how greatly Stuart was exhausted by the strain and fatigue of sleepless days and nights during this unfortunate campaign. For more than two weeks, he had been almost constantly in the saddle, using both mind and body in the effort to save his command and to bring the Confederate army back to Virginia without serious disaster.

On July 13, the waters had subsided so much

that General Lee gave orders for the army to cross the river that night. By one o'clock the next afternoon, the southern army was again in Virginia, General Stuart's command bringing up the rear.

The Federals, strange to say, offered little opposition and the crossing was a complete success. The Federal government and the northern people were much disappointed when they learned that General Lee had so skillfully led his army out of its perilous position. They had expected that General Meade would destroy it, hemmed in between the flooded Potomac and the Federal army so superior in numbers. Lee now moved back to Bunker Hill near Winchester. Stuart repelled an advance of the Federal cavalry and drove it steadily back to within a mile of Shepherdstown. Here a large number of the troopers were dismounted and advanced in line of battle. The Federals retreated slowly until dark when they withdrew from the contest in the direction of Harper's Ferry, having lost heavily in killed and wounded.

## CHAPTER XII

# FINAL CAMPAIGNS AND DEATH

## 1863-'64

GENERAL MEADE now advanced into Virginia and attempted to follow General Lee and cut him off from Richmond. Lee being at once informed by Stuart of the movement, skillfully eluded his foe and by the first of August, had placed his army behind the Rappahannock river, between Meade and Richmond.

The cavalry now had a short period of rest. The whole force was reorganized, and Hampton and Fitz Lee were promoted to the rank of major general. This much-needed rest was broken on September 13, by the advance of the Federals into Culpeper county. Stuart had been warned of their forward movement, and at once started his wagons and disabled horses toward Rapidan Station. General Lee supposing that General Meade was advancing in force, had already retired behind the Rapidan river and placed his army in a very strong position.

Early on the morning of Sept. 13, the Federal cavalry advanced in large numbers to the fords of the Rappahannock. As Lee did not intend to hold Culpeper county, Stuart retired toward Rapidan Station, keeping up a running fight as he withdrew.

A few days later, Stuart came in touch with Buford's cavalry near Jack's Shop in Madison county, and attacked them in several spirited charges. He was unable, however, to drive back these forces. Unwilling to retreat, he advanced and was engaged in a furious combat when he was informed that Kilpatrick's command was in his rear. As he withdrew to meet this unexpected foe, Buford pressed forward and it seemed for a time that Stuart had at last been caught in a place from which he could not escape.

Kilpatrick had already thrown a large force of dismounted men between Stuart and the river, and he was thus enclosed between two large forces of finely-mounted men. Buford pressed forward until the battle was brought into a field in the center of which a small hill afforded a good position for Stuart's artillery. He now divided his regiments and guns—some to fight Buford, some to fight Kilpatrick. At last, Kilpatrick's main force was driven back and one of Stuart's regiments dashed up to the fence behind which Kilpatrick's dismounted men were firing, threw it down, and made way for Stuart to retire. Withdrawing rapidly, Stuart then crossed the ford at Liberty Mills where he was very soon reenforced.

On October 9, General Lee commenced the movement around the right of General Meade's army which is called the "Bristoe Campaign." In this campaign, the cavalry was sorely tried. Fitz Lee—who, as you have been told, had been promoted to the rank of major general—was left at Raccoon Ford, supported by two brigades of infantry, to hold Lee's line and to make Meade believe that Lee's whole army was still encamped at that place. Stuart with Hampton's division moved to the right of Lee's army as it again marched northward; it was his duty to prevent the Federals from finding out Lee's movements and to protect the army from attacks.

Now followed a series of sharp engagements between the cavalry of the two armies. There was a skirmish near James City after which the Federals retired toward Culpeper Courthouse. The next morning, Stuart followed them. Three miles from the Courthouse, he met and drove in the Federal pickets. But he now found out that Meade was retreating from the Rappahannock and that Fitz Lee, who had fought a battle at Raccoon Ford, was advancing towards Brandy Station,—fighting Buford as he marched.

Stuart knew that Kilpatrick was at Culpeper Courthouse awaiting his attack, but on receiving this news he turned at once northward toward Brandy Station, hoping to join Fitz Lee and get possession of Fleetwood Hill from which he had driven the Federal cavalry in June. If he could carry out this plan, he would cut off Kilpatrick from Buford. Kilpatrick, who had massed his force of about four thousand men on the open space east of the Courthouse at Culpeper waiting the attack of Stuart, soon found out that the latter had eluded him and was hurrying toward Brandy Station. He, therefore, began a race for the same position.

Unfortunately, Stuart was delayed by a skirmish with Federal forces and when he came in sight of Brandy Station, he saw that Kilpatrick had beaten him in the race. Buford, who was being pursued by Fitz Lee, had already taken possession of Fleetwood Hill and placed his artillery upon its crest. Stuart had moved so rapidly that he had left his artillery far behind, but Fitz Lee's guns were booming as he came into position.

Fitz Lee joined Stuart and they at once attacked Kilpatrick's and Buford's forces, now under the command of Major-General Pleasanton. The Federals fought bravely, but they were steadily pushed toward their position on Fleetwood Hill. It was now late in the afternoon, and Stuart, declining to attack them in their strong position, sent Fitz Lee to the left as if to cut off the Federals from the river. As soon as Pleasanton perceived this flanking movement, he withdrew from Fleetwood Hill and, protected by his artillery, crossed the river. Stuart's weary troopers camped that night once more around Brandy Station, well pleased at having gained a decided victory over such large forces.

Two days later, Stuart reached Warrenton where the whole army was encamped and he immediately received orders to proceed toward Catlett's Station with two thousand men and seven guns, for the purpose of gaining accurate information about the position of Meade's army.

General Meade had started his forces back toward Culpeper Courthouse to engage General Lee in battle, but he found out that Lee was marching around his right, so as to get between him and Washington city. On receiving this information, Meade at once recalled his forces.

These movements and countermovements came near resulting disastrously to Stuart who was caught between the advancing and retreating divisions of the Federals.

When he reached Catlett's Station, he found that a column of Federal infantry was moving toward that place. He at once fell back on the road to Warrenton and found another Federal corps in his rear. His situation was now one of great peril. It seemed that his force would either be captured or cut to pieces.

Fortunately, when Stuart perceived his danger he was emerging from a piece of woods and night was closing in. He at once retired his command to the depths of the woods and called a council of his officers. They were so near the enemy that the neighing of a horse or the clash of a saber could be heard, and to make retreat impossible, they were hemmed in on one side by a swollen stream and on the other side by a forest. At first, it was proposed to leave the seven guns and cut their way out. Stuart, however, would not agree to abandon his artillery. At last, officers went through the command and ordered each man to stand by his horse's head, and to make no sound himself nor let his horse make any.

As soon as it was dark, Stuart ordered four

trusted men to make their way to General Lee at Culpeper Courthouse. They were to inform him of the dangerous position of the cavalry and ask him to send aid as soon as possible. Then followed long hours of anxious waiting. During the night, a Federal corps marched past the front of Stuart's position, but fortunately the noise of the moving column prevented the Federals from detecting the presence of the Confederates within the woods.

At the first peep of day, the Confederates discovered that a large force of Federal infantry had halted near, had stacked arms, and were getting breakfast. They were so near the Confederates that several of their officers who strayed into the woods were captured. In the dim light of morning, each soldier in gray tightened the girth of his hungry, weary steed and mounted silently, with weapons ready for the charge. The seven guns were parked near the west of the hill, just opposite the feasting Federals. Then the men waited,—waited either to be discovered by the Federals when the bright sunlight should flash upon their gray coats or to hear Lee's guns as a signal for them to attack.

At last! There was firing from toward Warrenton. Aid was approaching and the time had come to cut their way out. In an instant, the seven guns were pouring shot and shell upon the surprised Federals. The horsemen then charged upon the infantry regiments which had hastily formed in line of battle and were advancing upon the guns. A fierce combat now ensued in which the Federals were driven back. The artillery and wagons, followed closely by the horsemen, passed behind the rear of the Federals and thus the whole command escaped from its perilous position.

General Meade now fell back to Centerville and General Lee, having failed to cut off General Meade from Washington, retired again to the line of the Rappahannock. Stuart continued to follow the Federal cavalry, having skirmishes at Bull Run, Groveton, and Frying Pan Church.

A few days later, the Confederate cavalry defeated a large force of infantry near Buckland, in a battle that is known as the "Buckland Races." After a sharp skirmish, Stuart fell back slowly toward Warrenton in order to draw the Federals after him; for Fitz Lee was moving forward from Warrenton to attack them in the rear. Stuart, as soon as he heard the sound of Fitz Lee's guns, turned suddenly upon the Federals with so furious a charge that their lines were broken and put to flight. Stuart chased

them for five miles and captured two hundred
and fifty prisoners and eight wagons and ambu-
lances.  Thus he may be said to have fairly won
the race back to Buckland.

Soon after this, both armies went into winter
quarters.  The Federal soldiers had comforts
and even luxuries, while the Confederates were
poorly clothed and fed.  Their sufferings during
this bitter cold winter could not have been endured but for the food and clothing sent from
their homes.  Officers and men fared alike; the
resources of the Confederacy were at a low ebb.

Mrs. Stuart was boarding at Orange Courthouse, and, as General Stuart's headquarters
were near by, he was able to spend some time
with his family again.  And a very happy family
it was now, for on the ninth of the previous
October, the very day that began Stuart's heavy
work in the Bristoe Campaign, a daughter had
come to comfort him and Mrs. Stuart for the
loss of their little Flora.  The devoted father
named this little baby Virginia Pelham, in honor
of his beloved state and in memory of the gallant
young leader of the Stuart Horse Artillery whom
he had loved so well.  The members of General
Stuart's staff were all devoted to this new
member of the family, and General Lee, whose
headquarters were not far distant, came more

than once to visit Mrs. Stuart and "Miss Virginia," as he called the little lady. The admiration paid his little daughter gave Stuart great delight.

Late in February, 1864, the Federal cavalry made an attempt to take Richmond. This movement was known as "Dahlgren's Raid" and the large Federal forces were fitted out with great care. But in spite of their superior numbers, they were driven back by Stuart's cavalry.

On March 17, General U. S. Grant was placed in command of all the Federal armies. As it was evident that the great struggle of the year would take place in Virginia, he took charge of General Meade's army and prepared it for the coming campaign. He had an army of 125,000 men, fully equipped, and with all that money could buy.

At midnight on May 3, the Federal army began to advance. General Lee permitted it to cross the Rapidan and march into the Wilderness where the battle of Chancellorsville had been fought the year before. In this jungle, it would be difficult for the Federals to use their artillery and they would be compelled to fight at a disadvantage. General Grant expected General Lee to retreat to a line nearer Richmond, and he was surprised when his troops plunged into the dense woods and thickets of the Wilderness to find General Lee ready to fight on ground of his own choosing.

As soon as the news was received at the cavalry headquarters that the Federals had crossed the fords of the Rapidan, Stuart set out for his picket line. He conducted in person the advances of the infantry until the lines of the enemy were reached, and on May 6 and 7 the great Battle of the Wilderness raged furiously.

The cavalry did heavy work on the Confederate right. Gunner Neese, in his diary, tells an interesting anecdote of Stuart on the morning of the second day's battle.

He says: "Our orders to hasten to the front this morning at daylight were pressing and urgent, and we had no time to prepare or eat breakfast, which greatly ruffled some of our drivers. When we drew near to the enemy's line we awaited orders, and one of our drivers was still going through baby acts about something to eat and having no breakfast. Just then General Stuart and staff came along and halted a moment right in the road where we were and heard the grumbling and childish murmuring of our hungry man, and the general rode up to him and gave him two biscuits out of his own haversack."

On the night of May 7, Grant began to move his army by the left flank to get between Lee and Richmond, but the movement was discovered at once and Fitz Lee's cavalry was sent forward to delay the Federals until Longstreet's infantry could come up. Fitz Lee's men were at times dismounted, and they fought so stubbornly that Grant's forces were held in check until the infantry by a rapid night march reached the entrenchments which had been hastily thrown up near Spotsylvania Courthouse.

I am going to tell you about the arrival of the infantry and the beginning of the next morning's battle in the words of a private of the First Virginia cavalry.

He says: "We had been fighting and retreating all night, and at last, when near Spotsylvania Courthouse had thrown up slight entrenchments. Protected by Breathed's guns, we were awaiting another attack. Suddenly we heard the steady march of infantry coming in our rear. The old fellows came swinging along in the moonlight, each one with his camp-kettle on his back and his long musket with its gleaming bayonet resting easily on his shoulder. Each man settled down by a dismounted trooper, glad to rest a little while, but full of quips and jokes. 'Look here sonny,' said one to me, picking up my carbine, 'what's this here thing for? Ef I was you I'd be feared of it; it might hurt somebody!' But even talking was not permitted. Officers passed along, enjoining silence and ordering us not to fire until we could see the whites of the Yankees' eyes.

"About daylight we heard loud cheering. Major Breathed had brought off one of his guns in the face of thousands of the enemy, and they were cheering! On came a blue line of battle eight deep calling out, 'Come out, you dismounted cavalry! We know you are there.'

"Silence reigned behind the earthworks, but every gun was ready. When the Federals were well over the crest of the hill, the order rang along the line—'Steady, aim, fire!' Bang! went the carbines and muskets, and with piercing yells the Confederates leaped out of the works and rushed with gleaming bayonets upon the already retreating foe. The veterans had delivered so fierce and so well-directed a fire that the attack was not renewed at that position."

A short while afterward, Stuart arrived with reenforcements. Major McClellan was the only member of General Stuart's staff present during the brisk skirmishes of the morning. He says that Stuart exposed himself recklessly to the fire of the Federals, in spite of the earnest request of the infantry officers that he would retire to a safer position.

He sent Major McClellan on such seemingly unnecessary messages that after a while that officer thought that General Stuart was trying to shield him from danger, so he said, "General, my horse is weary. You are exposing yourself and you are alone. Please let me remain with you."

But Stuart merely smiled kindly and sent him with another message.

When Grant reached Spotsylvania Courthouse, he decided to send a corps of cavalry forward on a raid toward Richmond. This force was to cut Lee's communication, take Richmond, and be in position to attack the rear of Lee's army after Grant crushed him at Spotsylvania. General Sheridan commanded these troops that started for Richmond, along the Telegraph Road.

General Fitz Lee who saw them, says: "Ten thousand horsemen riding in a single road in column of fours made a column thirteen miles in length; and with flashing sabers and fluttering guidons were an imposing array."

To contend with this force, Stuart had only three small brigades, yet on him depended the safety of Richmond and the protection of the rear of Lee's army. At Jarrold's Mill, Wickham's brigade had a sharp skirmish with Sheridan's rear guard and captured a number of prisoners. Yet on and on marched Sheridan, leaving the Telegraph Road, and going toward Beaver Dam Station. At Mitchell's Shop, Sheridan's rear guard having been reënforced, made another stand. Wickham attacked again, but would have been forced back by the greatly-superior numbers of the Federals had not Stuart and Fitz Lee come up with reenforcements and the Federals passed on.

At Beaver Dam Station, Stuart left his command a short while to see if his wife and children, who were near by at the home of Mr. Edmund Fontaine, had escaped annoyance from the Federals. Having found them safe and well, he pressed on toward Hanover Junction to place his forces between Sheridan and Richmond.

Hanover Junction was reached after dark and Stuart proposed an all-night march. Fitz Lee's men, however, were worn out with fighting and marching and, at the request of their commander, Stuart at last consented that the troopers should rest until one o'clock. He directed that his trusted adjutant, Major McClellan, should remain awake to arouse the sleeping men, and to see them mounted and on the march at the time mentioned.

Major McClellan in his *Life of Stuart*, says: "When the troops had moved out, I returned to Stuart and awoke him and his staff. While they were preparing to move, I lay down to catch, if possible, a few moments' rest. The party rode off as I lay in a half-conscious condition, and I heard some one say, 'General, here's McClellan fast asleep. Must I wake him?' 'No' he replied, 'he has been watching while we were asleep. Leave a courier with him and tell him to come on when his nap is out.' "

After taking a short rest, Major McClellan rejoined General Stuart just as he passed the road leading to Ashland. A squadron of Confederate cavalry had come upon a force of Federal cavalry in that town, and had dispersed it with great loss to the latter.

Stuart reached Yellow Tavern, about eight miles from Richmond, about ten o'clock on the morning of May 11. He had beaten Sheridan in the race to Richmond and placed himself between that city and Sheridan's forces. He at once posted his small force to meet the Federal advance. Wickham was placed on the right of the Telegraph Road and Lomax on the

left.    Two guns were placed in the road and one
farther to the left.    The whole force was dismounted, except a portion of the cavalry which
was held in reserve.

General Stuart then sent Major McClellan
into Richmond to find out the condition of affairs in the city.    General Bragg, in charge of the
defense, replied that he had enough men to hold
the trenches and that he was hourly expecting
reenforcements from Petersburg—that he wished
General Stuart to remain on the Federal flank
and to retard its progress as much as possible.

General Stuart's last official dispatch written
on the morning of May 11, the day that he was
wounded, showed his wonderful determination
and unfailing cheerfulness in the face of danger
and difficulty, and was also a tribute to the men
who fought under him.

He wrote:    "May 11th, 1864, 6:30 A. M.
Fighting against immense odds of Sheridan—
my men and horses are tired, hungry, and
jaded, *but all right.*"

About four o'clock that same day, Sheridan
attacked the whole line, throwing a brigade of
cavalry upon the left.    Stuart galloped to this
point, and found that the Federals had captured
his two guns and had driven back almost the
entire left.    He at once ordered a reserve

squadron to charge the advancing Federals. Just as the latter were being driven back in a hand-to-hand combat, General Stuart rode up to where Captain Dorsey and about eighty dismounted men who had collected on the Telegraph Road, were firing at the retreating Federals. As the struggling mass fell back, one of the Federals who had been unhorsed in the fight, turned and fired his pistol directly at General Stuart. The fatal shot entered his body just above the sword-belt.

Captain Dorsey saw that the general was wounded and hurried to his assistance. He tried to lead the general's horse to a safer place, but it became very unruly. General Stuart insisted on being lifted off and allowed to rest against a tree. Then he ordered the captain to go back to his men, but Captain Dorsey refused to do so until his general had been taken to the rear. There were now only a few of Stuart's men between him and the Federals and for a few moments there was great danger of his being captured.

But soon another horse was brought, and the general was taken to a safer place by Captain Dorsey and put in charge of Private Wheatley. Wheatley speedily procured an ambulance, and took the general to the rear. Here Dr. Fontaine and two of the general's aides, Venable and Hullihen, took charge of their wounded chief and started at once to Richmond.

As the ambulance passed through the disordered Confederate ranks the general called to his men, "Go back! go back and do your duty as I have done, and our country will be safe. Go back! go back! I had rather die than be whipped."

These were his last words upon the battlefield, and they carried to his men a message, full of the spirit of their beloved chief. They did 'go back,' and fought so well that Sheridan was finally driven from Richmond.

The ambulance had to take a rough and roundabout way, in order to avoid the Federals, and it did not reach Richmond until after dark. The general was taken to the home of his brother-in-law, Dr. Charles Brewer. He had suffered greatly on the trip, but had borne the pain with fortitude and cheerfulness.

The next morning, Major McClellan, who according to Stuart's orders had remained on the battlefield, rode into the city to deliver to General Bragg a message from General Fitz Lee now in command of the cavalry. As soon as he had delivered his message, he went at once to the bedside of his wounded general. Inflammation had set in, and the doctors said there was no hope of Stuart's recovery. I shall let Mc-Clellan tell you in his own words about the general's last hours.

He says: "After delivering General Fitz Lee's message to General Bragg, I repaired to the bedside of my dying chief. He was calm and

THE HOUSE IN WHICH STUART DIED

This house has been torn down. The building erected on its site bears a tablet in memory of Stuart.

composed, in the full possession of his mind. Our conversation was, however, interrupted by paroxysms of suffering. He directed me to make the proper disposal of his official papers, and to send his personal effects to his wife.

"He then said: 'I wish you to take one of my

horses and Venable the other.  Which is the heavier rider?'

"I replied that I thought Venable was.

" 'Then,' he said, 'let Venable have the gray horse and you take the bay.'

"Soon he spoke again: 'You will find in my hat a small Confederate flag, which a lady of Columbia, South Carolina, sent me, with the request that I would wear it upon my horse in a battle and then return it to her.  Send it to her.' "

Later, Major McClellan found the flag inside the lining of the general's hat.  Among his papers was the letter conveying the lady's request.

"Again he said: 'My spurs which I have always worn in battle, I promised to give to Mrs. Lilly Lee, of Shepherdstown, Virginia. My sword I leave to my son.'

"While I sat by his bed, the sound of cannon outside the city was heard.  He turned to me eagerly and inquired what it meant.  I explained that Gracey's brigade and other troops had moved out against the rear of the enemy on the Brooke turnpike and that Fitz Lee would endeavor to oppose their advance at Meadow Bridge.

"He turned his eyes upward, and exclaimed earnestly, 'God g ant that they may be successful.' Then turning his head aside, he said with a sigh: 'But I must be prepared for another world.'

"The thought of duty was ever uppermost in his mind, and after listening to the distant cannonading for a few moments, he said, 'Major, Fitz Lee may need you.' I understood his meaning and pressed his hand in a last farewell. As I left his chamber, President Davis entered.

"Taking the general's hand he asked: 'General, how do you feel?'

"He replied: 'Easy, but willing to die if God and my country think I have fulfilled my destiny, and done my duty.'"

"The Rev. Dr. Peterkin visited him, and prayed with him. He requested Dr. Peterkin to sing 'Rock of Ages,' and joined in the singing of the hymn.

"During the afternoon, he asked Dr. Brewer whether it were not possible for him to survive the night. The doctor frankly told him that death was close at hand.

"He then said: 'I am resigned if it be God's will; but I would like to see my wife. But God's will be done.'

"Again he said to Dr. Brewer: 'I am going fast now; I am resigned. God's will be done.'"

Major Von Borcke, General Stuart's former aide who had not yet recovered from his severe wound, was also in Richmond. After McClellan went away, Von Borcke remained at his chieftain's side. He tells us that he sat on the bed, holding the general's hand and handing him crushed ice which he ate in great abundance and which was applied to cool his burning wound. Everyone was hoping that Mrs. Stuart would arrive in time to be with him before he passed from earth.

Finally the general drew Von Borcke to him, and after bidding him farewell said, "Look after my family after I am gone and be the same true friend to my wife and children that you have been to me." These were his last connected words.

At eight o'clock the end came, and it was three hours later before Mrs. Stuart arrived. The destruction of bridges and a fearful storm had caused delay in the trip from Beaver Dam. Owing to the telegraph lines being broken, the tidings that General Stuart was wounded did not reach his wife until noon on May 12.

At the time of his death, May 12, Stuart was just thirty-one years old. Yet through his high ideals, his devotion to duty, and his military genius, he had risen to a position of great trust and honor in the service of his country for which he laid down his life. Such a death, crowning such a life, is glorious and inspiring. One feels that Horatius, the noble Roman, indeed spoke truly when he said:

"And how can man die better,
    Than by facing fearful odds,
For the ashes of his fathers
    And the temples of his gods?"

## CHAPTER XIII

## SOME TRIBUTES TO STUART

WHILE General Stuart's life was ebbing away, General Sheridan retired from the attack on Richmond. The delay at Ashland and the all-day fight at Yellow Tavern in which two brigades of Stuart's cavalry had detained the ten thousand men of Sheridan's command, had given the authorities at Richmond time to collect forces for the defense of the city.

General Fitz Lee who now commanded the cavalry, harassed the retreat of Sheridan for a while, but his men and horses were too worn-out to attempt to cut off so large a force. Sheridan, therefore, marched through the swamps of the Chickahominy river to the Pamunkey, and after an absence of more than two weeks, rejoined Grant's army which was still vainly attempting to get between Lee and Richmond.

General Fitz Lee in his *Life of General Robert E. Lee*, says: "Sheridan's raid would have been the usual record of nothing accomplished and a broken-down command except that at Yellow Tavern the Confederate cavalry chieftain was mortally wounded and died the next day in Richmond. This sad occurrence was of more value to the Federal cause than anything that could have happened, and his loss to Lee was irreparable. He was the army's eyes and ears— vigilant always, bold to a fault, of great vigor and ceaseless activity. He had a heart ever loyal to his superior, and duty, was to him the 'sublimest word in the language.' "

In a letter to his wife a few days after General Stuart's death, General Robert E. Lee said: "As I write, I expect to hear the sound of guns every moment. I grieve for the loss of the gallant officers and men, and miss their aid and sympathy. A more zealous, ardent, brave, and devoted soldier than Stuart the Confederacy cannot have."

General Lee's order to the army announcing the death of Stuart was as follows: "Among the gallant soldiers who have fallen in the war, General Stuart was second to none in valor, in zeal, and in unflinching devotion to his country. His achievements form a conspicuous part of the history of this army, with which his name and services will be forever associated. To military capacity of a high order, he added the brighter graces of a pure life guided and sustained by the Christian's faith and hope. The mysterious

hand of an all-wise God has removed him from
the scene of his usefulness and fame. His grateful countrymen will mourn his loss and cherish
his memory. To his comrades in arms he has
left the proud recollection of his deeds and the
inspiring influence of his example."

General Wade Hampton's order to his cavalry
corps was also an eloquent tribute to the great
cavalry leader. It was as follows:

"In the midst of rejoicing over the success of
our arms, the sad tidings come to us from
Richmond of the death of our distinguished
Chief of Cavalry. Death has at last accepted
the offering of a life, which before the admiring
eyes of the Army, has been so often, so freely
and so nobly offered, on almost every battle-
field of Virginia. In the death of Major-General
J. E. B. Stuart the Army of Northern Virginia
has lost one of its most brilliant, enthusiastic
and zealous military leaders, the Southern cause
one of its earliest, most untiring and devoted
supporters, and the Cavalry arm of the service
a chieftain who first gave it prominence and
value, and whose dazzling achievements have
attracted the wonder and applause of distant
nations. His spirit shone as bright and brave
in the still chamber of death, as amid the
storm of the battlefield, and he passed out of

life the same buoyant hero he had lived. Blessed through a short but glorious career with many instances of almost miraculous good fortune, it was his great privilege to die with the consciousness of having performed his whole duty to his country. To his children he leaves the rich legacy of a name which has become identified with the brightest acts of our military history and, when the panorama of our battles shall be unfolded to posterity, in almost every picture will be seen the form of our gallant leader. His name will be associated with almost every scene of danger and of glory, in which the Cavalry of the Virginia Army has borne a part, and they will recount the exploits of Stuart with the pride which men feel in their own honorable records.

"The Major General commanding hopes that this division will show by their own noble conduct their high appreciation of the character of their lost commander, and when the danger thickens around them and the cause of their country calls for heroic efforts they will remember the example of Stuart. No leader ever set a more glorious example to his soldiers on the battlefield than he did, and it becomes the men he has so often led, while they mourn his fall, to emulate his courage, to imitate his heroic devotion to duty and to avenge his death."

While General Lee and his army continued to wrestle with the hosts of Grant, the city of Richmond was in deep gloom and mourning. Once more the tide of battle had come near her gates; and this time the beloved and gallant Stuart had fallen. He had been the pride of her heart, her brave and chivalrous defender. But Stuart was to sleep his last long sleep upon her bosom, in beautiful Hollywood around whose promontories sweep the waters of the James as they rush onward to the Chesapeake and where the tall pine trees whisper of the life eternal. The city aroused herself from her grief to do homage to the noble dead.

The City Council of Richmond passed resolutions of respect and sympathy for the family of General Stuart and asked that the body of him who "yielded up his heroic spirit in the immediate defense of their city, and the successful effort to purchase their safety by the sacrifice of his own life," might "be permitted to rest under the eye and guardianship of the people of Richmond and that they might be allowed to commemorate by a suitable monument their gratitude and his services."

At five o'clock on the afternoon of May 13, the funeral of General Stuart took place from old St. James Church in Richmond. The coffin con-

taining the remains of the brave soldier was
carried up the aisle and, covered with wreaths
and flowers, was placed before
the altar.

The funeral service was conducted by Reverend Dr. Peterkin who had been with General
Stuart during his last hours.
The church was filled with officials of the Confederate government and citizens of Richmond.
President Davis sat near the
front, with a look of great sadness upon his careworn face.
His cabinet officers were around
him and on either side of the
church were the senators and
representatives of the Confederate Congress.   But the cavalry
officers and soldiers who loved
and followed Stuart were all
absent.   They were on the firing
line, either in the Wilderness or
on the Chickahominy,—fighting
in defense of Richmond which
he had died to save.

MONUMENT
Marking Stuart's grave in
Hollywood Cemetery,
Richmond, Va.

No military escort could be

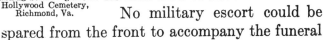

spared from the front to accompany the funeral

procession to Hollywood or to fire the usual
parting salute to the dead commander.  But
as the body was lowered into the grave, the
earth trembled with the roar of artillery from
the battlefield where his old troops were obeying his last command and driving back the
Federals.  No better salute could have been
given the gallant leader.

Leaving the body of their brave defender
beneath the pines of Hollywood, the officials and
citizens of Richmond returned to their homes
to meet other sorrows.  Before a year passed, the
devoted city was overtaken by the fate which
Stuart had so ably aided Lee in averting.
Richmond fell into the hands of the Federals,
General Lee surrendered, and the southern Confederacy was no more.

When the city arose from her ashes and
again put on the garb of peace, one of her first
works was to erect memorials in honor of
the men who had fought so nobly in her defense.

In 1888, a monument was erected by some of
Stuart's comrades to mark the place at Yellow
Tavern where he received his mortal wound.
Governor Fitzhugh Lee was the orator of the
occasion.  He had been one of Stuart's most
trusted brigadier generals, and had known him

since they were cadets together at West Point. In beautiful and touching language, he re-

MONUMENT AT YELLOW TAVERN
Marking the place where Stuart was wounded

viewed the chief events of Stuart's life, his brilliant campaigns, and his last hours.

The shaft at Yellow Tavern is twenty-two feet high and stands on a knoll about thirty feet from the spot where Stuart was wounded. Upon it are the following inscriptions:

*Face:* Upon this field, Major-Genl. J. E. B. Stuart, Commander Confederate Cavalry A. N. Va., received his mortal wound, May 11, 1864.

*Right:* He was fearless and faithful, pure and powerful, tender and true.

*Left:* This stone is erected by some of his comrades to commemorate his valor.

*Rear:* He saved Richmond, but he gave his life.
Born Feb. 6, 1833, died May 12, 1864.

In 1891, the "Veteran Cavalry Association of the Army of Northern Virginia" was organized for the purpose of marking the grave of General Stuart with a suitable monument; but it was afterwards decided that, with the aid of the city of Richmond, the association would erect an equestrian statue. The city donated the site on Monument avenue, near the equestrian statue of General Lee, and also contributed a large sum of money, so that the association was enabled to erect the statue.

The sculptor, Mr. Fred Moynihan, designed and executed a statue, which is an excellent likeness of General Stuart and a striking example of the sculptor's skill. In 1907, the memorial was unveiled in the presence of an immense concourse of people, including large numbers of veterans from all parts of the South. Chief among the guests of honor were Miss Mary Custis Lee, Mrs. Stonewall Jackson, and Mrs. J. E. B. Stuart.

Fully ten thousand men marched in the column which took over an hour to pass a given point. Veterans who were too feeble to endure the fatigue of the march went early to the monument, and joined the great multitude that crowded the sidewalks and even the house-tops.

When the parade reached the monument, the crowd was so dense that it was with difficulty that the police made way for the orator and distinguished guests. The multitude was called to order by Major Andrew R. Venable, of Farmville, Virginia, a member of the staff of General Stuart, who introduced Rev. Walter Q. Hullihen, of Staunton, Virginia, another member of Stuart's staff, who made the dedicatory prayer. Major Venable then introduced the orator of the day, Judge Theodore S. Garnett of Norfolk, Virginia, another member of the staff of General Stuart.

It was indeed a remarkable incident that three of General Stuart's staff officers presided at the unveiling of his statue forty-three years after his death.

Judge Garnett in an eloquent speech reviewed the life and campaigns of Stuart, paying glowing tributes to the general, to the "ever-glorious and gallant" Stuart Horse Artillery, and to his comrades of Mosby's Battalion. He closed with these words: "To the city of Richmond, as its faithful guardian, we commit this monument, in whose care and keeping it will henceforth stand in token of a people's gratitude and in perpetual memory of his heroic name."

The veil was then drawn from the monument

STUART STATUE
On Monument Avenue, Richmond, Va.

[ 201 ]

by the hand of little Virginia Stuart Waller, General Stuart's granddaughter.   As the canvas fell from the heroic figure of General Stuart mounted on his powerful horse, the guns of the Howitzers boomed a salute and the cheering of the vast throng arose in billows of sound.

"Stuart was again riding with Lee."

# SUGGESTIVE QUESTIONS

## CHAPTER I

Give three incidents to prove that Stuart inherited his spirit of patriotism and devotion to duty.

Tell an interesting story connected with his grandmother, Bethenia Letcher Pannill.

What do you know of Stuart's life at Laurel Hill?

Tell what you can about his early education.

Give an account of his life at West Point.

What do you know of his religious feelings and convictions?

Tell about his choice of a profession and his equipment for it.

## CHAPTER II

How did Stuart win distinction in his first military service?

What good qualities for a soldier and leader did he show in this adventure?

What two events of deep personal interest happened to Stuart in the fall of 1855?

Tell about the political trouble in Kansas at this time.

Who was "Ossawatomie" Brown?

Tell about Stuart's being wounded in a fight with Indians.

What qualities did he show in leading the party back to Fort Kearny?

What was the reason for his visit to Washington in 1859?

What interesting and important outcome did this visit have?

What feelings were aroused in the country by the John Brown Raid and the hanging of Brown?

## CHAPTER III

What was Stuart's first cavalry commission under the Confederate government?

What kind of troops did he have, and what was his work?

Tell about his wonderful capture at Falling Waters.

What did General Joseph E. Johnston say about Stuart?

Tell about Stuart's part in the First Battle of Manassas.

Tell about the visits paid Stuart by his family at his outpost near Washington.

What did General Longstreet write President Davis about Stuart?

## CHAPTER IV

See if you can paint a word-picture of Stuart when he was made a brigadier general.

Why did the soldiers still keep their confidence in Stuart after his defeat at the battle of Dranesville?

What was the Peninsular Campaign? What was Stuart's part in it, up to the time that General Lee was made commander of the Army of Northern Virginia?

Describe the Chickahominy Raid. Why is this raid one of the most wonderful cavalry achievements in history?

Tell two interesting incidents connected with the capture of the Federal supply depot at the White House.

Tell about the close of the Peninsular Campaign.

### CHAPTER V

What was Stuart's reward for his services in the Peninsular Campaign?

Tell about the reörganization of the cavalry.

Give an account of life at Dundee. What brought it to a close?

Tell about the capture of Stuart's hat.

Give an account of the adventure in which he "made the Yankees pay for that hat."

What was Stuart's part in the Second Battle of Manassas?

### CHAPTER VI

Tell about the capture of Fairfax Courthouse.

Tell a story to show how the people of this section felt toward General Stuart and the cause for which he fought.

Describe the crossing of the cavalry into Maryland.

Do you think the Maryland people were glad to welcome the Confederates into their State? Why?

Tell about the ball at Urbana.

How did the Confederates treat the Unionists in Frederick?

Describe Stuart's retreat from Frederick to South Mountain.

What were the principal mountain passes and why was it necessary for the cavalry to hold them until the capture of Harper's Ferry?

What did General Jackson say about General Stuart at the battle of Antietam?

How did the cavalry help General Lee to get his army back safely into Virginia?

Tell about "the girl of Williamsport."

Tell about Stuart and Von Borcke's narrow escape from being captured on a reconnoitering expedition.

Tell about Bob Sweeny and camp life at The Bower.

## CHAPTER VII

Would you have been proud of being one of the soldiers chosen by Stuart to accompany him on the Chambersburg Raid? Why?

Give a brief account of the raid.

To whom did Stuart assign all the glory and honor?

What was the effect of the raid on the North? On the South?

Why was Stuart sometimes called "Knight of the Golden Spurs?"

## CHAPTER VIII

Tell about McClellan's campaign in the autumn of 1862 and the retreat of the cavalry toward Culpeper.

What exciting adventure did Stuart have at Ashby's Gap?

What qualities as a man and a soldier did Stuart show during the illness and after the death of his "little Flora"?

When and how did Stuart lose a part of his mustache?

What was the condition of Stuart's cavalry at the time that Burnside took McClellan's place as commander of the Federal army?

Tell about the snowball fight in the Confederate camp at Fredericksburg.

What part did Stuart and his cavalry take in the battle of Fredericksburg?

How did Pelham, the young chief of the Stuart Horse Artillery, distinguish himself in this battle?

Tell about the Dumfries Raid and the joke that Stuart played on the Federal quartermaster at Washington.

Tell about the friendship between Stuart and Jackson.

What changes took place in the Federal army in the early spring of 1863?

## CHAPTER IX

Tell about the death of young Pelham and Stuart's love for him.

Give an account of Stuart's encounters with the Federal cavalry just before the battle of Chancellorsville.

How did Stuart and his cavalry assist Jackson in surprising the Federal left flank?

When Jackson was wounded, what did he say about Stuart?

How did Stuart fulfill Jackson's trust?

Tell about Stoneman's raid and its result.

## CHAPTER X

Describe the Culpeper cavalry review.

Draw a diagram showing how the Federals gave Stuart a double surprise in the battle of Fleetwood Hill, or Brandy Station, attacking him from both the front and the rear.

Describe the final combat for the possession of the hill.

## CHAPTER XI

Why did Lee's plan prevent Stuart's following up Pleasanton's retreat?

Why did not Stuart follow the route of the remainder

of the army when he started into Pennsylvania to join Early at York?

Describe his march from Seneca Ford to Carlisle.

In the light of what he knew, would it have been wise for Stuart to abandon his captured wagons? Give a reason for your opinion.

How long did his saving the wagons delay his march?

Do you think that he would have kept the wagons if he had known what was happening at Gettysburg?

What part did Stuart and his cavalry take in the third day's battle?

Tell about the work of Stuart and his cavalry in covering the retreat of General Lee's army.

Tell the incident about Stuart and the hard-boiled eggs. Explain his conduct on this occasion.

## CHAPTER XII

Tell about General Lee's position and Stuart's encounter with Buford and Kilpatrick at Jack's Shop.

What was the "Bristoe Campaign?"

Tell how Stuart drove the Federals a second time from Fleetwood Hill.

What narrow escape did Stuart and his cavalry have near Catlett's Station?

Tell about Virginia Pelham Stuart.

What northern general took command of all the Federal armies in the spring of 1864?

Tell about the Battle of the Wilderness. What interesting anecdote is told about Stuart when he was on his way to this battle?

Tell about the battle of Spotsylvania Courthouse.

How did General Stuart try to save Major McClellan from danger in this battle?

Describe the cavalry raid that General Grant planned in order to take Richmond.

How did Stuart beat Sheridan in the race to Yellow Tavern?

Tell about Stuart's being wounded and borne from the field.

What was his last command to his men?

What impressed you most when you read the account of Stuart's death?

Why is such a death as this glorious and inspiring?

Repeat the lines from "Horatius" that apply to the death of Stuart.

## Chapter XIII

What tribute did Fitz Lee pay his dead commander?

What private and public tributes were paid by General Robert E. Lee?

How did the city of Richmond show her grief at the time of Stuart's death?

What later tributes has she given to her hero and defender?

# THE ORGANIZATION OF AN ARMY

The Federal and Confederate armies in the War of Secession were organized in practically the same way. There were a few points of difference, and in active service the numbers and arrangement of military forces varied and were changed.

## INFANTRY

*Squad:* any small number of men, usually 7, under command of a corporal.

*Platoon:* a subdivision, usually half, of a company under a lieutenant.

*Company:* from 83 to 125 men under a captain.

*Battalion:* 2 or more, usually four, companies under a major.

*Regiment:* 10 companies—or 3 battalions of 4 companies each—under a colonel or a lieutenant-colonel.

*Brigade:* 3 to 5 regiments under a brigadier-general.

*Division:* 2 to 5 brigades under a major-general.

*Army corps:* 2 or more divisions under a major-general or a lieutenant-general,—organized as a complete army and sufficient in itself for all the operations of war.

## CAVALRY

*Squad:* any small number of men, usually 7, under a corporal.

*Platoon:* a sub-division, usually half, of a company under a lieutenant.

*Troop:* 2 to 6 platoons, 76 to 100 men, under a captain.

*Squadron:* 2 to 4 troops under a senior captain or a major.

*Regiment:* 10 troops—or 4 to 6 squadrons—under a colonel.

*Brigade:* 3 or 4 regiments under a brigadier-general.

*Division:* 2 to 4 brigades under a major-general.

## ARTILLERY

*Battery:* usually 144 men with 4 guns and 2 howitzers, under a captain.

*Battalion:* 3 to 4 batteries under a major.

*Regiment:* 2 to 8 battalions under a colonel.

When infantry regiments are combined into brigades, brigades into divisions, and divisions into army corps,—cavalry, artillery, and certain other auxiliary troops, such as engineers, signal corps, etc., are joined with them in such proportions as are necessary. Every unit, from the company up, has its own supply and ammunition wagons, field hospitals, etc.

# WORD LIST

**Ab o li'tion party:** a political party, founded by Garrison about 1833, the object of which was to free all slaves in the United States.

**ad vånçe':** forward movement of a military force.

**advance guard:** t r o o p s which march in front, in order to secure a military force against surprise.

**āid'-dē-cǎmp:** an officer who assists a general by sending orders, collecting information, etc.

**āide:** a military or naval officer who assists a superior officer.

**A på'chę:** a warlike Indian tribe originally located in New Mexico and Arizona.

**är'se nal:** a place for the storage or manufacture of arms and military equipment.

**ar til'ler y:** cannon, large or small; that branch of the service which handles the cannon.

**as saųlt':** attack of a military force on the works or position of an enemy, in the effort to carry it by a single charge.

**bāse:** a place from which the operations of an army proceed, forward movements are made, supplies are furnished, etc.

**bat tǎl'ion:** See page 210.

**bat'ter y:** See page 210.

**bǐv'ouac (-wǎk):** a temporary encampment of soldiers, usually without tents.

**bri gāde':** See page 210.

**brǔnt:** the shock of an attack or onset.

**buoy'ant:** cheerful, lighthearted.

**cāis'son:** a strong four-wheeled wagon, consisting of two parts, the body and the limber, that carries ammunition chests or boxes.

**căn'is ter:** cannon shot consisting of a metal cylinder which bursts when fired, discharging the bullets with which it is filled.

**căr'bine:** a short, light rifle used chiefly by cavalry.

**căs'ca bel:** a knob or projection in the rear of the breech of a muzzle-loading cannon.

**căv'al ry:** that part of the army consisting of mounted soldiers.

**Cheȳ ĕnne':** an Indian tribe formerly inhabiting South Dakota, Wyoming, and Nevada.

**com man dänt':** the commanding officer of a place or of a body of men.

**côm'pa ny:** See page 210.

**corps** (cōr): See page 210.

**coun'ter movement:** a movement by which a body of troops marches back over ground it has recently occupied or marched over.

**cŭl'mi nat ed:** reached a final result

**di vī'sion:** See page 210.

**en cămped:** formed a camp.

**en trĕnch':** fortify with defensive works as with a trench or ditch and a wall.

**en trĕnch'ments:** fortifications consisting of a parapet of earth and the ditch or trench from which the earth was taken.

**flănk:** the side of an army, either in column or in line.

**grāpe'shŏt:** a cluster of iron balls arranged in an iron framework to be discharged from a cannon. Formerly grapeshot was inclosed in a canvas bag so quilted as to look like a bunch of grapes.

**guī'dons:** small flags carried by cavalry and field artillery.

hăv′er sack: a bag or case in which a soldier carries provisions on a march.

Ho rā′tius: a hero of ancient Rome who with two others defended the bridge across the Tiber against an advancing army. Read Lord Macaulay's poem "Horatius."

how′itz er: a cannon for throwing shells.

ĭm′mi nent: threatening; dangerous and close at hand.

in dŏm′i ta ble: unyielding; unconquerable.

ĭn′fan try: foot soldiers armed with rifles and bayonets; one of the three chief divisions of an army, the other two being cavalry and artillery.

in vĕst′ing: surrounding with troops; laying siege to.

ir rĕp′a ra ble: not capable of being repaired or remedied.

lăr′i at: a long, small rope used for catching or for picketing cattle or horses.

lĭm′ber: the fore part of a gun carriage, consisting of a chest mounted on two wheels and having a pole for the horses. See *caisson*.

ma neū′vers: movements or changes of position of troops or war-vessels for tactical purposes or for display.

ma rïnes′: naval troops; soldiers serving on war-vessels.

mär′tial law: the military administration which when proclaimed takes the place of civil law in time of war or disorder.

mĭl′i ta ry law: the laws by which an army and its affairs are governed. Military law differs from martial law in that the former is a permanent code for the government of the army and the latter is the application of the laws of war to all the people in a certain district.

**mīne:** an explosive charge, sunken in the earth or under water, for the purpose of destroying an enemy passing over it,— formerly exploded by contact or by a fuse, but now usually exploded by electricity.

**ôrd'nance:** military supplies.

**ŏr'i flămme:** a standard or ensign in battle, especially the ancient royal banner of France.

**out'post:** a post or station outside the limits of a camp, for observation or to guard against surprise.

**'pa rōled':** set at liberty on parole, or word of honor not to bear arms against the captors.

**pĕr'emp to ry:** authoritative; not admitting of debate or question.

**pĭck'ets:** soldiers stationed on the outskirts of a camp to warn against the enemy's approach.

**pīkes:** soldiers' weapons, consisting of wooden staves with steel points. In recent warfare, pikes have been superceded by bayonets.

**pla tōōn':** See page 210.

**pon tōōn':** a vessel, such as a flat-bottomed boat or a canvas - covered frame, used in the construction of a floating bridge.

**pre dĭc'a ment:** a difficult or trying condition or situation.

**prō'vost** (vō) **guard:** a body of soldiers detailed for police duties.

**quạr'ter master:** a staff officer of a regiment or other body of troops, whose duty it is to provide quarters, arrange transportation, and provide and issue food, clothing, and other supplies.

**rănk:** grade of official standing in the army or navy.

**rēar guard:** troops which

march in the rear of a body of forces in order to protect it.

rḛ cŏn'nȧis sȧnçe: an examination of territory or of an enemy's position for the purpose of gaining information,—sometimes involving an attack for the purpose of discovering the enemy's position and strength.

rĕg'i.ment: See page 210.

re trēat': the withdrawal, especially in an orderly manner, of troops from an exposed or dangerous position.

rī'fled: having the bore rifled, or grooved spirally, in order to give a rotary motion to the bullet.

shĕll: a hollow projectile for cannon, which contains an explosive charge.

side arms: weapons worn at the side or in the belt, as sword, pistol, bayonet, etc., especially sword.

Sĭd'ney, Sir Philip: a famous English soldier and author of the sixteenth century, the model of unselfish courage. He was mortally wounded in battle of Zulphen, in 1586.

sī mul tā'ne ous: happening at the same time.

spȳ: a soldier not in uniform who penetrates the enemy's camp or zone of operations, for the purpose of gaining information.

tăl'ma: a style of long cape or cloak worn by men and women during the first half of the nineteenth century.

un lĭm'ber ed: removed from the limber. See *limber* and *caisson*.

Zou̯ äves': infantry wearing a͓ brilliant oriental uniform, consisting of leggins, baggy trousers, short jacket, and tasselled cap or turban.